AF361607

Hunting and Fishing in the New South

Hunting and Fishing
in the New South

Black Labor and White Leisure after the Civil War

SCOTT E. GILTNER

The Johns Hopkins University Press
Baltimore

2 4 6 8 9 7 5 3 1

The Johns Hopkins University Press
2715 North Charles Street
Baltimore, Maryland 21218-4363
www.press.jhu.edu

Library of Congress Cataloging-in-Publication Data
Giltner, Scott E., 1973–
Hunting and fishing in the new South : black labor and white leisure after
the Civil War / Scott E. Giltner.
p. cm. — (Johns Hopkins University studies in historical and
political science)
Includes bibliographical references and index.
ISBN-13: 978-0-8018-9023-9 (hardcover : alk. paper)
ISBN-10: 0-8018-9023-3 (hardcover : alk. paper)
1. Hunting — Social aspects — Southern States — History — 19th century.
2. Hunting — Social aspects — Southern States — History — 20th century.
3. Fishing — Social aspects — Southern States — History — 19th century.
4. Fishing — Social aspects — Southern States — History — 20th century.
5. Men, White — Southern States — Social conditions.   6. Hunters —
Southern States — History.   7. African American men — Southern
States — Social conditions.   8. Hunting guides — Southern States —
History.   9. Southern States — Race relations.
10. Southern States — History — 1865–1951.   I. Title.
SK43.G55 2008
799.0973 — dc22   2008007845
A catalog record for this book is available from the British Library.

*Special discounts are available for bulk purchases of this book. For more
information, please contact Special Sales at 410-516-6936 or
specialsales@press.jhu.edu.*

The Johns Hopkins University Press uses environmentally friendly book
materials, including recycled text paper that is composed of at least 30
percent post-consumer waste, whenever possible. All of our book papers
are acid-free, and our jackets and covers are printed on paper with
recycled content.

Contents

Hunting and Fishing in the New South

Introduction

Hunting, Fishing, and Freedom

In 1937, former Alabama slave Heywood Ford recounted to a Works Progress Administration interviewer the escape of a fellow slave named Jake Williams. For Williams, who hated their plantation's overseer "case he was so mean an' useta try to think up things to whup us for," the last straw came one day when the overseer, after seeing him playing with his "ole red-bone houn" dog Belle instead of working, sternly reproached him and hit the dog sharply with a rock. That night Williams told Ford he was running away and begged a favor. "I wish you'd look after my houn' Belle," he requested. "Feed her an' keep her de bes' you kin. She a mighty good possum an' coon dog. I hates to part wid her, but I knows dat you is de bes' pusson I could leave her wid." With that, Williams slipped out of the cabin and escaped into a nearby swamp.

It did not take long for the overseer to notice the slave's absence and set after him with a pack of hounds. They soon caught up with Williams, who climbed a tree to avoid his pursuers. When the overseer climbed up after him, Williams, in desperation, kicked him to the ground. What happened next astonished the terrified runaway. On hitting the ground, the overseer was immediately set upon by the hounds, who "to' dat man all to pieces." An even greater shock came when Williams realized the identity of the lead dog. "De leader of dat pack of houn's, white folks, warn't no blood houn," asserted Ford. In fact, a "plain old red-bone possum an' coon dog" had led the pack. It was none other than Williams's own Belle.

Ford heard this remarkable tale from Jake Williams himself, who fled with the loyal hound after the incident described above. "I seed Jake after us niggers was freed," Ford recalled. "Dats how come I knowed all 'bout it. It must have been six

years after dey killed de oberseer." By pure chance, the two friends reunited in
Kentucky. "He was a-sittin' on some steps of a nigger cabin. A houn' dog was
a-sittin' at his side." Ford told Williams how glad he was to see him and asked if
the dog was Belle. "'Naw,' Jake answers, 'Dis her puppy!' Den he tol' me de whole
story."[1]

Ford's account, which the interviewer tellingly titled "Heywood Ford Tells a
Story," is no doubt embellished or fictionalized.[2] But even if only a colorful tale
to please the interviewer, it nonetheless reveals important facts about blacks' life
in the rural South before and after Emancipation. First, as evidenced by Jake
Williams's attachment to Belle, African Americans depended on independent
economic activities such as hunting to survive the rigors of bondage. Second, as
demonstrated by Williams's flight following the overseer's implicit threat to his use
of Belle to meet his needs, slaves protected such activities as best they could and
resisted attempts to deny them. Finally, as shown by Ford's reunion with Williams,
Belle's puppy happily sitting by his side, the reliance on traditions such as hunting, or on loyal hunting dogs, did not end with Emancipation.

Since the early colonial period, from tidewater Maryland to the Mississippi
Delta, from the South Carolina Lowcountry to the Alabama frontier, Southerners had hunted and fished for food, market, or sport. For both blacks and whites,
exploitation of the sporting field became a key marker of racial and class status.
For well-to-do whites, the ability to hunt and fish freely, to use certain methods
and equipment, and to employ black laborers to attend their excursions became
ways to publicly display their wealth and social standing. The pursuit of fish and
game became purely a sporting activity, unburdened by the specter of necessity
that drove others' hunting and fishing. For African Americans, particularly slaves,
hunting and fishing were vivid symbols of an economic, cultural, and spatial separation from whites that reflected the struggle for control over their own lives and
labors. Hunting and fishing became forms of work that demonstrated not aristocratic pretension but the pressing need for food and income.

Hunting and fishing remained deeply rooted traditions that reflected Southerners' aspirations and reinforced their identities. Yet it is essential to note that the
hunting and fishing traditions of blacks and whites developed in opposition to
each other. Elite whites followed established sporting codes carried over from European aristocracy and reveled in hunting and fishing in ways that those in lower
social strata could not. African-American hunters and fishermen had no such pretension. In earning a part of their living away from agricultural labor in the service of whites, and confounding expectations of proper behavior for people of

color, they sought to maximize their independence and thereby challenged the Southern racial hierarchy.

This examination of the connection between hunting and fishing and Southern race relations began as a proposal for a master's thesis on the role of hunting and fishing in plantation slave communities. A cursory examination of the logical starting point for such a study—slave narratives, including those compiled in the 1930s by the Federal Writers' Project—revealed that many former slaves enthusiastically recalled stalking through the woods or fishing at a nearby creek and that such activities stood out as rare high points in a cold, capricious system based on brutal exploitation. Their descriptions, moreover, indicated that hunting and fishing as sport or recreation was at best a secondary consideration for slaves. Hunting and fishing served more vital functions. When former slaves described the primary benefits of these activities, they recalled not only recreation but, more significantly, the crucial ability to feed themselves when sufficient food was denied them, the feelings of pride that came with providing for themselves and their families in a system that sought to keep slaves in a state of dependency, and the valuable market activities, both simple and elaborate, that provided bond people and their families with much-needed cash and goods. Much more than fun or sport attended such abilities. As former slave Charles Ball remembered about the day he acquired an old musket for hunting, "I now began to live well, and to feel myself, in some measure, an independent man."[3]

The hundreds of narratives by former and runaway slaves indicated that hunting and fishing gave slaves greater control of their time and cultivated independence rather than mere recreation, a theme that ultimately formed the heart of my master's thesis.[4] Based mostly on former-slave narratives and elite whites' accounts of plantation life, the thesis argued that hunting and fishing strengthened slaves' nutritional and material condition, provided food, money, and material goods, and gave slaves time for family and community camaraderie. Hunting and fishing created and augmented feelings of independence among slaves and turned privileges granted by masters into customary rights that slaves expected. Once such privileges became established, slaves regarded them as part of a contract—informal, of course, yet important and worth defending. Moreover, just as some masters used hunting and fishing to solidify their hold on labor, slaves used these activities to make claims to their own time and cultivate opportunities to resist, subtly and overtly, the conditions of bondage. The thesis explained some of the ways in which slaves relied on the natural environment to ease the daily burdens of bondage. It identified hunting and fishing as sometimes contested activities inseparably linked to slavery and raised important, unanswered questions about the connections between hunting and fishing and race after Emancipation.

These numerous questions about African Americans' hunting and fishing in the postwar South ultimately gave rise to this book. I wondered how much former slaves relied on the natural environment after liberation and to what extent former slave owners approved of such activities. I wondered how much Emancipation—bringing African Americans greater physical mobility, more economic alternatives to agricultural labor, and (generally) increased access to firearms—altered the Southern sporting field. Most importantly, I wondered to what extent conflicts between whites and blacks over hunting and fishing, reports of which appeared occasionally in antebellum primary sources, increased with Emancipation. Perhaps unsurprisingly, I learned that such conflicts created far more controversy in the decades following the Civil War. Yet I was unprepared for the open hostility that the research revealed.

Hunting and fishing appeared regularly in postwar complaints about African Americans. Indeed, I could hardly read a white Southerner's description of post-Emancipation life without finding highly critical references to the practices. Far from decreasing after Emancipation, the number of such accounts that touched on issues of race expanded dramatically. These descriptions, moreover, often took on a decidedly different tone than similar reports on the Old South. Antebellum narratives of slaves' hunting and fishing reflected white Southerners' confident mastery over those in bondage, but postwar depictions often revealed a deep unease with black liberation and a growing anger over freed people's customary rights. Hunting and fishing, as sources of slave privilege and temporary independence, sometimes irritated and occasionally alarmed antebellum planters, but they did not view these activities as serious threats to their basic control. After liberation, however, white Southerners saw that those same activities, often performed free from white oversight, allowed African Americans to earn a living apart from regular labor in the service of whites, to challenge white sportsmen's monopoly over Southern hunting and fishing, and to create greater power and control over their own time and work.

This was the central question that propelled this study forward. How could such activities, common across the South for centuries for black and white Southerners, become such a source of open economic, cultural, and legal conflict in the decades after the Civil War? Why did white Southern elites, who often readily embraced slaves' hunting and fishing, so quickly and venomously decry these activities when performed by freed African Americans? What role did liberated African Americans play in Dixie's sporting field in the half-century after Emancipation? How, exactly, did freedom change the nature of Southern hunting and fishing? Answering these questions is the purpose of this book.

The study also raised important questions about the interplay of Southern hunting and fishing and class relations. Conflict over those traditions did not occur just between elite whites and African Americans; poor whites no doubt played a part in the story as well. Yet given the centrality of establishing the ways in which hunting and fishing reflected former slaves' struggle for greater independence, I chose not to focus on poor whites directly. Sources so rich for studying African Americans' relationship to hunting and fishing, moreover, often proved strangely silent on poor whites. African-American sources tended to focus exclusively on blacks' own sporting and subsistence activities. Elite white sources—particularly sportsmen and prosperous landowners—if they ventured beyond documenting their own connection to hunting and fishing, frequently discussed African Americans' contributions but seemed to ignore those of poor whites. Because so much of what made a sporting expedition authentically "Southern" to native and visiting elites depended on the presence of people of color, African Americans receive far more discussion than poor whites. Whether in the narratives of visiting sportsmen, the published accounts of native Southerners, or magazine articles discussing Southern sporting excursions, descriptions of hunting and fishing scenes and complaints about sporting abuses tended to focus on race.

Such questions as the relationship between poor whites and African Americans in the sporting field; the extent to which elites used the rhetoric of race, embedded in emerging efforts to restrict wildlife, to target both poor whites and blacks; and the degree to which elites succeeded in convincing lower-class whites to accept such wildlife restrictions as a way to control the black population—all are potentially revealing, but beyond the scope of this study. Focusing on poor whites might provide a better understanding of the inherent class conflicts reflected in Southern hunting and fishing in the late nineteenth and early twentieth centuries, but the limited sources suggest, in part by their scarcity, that poor whites played a limited role in constructing the larger contours of African Americans' relationship to those long traditions.

The sources consulted for this book also raised important questions about the geography of Southern hunting and fishing after Emancipation. J. William Harris, in his Pulitzer Prize–nominated *Deep Souths: Delta, Piedmont, and Sea Island Society in the Age of Segregation*, reminded us that "there is more than one South to tell about," and all scholars must be careful to avoid painting the whole region with too broad a brush.[5] Despite that caveat, this study poses a challenge to those who demand geographic specificity. Like the issue of poor whites, the question of geographic focus dogged the project from the outset, and, again, the nature of the sources would shape the finished product. Because specific sources concentrated in one particular state or region were lacking, and because the majority of the available material, particularly periodical literature, was not geographically specific beyond identifying the location of individual contributors, it became difficult to limit the discussion of Southern hunting and fishing to one part of the South or to identify regional variation in the topic, as Harris did so thoroughly in *Deep Souths*.

Nor was a geographically limited study possible. Articles in sporting periodicals, which often did not specifically discuss geography, became perhaps the key source for the study. In such sources, sportsmen often seemed much more willing to describe the acts of hunting and fishing or discuss their companions than to relate the location of their excursions. One can sometimes get a sense of overall sporting geography from the magazines and published sporting narratives, since part of the reason sportsmen wrote to these publications was, ostensibly, to share information and tips on good sport, but even that is uneven. Since many of the key sources for the study were national in nature, this book often deals with the national dialogue on hunting and fishing and the ways in which Southern hunting and fishing fit into it. This national dialogue, while excellent for understanding the intersection of hunting and fishing and race that became so central to both Northerners' and Southerners' views, does not provide specific sources for tracing geographic variation. I do not argue that African Americans' relationship to hunting and fishing was homogeneous across the region—in fact, I note regional variations where appropriate—but detailed discussion of geographic variation was not possible and would not have added substantially to the central argument.

The volume is not without a geographic focus, however. Thick description of hunting and fishing in specific parts of the South remained elusive, but the sources do provide something of a geographic framework for the study. Hunting and fishing, particularly for employment or marketing, or as part of the emerging sporting tourism industry, became contested in regions with large African-American populations. With some exceptions, most accounts came from areas with large black populations, including north-central North Carolina, coastal South Carolina and Georgia, north Florida, south-central Alabama, western and southern Mississippi, and southern Louisiana. These areas correspond to the "black belt" that snaked across the South between the 1860s and the 1920s. The fact that the majority of my evidence originates from such black belt areas allows me to demonstrate both that African Americans hunted and fished most substantially and effectively in areas where their numbers were high and that complaints about blacks' exploitation of those traditions drew the most criticism in areas where whites contended with a large black population.

This criticism encapsulated the many tensions inherent in the transition from slavery to freedom. The ability to hunt and fish provided freed people with privileges that clashed with whites', particularly agricultural employers', expectations of proper African-American behavior. Along with independent hunting and fishing came better control of subsistence, freer use of guns and dogs, and the ability to more easily avoid permanent labor in the service of whites. In the minds of white observers, these freedoms clashed with the future prosperity of the region. The increasingly bitter tone with which white Southerners discussed blacks' hunting and fishing in post-Emancipation sporting narratives indicates that those activities would continue to be key points of conflict in Southern life for decades. Indeed, as elite whites discovered, those customary traditions, born in slavery and later employed by freed people liberated from the master-servant relationship that had once characterized such activities, posed very real threats to their control.

Between the late 1860s and the mid-1920s, the role of hunting and fishing in Southern society changed. In addition to becoming a growing source of tension between elite whites and former slaves over freed blacks' privilege, subsistence, and labor, hunting and fishing also became increasingly important to the region's emerging tourism industry. The South's emergence as a leading sporting destination heralded economic and cultural reunion between North and South. Thousands of visitors from around the country and across the world journeyed to Dixie, seeking both ready supplies of fish and game and an "authentic" Southern experience, which included the presence of subordinate African Americans to complete the vision of a mythical antebellum South. Elite landowning Southerners thus had a direct vested interest in restricting former slaves' hunting and fishing even as the presence of blacks in the sporting field became more important to the region's fish and game industry. As sporting tourism garnered millions for the coffers of the leading resort and sporting states, Southerners' need to protect fish and game, preserving it for whites only, became more urgent. Like agricultural employers and landowners, sportsmen and tourism investors increasingly realized that independent hunting and fishing by African Americans was bad for business.

With time, a coalition of white Southern elites agreed on the need to control hunting and fishing in response to African-American liberation. For landowners and agricultural employers, former slaves' renewed ability to freely pursue fish and game challenged elite whites' quest for tractable labor and raised troubling questions about the harmful effects of independent black subsistence. For sportsmen, unrestricted hunting and fishing gave African Americans the ability both to capture valuable wildlife and to engage in sporting behavior that elite whites wished to retain as their exclusive purview. For those invested in sporting tourism, independent black hunters and fishermen not only competed with native and visiting sportsmen for the products of the chase, thereby damaging the remunerative potential of an increasingly lucrative industry, but also challenged the basic assumptions about black subordination that lay at the heart of the popularity of Southern tourism. For each of these groups, then, African Americans' hunting and fishing underscored the problems of black independence and presented immediate challenges to their economic and social positions. For decades, this coalition discussed, criticized, and forcefully attacked independent hunting and fishing by African Americans in order to limit these activities to those who followed codes of proper sportsmanship, to those who brought tourist and investment capital into the region, and to those whose labor did not bear the future of Southern economic prosperity. For elite whites, hunting and fishing might remain permanently biracial, but control of it could not.

Between Emancipation and the early twentieth century, then, sportsmen, landowners, and agricultural employers responded to black liberation by attacking blacks' customary rights. If they could circumscribe how former slaves supported themselves, they might compel tractable labor. If they could force people of color to adhere to codes of proper sportsmanship or remove themselves from the sporting field altogether, they might maintain elite whites' dominion over Southern fields, forests, and streams. And if they could use regulation of hunting and fishing to keep African Americans both more dependent on white employment and more susceptible to white control, they might simultaneously guarantee elite whites' future economic prosperity while preserving images of African-American inferiority for tourists. But the going was not easy. Before the coalition could effectively target those threats, they first had to convince a reluctant, poorer Southern public—long suspicious of restrictions on general access to fish and game—that the need to control an increasingly independent-minded black population far outweighed traditional hostility to legislative action targeting cherished customary rights.

By the 1920s, decades of vigorous public complaint from this coalition of white interests about African Americans' hunting and fishing had secured several important victories. With the explosion of sporting tourism, many Southerners began to understand the financial motivations for better protecting fish and game. With the rise of a national conservation movement, which by the late nineteenth century had penetrated even the reluctant South, sportsmen had begun to accept some limits on hunting and fishing as necessary measures to stop abuses by immoderate lower-class sportsmen. By the beginning of the Jim Crow period, both Southern and national audiences agreed that failure to control African Americans lay at the heart of the region's economic, social, and sporting problems. The time had finally arrived for a wide-ranging legislative attack on African Americans' right to hunt and fish.

"You Can't Starve a Negro"

*Hunting and Fishing and African Americans'
Subsistence in the Post-Emancipation South*

We try to treat them fairly, and to impress them with the
idea that we take an interest in them, which we really do.
Yet with all this, when fish bite, they will go fishing, no
matter how important their labor may be.
—Southern Planter and Farmer *editorial on the state
of African-American labor, 1872*

I ain't never stole a moufful somepin' t'eat for [my fam-
ily] in all my life. It's honest vittles dey et, and varmints
I's killed in de woods, 'ca'se us raised chillum fast, and us
had a heap of 'em, sixteen if I 'members right, and soon's
I found out dat I could help feed 'em dat way, I done a
heap of hunting. And everybody knows I's a good hunter.
—*Testimony of former slave Josh Horn to Works Progress
Administration interviewer*

In December 1900, farmer George Washington Trimble of Augusta County,
Virginia, received a letter from a fellow landowner voicing a complaint common
among landed Southerners in the decades after the Civil War: the difficulty in
keeping and managing African-American farm labor. The letter recounted an incident involving a laborer both men knew, William Carter. Mrs. Bell, a neighbor
of the letter writer, was looking for farmhands. Having employed Carter in the past,
Trimble's friend recommended him to Mrs. Bell—a gesture he came to regret.

Mrs. Bell hired Carter, gave him clothes, and agreed to a month's advance on his wages. Carter, on receiving the advance, *"like a nigger, . . . 'skipped by the light of the moon.'"* Carter used the advance to reclaim Jack (a hunting dog) from a Mr. Michael. After recovering the dog, Carter disappeared. "Where he went," Trimble's acquaintance wrote, "the lord only knows; but coon-hunting I guess." For the letter writer, this was the last straw. After years of frustration with the use of freedmen for labor, he vowed never to be taken in again. "[Carter] is one of the *very few* Negroes I would have recommended, but *now* there is *none*. I'll never, *never again*, endorse one of them to anybody for anything, under any circumstances."[1]

The story of William Carter, who abandoned a new job as a farmhand after getting enough money in advanced pay to recover his hunting dog (and, in the process, embarrassed the man who had recommended him for the job), echoes several important facts about life in the agricultural South in the decades after Emancipation. First, the "labor question," as Southern farmers often framed the problem of managing the labor of former slaves, became a central concern of landowners striving to recover from the economic dislocation of the war and the loss of slaves. Second, African Americans' ability to avoid laboring exclusively for whites became linked, as was well understood by employers such as Trimble and his friend, to their ability to find alternative subsistence options. Third, although farmers and landowners worked to establish an economic system that gave most former slaves little choice but to make their living through farm labor, hunting and fishing gave freed people alternative means for subsistence and income.[2] In the case of Carter, recovering his hunting dog enabled him to leave his job as hired farmhand, perhaps earn a portion of his living outside agricultural work, and perhaps escape the control and oversight of white employers. For African Americans, the long-cherished customary rights of hunting and fishing provided distance from white employers by cultivating additional economic and dietary options. For Southern landowners, these rights interfered with their economic success by making it more difficult to narrow former slaves' subsistence options and thus better dominate black labor.

It was clear to white Southerners, almost from the moment of Emancipation, that former slaves had no intention of abandoning their cherished customary rights to hunt and fish. Indeed, the frequency with which freed people of the rural South made fish and game crucial parts of their daily subsistence is confirmed by a virtually limitless number of narrative descriptions from both white and black Southerners. And as demonstrated by the extent to which African Americans used fish and game to enter into a wide array of valuable market activities, former slaves exploited these time-honored survival strategies to the fullest. White Southerners recognized that hunting and fishing provided avenues for liberated African Americans to work toward, and sometimes achieve, a life away from the oversight and control of exclusive agricultural labor. These activities posed a serious and continuing problem for Southern landowners. Both African Americans' reliance on hunting and fishing and whites' consternation over such customs deepened as the subsistence and partial independence provided by fish and game became an increasing point of conflict in the decades after Emancipation.

Thus, at the close of the war, Southern planters faced not only humiliating defeat but also the possible loss of control over their entire labor supply. This great fear, although somewhat assuaged by Northern authorities who soon showed their intention to partially side with the landholding elite in matters of labor contracts, stayed with Southerners for decades. African-American labor could be temporarily forced, through "black codes" designed to limit former slaves' mobility and their ability to refuse laboring for their former masters. Yet most landowners realized by 1867–1868 that, given African Americans' resistance and the interference of federal authorities, a return to slavery—even quasi-slavery—had become impossible. The freedom that came with Emancipation, albeit not total, gave blacks the power to modify the Southern labor system. By the close of the 1860s, the planter's dream of a return to a system much like bondage and the former slave's dream of widespread fee-simple land ownership had melded into a compromise: contract labor, tenancy, and sharecropping. Former slaves, although largely unable to own land, could now migrate, withdraw their families from the field, begin work later in the day and quit earlier, control the pacing of their labor, and hunt and fish.

This serious challenge to Southern employers was a frequent topic in newspapers and agricultural journals. Because elite whites could no longer control the operation of labor, they needed to guarantee its supply. As one contributor noted in *Southern Planter and Farmer* in 1867, "the first and paramount necessity of the colored race within these States is *employment*—permanent and remunerative employment."[3] Planters soon became aware of a general drop in prices and production, which seemed to worsen in the years after the war. "The South is sparsely settled," a planter wrote in 1867, "is scarce of labor, and what [labor] they have, is so much demoralized, by a surfeit of *freedom* 'so called,' that two laborers now perform but little more than one accomplished a few years since, and the loss of a hand or two at a critical time, may lead to most serious loss to the owner of the soil."[4] Planters argued that laborers had become too independent and had too much control over their own workday. According to the "Essay on the Subject of

Labor" by the Goodwyn Agricultural Club, "the wild ardor of the freedmen in the first years of their emancipation, during which they seemed to regard their broken shackles as introducing them to an independence of work . . . left no opportunity to try conclusions or make choice of modes or terms of [labor's] employment."[5] Put simply, freed people had become too independent—they had options. Such independence, particularly former slaves' new capability of providing for themselves, remained the single greatest threat to landowners' ability to recover their wealth and prosperity.

Between Emancipation and the first decades of the twentieth century, hunting and fishing were important subsistence and market activities for African Americans, aiding in their struggle for greater freedom from white domination and for more personal control over their lives and labor. As long-standing customary activities that benefited slaves and free blacks across the South, hunting and fishing now joined other independent economic activities, such as gardening, self-hire, and marketing of homemade goods, through which African Americans loosened the hold of servitude. After the Civil War, hunting and fishing complemented such institutions as black churches, schools, and mutual aid societies as crucial ways in which freed people could guarantee subsistence and avoid falling into dependency on their former masters. Hunting and fishing thus demonstrate how former slaves turned to long-cherished survival strategies to meet the changing economic and social circumstances of life in the postwar South.

For slaves, hunting and fishing had long been critically important customary activities that strengthened their nutritional and material condition, provided food, money, and material goods, and gave them valuable time for family and community camaraderie. After Emancipation, as hunting and fishing became an important part of the transition from slavery to freedom, the tensions engendered by these activities increased—including controversy over freed people's use of firearms, ownership of dogs, use of traditionally scorned plebian sporting methods, entry into a variety of hunting- and fishing-related market activities, and, perhaps most important, ability to apply such traditions to supplement or replace agricultural labor.

Hunting and fishing in the South, before and after Emancipation, rested on a complex web of mutuality and interdependence. African Americans had long acquired fish and game far from the prying eyes of whites, but they had also, for centuries, taken to the field alongside, in service to, or with the full knowledge of whites. The Southern sporting field was racially integrated, a tradition that continued after Emancipation. Former masters and former slaves became well acquainted with each other's sporting aims and methods through decades of sharing common social and productive space. The many conflicts created by hunting and fishing helped define the nineteenth-century rural South, but deep traditions of cooperation often played a countervailing role.

In September 1863, with war still raging across the South, Edward Philbrick, a New Englander working with freedmen in Port Royal, South Carolina, wrote a letter to his friend William C. Gannett describing the fishing activities of two former slaves named Limus and 'Siah (whom both men knew). Philbrick, a devotee of local fish and game who often employed African Americans as oarsmen and laborers, noted that former slaves drew much of their subsistence from fishing. Uneasy with that fact, he was reluctant to order new seines (large fishing nets) requested by Limus and 'Siah. Thinking such equipment a poor investment, Philbrick had arranged for only one seine to be shipped (to Limus), opting to postpone 'Siah's in the hope that his fishing activities might diminish. "Moreover, entre nous, I do not believe it will do him ['Siah] any good to spend his time a-fishing," Philbrick wrote. "After the war the negroes will have to fall back upon field-labor for a living, and it will be better for them if in the meanwhile they do not acquire a distaste for steady labor and get vagrant habits." Many other Northern and Southern whites, confident that former slaves would abandon such means of survival, believed a quick return to agricultural labor would prevent them from developing such "vagrant habits" as fishing.[6]

Yet a letter from Gannett describing Limus's activities in more detail belied Philbrick's hope that freed people might exclusively "fall back upon field labor for a living." Describing Limus as "a black Yankee," someone who "has the energy and *'cuteness* and big eye for his own advantage of a born New Englander," Gannett documented just how substantial the freedman's business interests had become. According to Gannett, Limus owned substantial property, including "poultry-houses, pig-pens, and corn-houses" and "even a stable, for he made out some title to a horse," all of which he maintained through cotton farming and, more importantly, a fishing enterprise. "With a large boat which he owns," Gannett reported, "he usually makes weekly trips to Hilton Head, twenty miles distant, carrying passengers, produce, and fish." Limus had the use of a seine for which "he pays [the] Government by furnishing General Hunter [Major-General David Hunter][7] and staff with the finer specimens, and then has ten to twenty bushels for sale." With the money earned from fishing, combined with his other activities, Limus "is all ready to buy land, and I expect to see him in ten years a tolerably rich man." Gannett concluded by suggesting that such activities were not confined to just one industrious former slave. "Limus has, it is true, but few equals in the islands, and yet there are many who follow not far behind him."[8]

Some freed people, like the former slaves at Port Royal, clearly intended to meet the challenges of freedom through customary traditions that had served them so well under slavery. The ambitious fishing enterprise maintained by Limus suggests that despite the wishes of white observers such as Philbrick, African Americans would not give up such cherished practices in favor of the exclusive agricultural labor that whites saw as the sole path to the South's future prosperity. Former slaves would show tremendous determination and resourcefulness in earning subsistence and income in the decades after Emancipation, and they would work to do so on their own terms.

HUNTING, FISHING, AND SUBSISTENCE AFTER FREEDOM

African Americans intended to maintain old customary rights to meet the new challenges of the postwar South. Although slavery had disappeared, former slaves' nutritional, material, and cultural needs had not. When Robert Glenn, a former slave from Hillsboro, North Carolina, was asked by a WPA interviewer what he had done in 1865 and 1866, he replied simply, "I went back home [to the plantation] and stayed a year. During the year I hunted a lot at night and thoroughly enjoyed being free."[9] Likewise, former Alabama slave George Fortman asserted that after liberation he became a "roustabout," surviving by hunting, between bouts of employment. "There was much wild game to be had and the hunting season was always open," his WPA interviewer noted. "He also remembers many wolves, wild turkeys, catamounts [mountain lion], and deer in abundance near the Grand River."[10] African Americans' continued reliance on the region's wildlife even reached into popular literature. In George Washington Cable's *John March, Southerner*, Cable tells of a postwar meeting between former slaveholder General Halliday and his former slave Cornelius Leggett. Asked if he and his kin are still on the old plantation, Leggett replies: "they ain't ezac'ly on no plantation," admitting that he and his family are "mos'ly strewed round in the woods in pole cabins an' bresh [brush] arbors." Halliday asks if that means they survive by hunting and fishing. "Yaas, sah, livin' on game an' fish," the freedman replies.[11]

Hunting and fishing became natural remedies for the dislocations accompanying Emancipation. Many newly freed African Americans, lacking employment opportunities or sources of income, relied on fish and game to meet their needs. Numerous observers, Southern and Northern, commented on freed slaves' retention of such time-tested survival mechanisms. Immediately after Emancipation, many former slaves chose to eke out a living on the South's seemingly limitless supply of abandoned or unoccupied land rather than work for their former masters. One-time Virginia slave Minnie Fulkes noted how freed people "stay in de woods an' git long best way dey could after freedom done bin 'clared," an ability that angered many white Southerners.[12] As indicated in 1866 letters between farmer and physician James Philip Jones of North Carolina and his cousin, farmer and physician Ethelred Philips of Marianna, Florida, landowners disapproved of such activity. "The negroes are so fond of living off of public lands to themselves and stealing for a subsistence, I don't know who will work next year," the Floridian noted. "The most sanguine among us who early in the spring were hopeful of good crops, have changed their opinions now."[13] His Carolina cousin described a similar type of squatting in the Old North State, noting that "the negroes settled on the public lands will soon not have a squirrel or possum left and then there will be trouble . . . I get a more unfavorable opinion of our future every year."[14] Alarmed by the prospect of former slaves living by means other than white-controlled labor, farmers such as Jones grew uneasy with freed people's ability to hunt and fish.

Many white observers noted the omnipresence of hunting and fishing by freedmen. Ruth McEnery Stuart, in her recollection of nineteenth-century Simpkinsville, Arkansas, described former slave Old Proph (shortened from "Jeremy the Prophet") as someone who "never done nothin' sence freedom but what he had a mind to," but was nevertheless renowned as a woodsman. "They was only one thing Proph' was, to say, good for. Proph' was a capital A-1 hunter—shorest shot in the State, in my opinion, and when he'd take a notion he could go out where nobody wouldn't sight a bird or a squir'l all day long, and he'd fill his game-bag."[15] According to South Carolina's first poet laureate, Archibald Hamilton Rutledge, such sportsmen ranked among the best, and most often overlooked, in the country. "And here I wish to mention perhaps the least known of all American hunters: I mean the Negro," Rutledge declared. "Passing through the South in the autumn or the winter, you recall that you noticed as one of the standard features of the landscape a tattered Negro, with a battered gun under his arm, following a more or less physically shattered cur with no social background whatsoever."[16] It seems white observers could hardly write about the region without commenting on African Americans' hunting and fishing.

Scribner's Monthly correspondent Edward King gave perhaps the best account of the ubiquity of blacks' pursuit of fish and game. Across the South, former slaves expanded their traditional reliance on hunting and fishing. In San Antonio, Texas, King watched "the negro fisherman as he throws his line horizonward, to see it swirl and fall in the retreating surf to come up laden with scaly treasure." In a freed person's community near Beaufort, South Carolina, King noted that "most of the men are armed; they manage to secure a pistol or a gun, and are as fond of hunting as their white employers." Along Alabama's Mobile Bay, King ran across "a negro woman [who] fished silently in a little pool made by the tide." And along the banks of the Savannah River in Georgia, he saw that "[former slaves] are fond of the same pleasures which their late masters give themselves so freely—hunting, fishing, and lounging; pastimes which the superb forests, the noble streams, the charming climate minister to very strongly."[17] For King and other Northerners, a tour of the Reconstruction South left no doubt that hunting and fishing survived the end of slavery and remained important traditions for liberated African Americans.

To slaves, hunting and fishing had been first and foremost sources of food. As slave narratives make clear, masters rarely provided sufficient nourishment. Despite laws requiring minimum food allotments and despite claims by some ex-slaves about adequate diets under slavery, it is clear that many wanted more and better food. As former Texas slave Mary Reynolds put it, "We prays for the end of Trib'lation and the end of beatin's and for shoes that fit our feet. We prayed that us niggers could have all we wanted to eat and special for fresh meat."[18] This deficiency, whether induced by poverty or part of a purposeful strategy by white employers, continued after Emancipation. Life remained hard for former slaves in the rural South; they were often forced to survive on the meanest subsistence, particularly as, beginning in the 1880s, Southern agriculture became notoriously less efficient and more unpredictable.

Freed persons usually had to provide themselves with sufficient food, money, or material goods. Many turned to hunting and fishing. Former North Carolina slave John Evans, for example, "a well-known character for fifty years among the summer residents along the sounds and on Wrightsville Beach," earned a solid living, according to his WPA interviewer, as a "fisherman and huckster in his palmy days." Evans took advantage of coastal Carolina tourism after the war, noting that "when I growed up my job was fishin'. I made enough sellin' fish to the summer folks all along Wrightsville and Greenville sounds to keep me all winter."[19] Former Florida slave Christine Mitchell described life on Amelia Island, a small coastal barrier island near Jacksonville, Florida, that is still a tourist draw for its resorts and fine fishing. According to Mitchell, former slaves turned the island into a community that was "practically self-sustaining, its residents raising their own food, meats, and other commodities. Fishing was a favorite vocation with them, and some of them established themselves as small merchants of sea foods."[20] Like other aspects of slave culture redeployed after liberation, hunting and fishing became two dependable ways in which former slaves could mend the dislocation of Emancipation.

Josh Horn, former slave of Sumter County, Alabama, reportedly won renown as a hunter and guide. "Josh's granddaughters still marvel at his proficiency with a gun," the WPA interviewer noted. "The Horn family grew up eating the raccoons, rabbits, opossums, and deer that Josh had shot . . . The most important meal of the week—Sunday dinner—consisted of possum, deer, or raccoons served with potatoes, collard greens and yeast bread."[21] For Horn, this ability to stretch meager means into certain subsistence was a badge of honor. "I ain't never stole a moufful somepin' t'eat for [my family] in all my life," Horn declared. "It's honest vittles dey et, and varmints I's killed in de woods . . . And everybody knows I's a good hunter." Even years later, Horn still spoke proudly of that ability. "So I went every Friday night and went in de week too, and dat help a lot to feed de chillum," he concluded. "I don't owe nobody, not a nickel."[22]

Freedmen such as Josh Horn plied their skills in a fish and game region that was the equal of any, save perhaps the largely unspoiled American West. "That country was full of varmints—just full," another former slave recalled in the 1930s. "A man could go out and kill a dozen squirrels, they was that thick. Pigeons were thick too, thicker than hens and chickens. They would come over at night, and they would darken the sun, there were so many. Wild ducks were numerous; wild ducks came in droves."[23] Such richness made hunting and fishing obvious options for supplementing poor diets. Former South Carolina slaves Toby Jones and his wife, Govie, who emigrated to Texas in 1869, met the poverty of their hardscrabble existence by using hunting to supplement meager corn harvests. "We didn't plant cotton, 'cause we couldn't eat that," Jones recalled. "I made bows and arrows to kill wild game with, and we never went to a store for nothing. We made our clothes out of animal skins."[24]

Generations of bondage taught former slaves that while customary rights could not guarantee material comfort, they could mean the difference between a degree of economic freedom and continuing dependence on labor in the service of whites. As late as the 1920s, according to James Henry Rice Jr., secretary of the South Carolina Audubon Society, African Americans on St. Helena Island (a small island north of Hilton Head populated by former slaves in the early years of freedom) guaranteed their living by fishing for mullet, oystering, and digging clams.[25] Northerner Julian Ralph, who toured the South when preparing to write his nostalgic *Dixie; or Southern Scenes and Sketches*, asserted that African Americans dominated fishing in New Orleans along the Mississippi shores. "Somebody

An African-American fisherman from Saint James Parish, Louisiana, surrounded by his nets, shows off part of his catch in this photograph from the early 1900s. More than just a valuable source of food, this fishing tradition, as many white complainants noted, helped provide money and economic distance from exclusive labor in the service of white employers. (The Louisiana Collection, State Library of Louisiana, Baton Rouge, Louisiana)

has called fishing 'idle time not idly spent,' and that must be how the Southern colored people regard it, for they seem to be eternally at it wherever they and any piece of water, no matter how small, are thrown together." To Ralph, African Americans' reliance on fishing seemed somehow natural. "After one has seen a few darkies putting their whole souls into fishing it is painful to see a white man with a rod and a line," he concluded. "The white man always looks like an imitation and a fraud."[26]

These narratives are supported by an 1895 study of the dietary habits of African Americans in Eastern Virginia, presented to the U.S. Department of Agriculture (USDA) by Hampton Normal Institute President H. B. Frissell and Lake Erie College chemistry professor Isabel Bevier. The study, "confined to families living in the region bordering the Dismal Swamp, where the style of living was very primitive and the income usually quite limited," found that hunting and fishing contributed substantially to many families' nutritional intake.[27] "Family #211," for example, living near Franklin, Virginia, depended heavily on game provided by a son who supplemented his parents' income from odd jobs and midwifery. "The family used little or no beef, mutton or other lean meats," the study found. "Muskrat, opossum, raccoon, and other game, fish, frogs, turtle, and even snakes in certain seasons, furnished part of their diet." Fishing in the freshwater of the Great Dismal Swamp and the saltwater of the Atlantic proved even more important for the typically impoverished families. The study found the average protein in the typical African-American family's diet was comparable to that of white persons "in moderately comfortable circumstances, such as families of mechanics and families of professional men." The reason was the proximity of fish for food. Of the nineteen families examined near Hampton, Virginia, only two failed to eat a meal of fish during the study. For one family, fish accounted for more than fifty percent of its total dietary protein.[28]

This dependence did not go away as the nineteenth century passed into the twentieth. A 1922 North Carolina State Cooperative Extension Service study, "How Farm Tenants Live," documented the subsistence of Old North State tenants. In the fifty-one tenant households studied, researchers found fifty guns and forty-six dogs.[29] Crediting this high number to the long relationship between farm tenants and the natural bounty of North Carolina, the study's authors declared: "it is impossible to starve or freeze in the country regions of North Carolina. God almighty made the state a paradise for poor folks."[30]

Of course, the degree to which African Americans in the rural South could even partially liberate themselves from regular labor in the service of whites depended heavily on geography. African Americans, like all Southerners, hunted and fished for food, market, and sport across the South, but those in the richer fish and game regions found themselves better positioned to do so. Coastal, riverine, and densely forested and thicketed parts of the South, areas with sufficient wilderness and cover for wildlife propagation, provided former slaves with a bounty of game animals and seafood that created greater independence from whites. As J. William Harris argues, for former slaves along the Georgia coast, the area's rich wildlife, in addition to its cheap, accessible pineland not far from coastal plantations, allowed them to resist wage labor, better pursue independent farming, and become "in effect peasants, centered on their own family farms."[31] Certainly the ability to hunt and fish proved a boon to freed African Americans anywhere, but the more readily available the wildlife, the greater the potential for creating economic alternatives.

The natural bounty of the South may have made it a "paradise for poor folks," especially former slaves, but only because they were innovative in meeting their subsistence requirements. Resourcefulness and opportunism became necessary hallmarks of African Americans' hunting and fishing in the late nineteenth century. Under slavery, individual masters and local and state governments prohibited slaves' ownership of potentially harmful weapons, particularly firearms, and often circumscribed their hunting and fishing.[32] With Emancipation, former slaves found that the problem of obtaining the time, equipment, and financial resources to hunt and fish effectively did not disappear. Guns, for example, though more widely and legally available to African Americans, remained difficult to obtain. White Southerners created barriers such as the various "black codes" implemented across the South in 1866. Prohibitions against gun ownership were added to laws that regulated contract-breaking, restricted mobility, established apprenticeship systems, cracked down on vagrancy, and required African Americans to show proof of employment—all as attempts to return former slaves to semi-servitude. In some Southern states, African Americans even needed licenses to hunt and fish.[33] Whites' fear of an armed black population lurked behind such measures, but firearm restrictions also targeted hunting—a troubling source of subsistence and income that did not require African Americans to be employed by whites.

African Americans obtained guns despite these efforts. The federal government, to the chagrin of Southerners, provided many firearms after the war—a subject of frequent, angry editorials in sporting periodicals. The government's sale of tens of thousands of surplus firearms to anyone who could afford them put many military-grade, albeit often obsolete, firearms into the hands of African Americans. An anonymous 1886 editorial in the New Orleans *Times-Democrat*, for example, blamed the federal government for Louisiana's game depletion, noting that "after the war the government sold about a hundred thousands, more or less, condemned muskets here, at prices that placed them within reach of the lowliest Nimrod in the land."[34] Attorney and renowned turkey hunter Henry Edwards Davis recalled a similar development in the South Carolina Lowcountry, which after the war was "flooded with old smooth-bore army muskets" that reached the hands of local merchants. Davis noted that these surplus weapons "were quickly snapped up by local negroes" at a price of, to his recollection, $3.50 each.[35] With the demise of black codes, the states loosened the legal restrictions on African Americans' gun ownership just as the national government provided surplus weapons. According to one angry Mississippian, "the man and brother, liberated from his shackles, soon scraped up $8 and invested in a pot metal blunderbuss, or an old 'war gun.'"[36]

Despite this wider availability of guns, African Americans still had to get the money to own and use such weapons. Even cheap guns could be out of reach for the poorest people in the cash-strapped rural South. Former Alabama slave Mingo White overcame this by sharing a gun with other former slaves, in particular his friend Ed Davis.[37] It is likely that many financially burdened African Americans acquired the use of a gun in that way.[38] Henry Edwards Davis recalled that the mate of his favorite hunting gun, which had "always been known as the John Gordon gun, as it was one of a matched pair owned by the two brothers John Gordon and Captain Ervin Gordon," made its way into African-American hands in this fashion. "After he bought a good double breech loader, Captain Gordon gave the mate to his son and namesake," Davis recalled, "and it was subsequently acquired by a negro and thus passed into oblivion."[39] Some African Americans worked for years to acquire such valuable means of earning a living. "I always wanted a home and a gun," one former slave recalled, "and I got both of them, but my boy took my gun when they had the riot in St. Louis, and I never did buy another one."[40]

If aggrieved whites can be believed, African Americans made good use of obsolete, damaged, or poor-quality guns. Former slaves loved even these shoddy weapons because they both greatly aided in hunting and, according to a Mississippian writing under the name Coahoma, testified to African Americans' liberation. Slaves relied on trapping or nighttime hunting because "they were not allowed to own guns," Coahoma observed, but since Emancipation "nearly every negro owns a pot-metal shotgun or old musket . . . but eschews possum hunting at night, of which we, who were the sons of slave owners in the old times, cherish fond recollections, as the youthful romances of old plantation life."[41] For those who long depended on hunting but had difficulty making the most of it, even a poor gun symbolized and guaranteed the potential of freedom.

The constant grumblings of white sportsmen about African Americans' weaponry suggests the importance of firearms to freed people. And no one, not even white critics, doubted the weapons' effectiveness. Southern sporting authority Alexander Hunter found an odd nobility in them. "The freedman's musket, battered and patched though it be," he asserted, "must look down upon the handsome, resplendent breech-loader, as a great orator upon the garrulous, loquacious youth who talks upon every subject at any time, and at any length, while he only opens his mouth to make knock-down arguments, or to utter words of great import that thrill and convince."[42] Archibald Rutledge also noted the gap between the appearance of these weapons and their deadly accuracy. Writing of his boyhood friend and hunting mentor Gabriel Myers, "as fine a hunter as any Masai," he recalled that "his weapon was a crude, single-barreled affair, but in this woodman's hands it was deadly."[43] Many former slaves clearly found ways to obtain reliable guns and make the most of them.

In addition to firearms, freedmen also needed powder and shot or cartridges. To deal with this demand, African-American hunters relied on a combination of conservation and cooperation. Ammunition, African Americans had learned under bondage, could not be wasted. Former slave Sylvia King, for example, recalled the extreme care that her fellow slaves used in hunting: "dey didn't shoot if dey could catch it some other way, 'cause powder and lead am scarce."[44] Out of necessity, this frugality continued after Emancipation. Alexander Hunter reported a conversation with a "weather-beaten old darkey" who always took the most careful aim for fear of wasting his ammunition. "It dun cos' me nearly five cents to load that air musket, countin' powder, caps, shot, and everythin'," the pragmatic freedman recalled, "an' I ain't gwine to let er off 'less I knows I'se sartin to make by de shot."[45]

Before conserving their ammunition in such a fashion, African-American sportsmen first had to secure it. And if they could not raise the money, they made other arrangements. A former slave named Uncle Ned used borrowed ammunition to celebrate his wedding, after nearly eighty years on the same plantation. Determined to use his own skill to help feed his wedding guests, Uncle Ned visited a local white "on a borrowing expedition," according to a contributor to *Forest and Stream*. Thus armed with powder and shot, Ned secured five rabbits for the feast.[46] Likewise a *Forest and Stream* contributor calling himself Will Scribbler traded ammunition for information from an African-American sportsman while on a plantation hunt. "Further on we met a native hunting rabbits with a hound and musket who volunteered to show a covey if we would repay his pains with a 'load er two,'" Scribbler recalled. "The terms were easy and we quickly emptied shells enough to satisfy his avarice, demanding that he lead us to the slaughter."[47] Information and experience were something black sportsmen had in abundance, but they often lacked the financial means to obtain proper equipment and so depended on such exchanges to improve their hunting.

Because of the difficulty in acquiring, equipping, and maintaining firearms, African Americans used many sporting methods that did not involve guns. To the necessities of conservation and cooperation in methods for pursuing fish and game we can add a third characteristic—creativity. Some African Americans could not afford firearms. For them, the essence of hunting and fishing became the necessity of doing so whenever and however they could.

Whether armed or unarmed, freed people made dogs an important part of their hunting practice. One of the most cherished traditions carried over from bondage, as demonstrated by Jake Williams and his dog Belle (as recounted in the Introduction), was slaves' reliance on dogs.[48] Because they both helped to provide meat and represented a part of life not dominated by the master, hunting dogs were ubiquitous in slave quarters. J. Vance Lewis, born a slave in Louisiana, noted this dual importance. "The slave loves his dog," he wrote. "They are constant companions. He talks with him by day and hunts with him by night . . . His dog is the only thing under the sun that he can call his own; for the master claims the woman that is called his wife, his offspring, his hut, his pig, his own body—his very soul."[49]

Renowned southern writer Charles H. Smith, writing under the pen name Bill Arp, reached a similar conclusion about the role of dogs in the lives of former slaves. "Dominion is the pride of man—dominion over something," Smith asserted. "A negro is proud if he owns a 'possum' dog."[50] Harry Worcester Smith, while on a Southern excursion, was awoken each morning by an African-American servant who regaled him with proud stories of his father's dogs and hunting prowess. "He told me the names of all the spaniels and how three of them would 'fetch' but he 'spected' the two younger ones would soon learn, that his papa could make a dog do anything," Smith recalled. "He told me the names of the Negroes and how one of them was death on coons and how his papa had killed a great big bear ever so big last fall and there was skin on the floor by my bedside."[51] Northerner Sarah Carter, traveling to Yorktown, Virginia, to teach at a freedman's school, encountered many dogs in a black community near Hampton. "From every house we passed there came out, at least, two, often three dogs. The houses were mostly back from the road, and the dogs ran along the lanes to meet us."[52] Such numbers could be found in black settlements across the South. Travel writer Clifton Johnson noted bluntly that "a nigger always has a dog, a poor nigger has two, and a desperately poor nigger has half a dozen."[53]

Such descriptions matched the reality of African-American life in the rural South that white observers knew all too well. Charles Hallock, describing his hunting of wild cattle on the Georgia coast, recalled a former slave named Sambo who, along with his loyal dog Sanch, led the hunts. According to Hallock, "the twain are officially recognized as law and gospel on all occasions, especially in matters appertaining to the hunting of beasts, the catching of fish, or the entrapping of birds."[54] Archibald Rutledge recounted another such relationship cultivated by his hunting mentor Gabriel Myers. According to Rutledge, Myers's bonds with his animals made him a great huntsman. "A more complete companionship between dog and man could not exist, for to it Gabe brought that strange, wise intimacy that he had with all animals, a peculiar fellowship and understanding that he shared with the creatures of the wild. This comprehension, turned to his account, was what made him the best trapper, hunter and general poaching rounder-up of game in all that country."[55]

Even without dogs and guns, black hunters and fishermen possessed the necessary skill and flexibility to meet their needs. Like slaves before them, freed people learned to catch fish and game through a variety of methods, from the commonplace to the extremely creative. Without guns or dogs, they often turned to trapping skills learned under bondage when, given the obvious time constraints, they depended on devices requiring little attention.[56] After Emancipation, a trap, snare, or other such device that, once set, required only daily or weekly checking and occasional repair was sure to have a permanent place in African Americans' hunting and fishing.

The trapping of game animals and fish not only provided subsistence but also struck at elite white ideals of sportsmanship. A *Forest and Stream* contributor noted the effectiveness of these methods, especially for small game. "I have never seen a trap of any kind set for one which . . . wouldn't catch a coon," the contributor recalled. "In my boyhood days I have seen them caught in boxes set for rabbits at holes in the fence; I have seen them [raccoons] caught by the score in log traps set across fallen trees in the swamp, and by the way that is the darky's favorite way of trapping them."[57] Sussex County, Virginia, resident "Chasseur," writing to *Forest and Stream* in 1875, provides some idea of the magnitude of former slaves' reliance on trapping. Out hunting one day, he came upon a trapping ground popular with African Americans, and "in this cornfield bordering the swamp . . . I counted sixty-eight log traps balled and set. They were placed at regular intervals of about ten yards distant; and this is just an instance—a thousand could be given."[58]

Freedmen also continued to rely on fire hunting, a universal tool of plebian and primitive hunters that was despised by elite sportsmen, who looked on it as dangerous and unsporting. Through the use of torches, hot coals, and even bonfires to illuminate the animals' eyes and make easy targets of potential prey, hunters greatly increased their productivity.[59] Slaves had fire-hunted for decades and, unsurprisingly, freed people carried the practice into the postwar period. Former Virginia slave Sarah Woods Burke recalled her father using fire to provide for the family. "The men folks would build a big fire, and I can remember my Pappy a settin' on top of the house at night with a old flint lock across his legs awaiting for one of these critters to come close enough so he could shoot it."[60] Likewise, John Fox Jr., in his *Blue-Grass and Rhododendron: Out-Doors in Old Kentucky*, described old Ash, "a darky coon-hunter who is known throughout the State," who typically hunted with fire. "In his pockets were matches to build a fire, that the fight could be seen; at his side hung a lantern with which 'to shine his eye' when

the coon was treed; and under him was a meal-sack for Br'er Possum."[61] Henry
William Ravenel noted that farm tenants "would go, two or three together with a
blazing torch, and a good supply of lightwood, into the swamps and thickets
within a mile or two of the plantation. I have often, when a boy, gone out on these
hunts."[62] Well-heeled sportsmen despised such methods, declaring them both destructive to Southern forests and emblematic of blacks' inferiority. Former slaves,
however, prevented by necessity from giving primacy to sportsmanship, embraced
any method that worked.

African Americans across the South employed hunting and fishing methods as
simple as crude wooden clubs and as complicated as intricate weirs. North Carolinian James Lee Love recalled fishing as a child with an older, former-slave companion using only "little hooks, baited with what we called 'fish worms'—now
called 'red-worms' or earth worms, or angle worms—the universal earth worm."[63]
Clifton Johnson witnessed small-game hunting that was decidedly not elaborate.
"If de 'possum git in a small tree, we knock him out, an' if de tree is large, we sometimes cut it down an' sometimes climb up it," one of his black companions noted,
making clear that catching fish or game often required no more than determination and a blunt instrument. "We mos' gener'ly ketch de 'possum alive. He'll bite
yo' if he can, an' we tote him home bu puttin' his tail in a split stick dat pinch it
tight an' keep him remind dat he is ketched."[64]

But not all hunting and fishing was so simple. Henry Edwards Davis, for example, recalled that while some "old gun-carrying negroes" focused on shooting
game on the ground because it was easier, "there were many negroes who were
real shots and hunters who specialized on squirrels and ducks by day, and on treed
raccoons and opossums by night. Most of the squirrels were taken at feed trees, especially oaks and hickories, and the ducks were shot on the water by hunters con-
cealed either in the canes or in the shrubbery bordering it, or in a camouflaged
boat."[65] The Reverend Peter Randolph, who hunted and fished as both slave and
freedman, noted in his *From Slave Cabin to the Pulpit* that fishing was also sometimes quite elaborate, as in the case of a fish trap "made by cutting oak wood into
very small strips, which are tied together with a great deal of ingenuity."[66] This
range of methods and devices confirms that function, not form, guided those who
lacked the luxury of conforming to white sporting ideals.

HUNTING AND FISHING AND MARKET RELATIONS

The ability to acquire fish and game through methods both commonplace and
creative ultimately had value for both former slaves and their employers. Like an-

tebellum planters who reduced costs by allowing slaves to hunt and fish, postwar agricultural employers, in many cases still responsible for feeding tenants and laborers, often provided fish and game to African-American farmhands. Simeon H. Duffer, overseer for Isaac Coles Carrington's Sylvan Hill plantation in Charlotte County, Virginia, relied on wild hogs to feed his laborers. Throughout November 1866, Duffer assigned between one and four farmhands the task of hunting hogs for the Southside plantation.[67] To provision farmhands on his Pampatike plantation in King William County, Virginia, Thomas Henry Carter relied on locally caught fish. His 1875 ledger shows that he bought substantial amounts of shad from employees. Between April 5 and May 13, Carter received 34 shad from Polk Gary, for which he paid a total of $2.80 plus credit on an order to Hay & Co., presumably a general goods company. Between April 6 and May 4, Carter received 41 shad from Jim Nelson, for which he paid a total of $4.30.[68] So cheaply could fish and game be obtained in some parts of the South that many employers enthusiastically adopted this practice.

Even as late as the first decade of the twentieth century, some planters made wildlife a substantial part of laborers' diets. B. F. Fly, for example, lauded his own ability to feed laborers on his Ogden, Arkansas, farm in this fashion. "In the fishing season . . . niggers are fed black bass in preference to 'sow belly' because I find it much cheaper," Fly wrote in a letter to the *National Sportsman*. During the winter, Fly fed his farmhands on a variety of fish and game, including "canvas backs, mallards, sprig tails, swan bills, butter balls, teals, wood ducks and the like for the same reason, now and then giving them venison, turkey, quail, squirrel, coon, possum and the like for appetizers." This generosity, according to Fly, gave him a strong reputation among area laborers. "The niggers all say that 'Mars Frank sho do feed his niggers good,'" he declared.[69]

It is likely, however, that employees' approval was not the central motivation for these additions to their diet. Much like antebellum masters who boasted about their benevolent treatment of well-fed, contented slaves, postwar landowners covered their drive to save money in a veneer of concern for laborers' well being. Although not legally bound, as were their antebellum counterparts, to feed laborers, many thought it good business. South Carolinian John Edwin Fripp, before selling his plantation to become overseer for the Chelsea Plantation Club (a Beaufort County sportsmen's association), fed his laborers on fish provided by local African Americans, many of whom were his own farmhands. Fripp's account books from 1872 to 1877 show that he regularly rented boats to laborers (including Glasgow, Greaves, Peter, and Tom) for between $1.00 and $1.50, and purchased the fish they caught.[70]

The plantation huntsman or fisherman, usually a trusted farmhand who provided meat and fish for storehouse or table, remained another holdover from the antebellum period.[71] Ambrose Gonzales, cofounder of the South Carolina daily *The State*, recalled the prowess of former slave Boatswain Smashum, or Bo'sun, who "became an expert horseman" and "as he was quick and intelligent" eventually became a loyal and trusted huntsman and deer-driver to a Major King.[72] South Carolinian Anne Simon Deas, in her Comingtee plantation memoir, described "old 'Josh Lovely,'" huntsman for Alwyn Ball as slave and freedman. According to Deas, Lovely was "as fond of hunting as his master, to whom he was much attached. He was a daring rider, and would risk anything when well mounted."[73]

The descriptions of Bo'sun and Lovely demonstrate how former slaves often spent as much time hunting alongside whites as hunting independently. One of the chief concerns of Texas slave J. Vance Lewis on liberation was dissolving his long-standing hunting relationship with his master's son, Cage Duncan. Lewis recalled that "there was also a very difficult problem for us to solve—we had three coon dogs which we jointly owned, and I did not see how to divide the dogs without hurting his feelings, my feelings or the dogs' feelings, without relinquishing my claims, which I was loathe to do."[74] After liberation, such sporting ties often continued. Louisianan B. H. Wilkins, whose family emigrated to Charles City County, Virginia, at the end of the war, recalled getting food secured by "a former slave named Robert," hired to both labor and procure meat.[75] "He was a good trapper, hunter, and woodcraftsman," Wilkins recalled, "and could guide us hunting or fishing through the woods and swamps, when the crops were laid by."[76] Likewise, Patti Jane Watkins Scott, diarist of the Charlotte County, Virginia, Bartees plantation, noted that her son often hunted or fished with hired hands. Entries such as "Embry has been out nearly the whole day putting up the geese & hunting with Mose," dated February 9, 1883, typify the way that whites used African-American sporting skill for their own benefit.[77]

Aside from hiring former slaves to hunt and fish for and with them, employers and landowners relied on freed people to protect their property from pests or predators. Some animals proved expensive nuisances; to counter such threats, most state or county governments offered cash bounties on certain birds and other animals, including, depending on the region, wolves, crows, hawks, and rattlesnakes.[78] Such bounties primarily served agricultural interests, but also helped sporting clubs protect wildlife supplies from predators.[79] While overseer and gamekeeper for the Chelsea Plantation Club, John Edwin Fripp offered bounties for hawks.[80] He recorded the bounties, paid when the claimant produced the head of each animal killed, in his daybook. At 15 cents per head, the bounties apparently became popular with area hunters. In 1904, the year Fripp most consistently kept track of such payouts, Charles Scott offered 58 hawks for a total of $8.70. At a time when unskilled laborers might receive between $6.00 and $15.00 per month, depending on the region, crop, and prices, such income was extremely valuable. Other local laborers also collected Chelsea bounties, including Rufus Brown ($1.80), "John Brown's Children" ($2.10), and brothers Charlie and Frank Palmer ($3.15). This extra money, which farmhands typically earned during free time, on days off, and over the winter months, provided a valuable source of income that white interests would most likely not begrudge.[81]

African-American hunters, aside from earning bounties for nuisance animals, also found employment protecting crops at harvest time. Marauding birds could devastate ripe rice, corn, and other crops. To meet this threat, planters sometimes employed bird-minders. According to Archibald Rutledge, "the only way to keep birds from ruining a crop is to send Negro bird-hunters into the rice after them."[82] Fletcher Coyne, writing for New York's *Frank Leslie's Popular Monthly*, asserted that "the 'bird-minders' formed a very important and happy throng during the season when birds made their onslaught on the rice crop." Squads of laborers took to the field each season when "it became necessary to keep the May-birds off at the early dawn, by the shooting of guns, the cracking of whips and the loud shouts of the merry 'bird-minders.'"[83] Former Arkansas slave Scott Bond also commented on this necessity, noting that "it was next to impossible to make a corn crop unless there was some one to hunt at night and guard the fields of ripening grain. If this was not done, the farms would be stripped of their corn."[84] The need to protect crops from birds proved a boon for the hired bird-minders. African Americans, if permitted, ate or marketed the birds, making bird-minding both popular and remunerative. James Henry Rice Jr. recalled that to drive bobolink (a small New World blackbird) from fields, "little negroes were given muskets and plenty of cheap black powder. In bird season there was a continuous rattle, sounding like a battle was in progress." Rice was careful to note, however, that real ammunition "was never given the negroes, because they would shoot down the birds and stop to pick them up, allowing others to devour rice," demonstrating that, if given the opportunity, African Americans would first meet their own needs.[85] Bounties and the income from bird-minding were just two more ways that former slaves reaped the financial benefits of fish and game.[86]

Hunting and fishing also proved invaluable ways for freedmen to enter into crucial market activities. This was a middle ground between cooperation and conflict that characterized Southern hunting and fishing, with the ability to market fish and game making those activities so valuable to African Americans and so irksome to whites. Marketing fish and game provided economic options for former slaves that white landowners sometimes could not control and often did not condone. Yet whites frequently employed African-American hunters and fishermen and often bought their fish and game. Without whites' involvement these market activities would not have been possible. It is ironic, then, that while white Southerners' role in and dependence on former slaves' hunting and fishing guaranteed that such activities would remain potentially lucrative for black Southerners, African Americans' marketing of fish and game guaranteed that these activities would remain a permanent source of conflict.

Most fish and game marketed by African Americans provided only supplementary income. Because hunting and fishing were seasonal and because most rural blacks farmed for a living, fish and game had to be caught and marketed wherever and however the opportunities arose. Clifton Johnson met an unnamed African-American tar burner who always took his gun and hounds with him on the way to and from his daily work.[87] Former Texas slave Virginia Bell recalled that "pappy used to catch rabbits and take them to town and sell them or trade them for somethin' to eat, and you know that wasn't much, 'cause you can't get much for a little ol' rabbit."[88] *Recreation* contributor Frank Farner described former slaves Gabe and his wife, Clare, who turned hunting into economic opportunities to which they both contributed. Gabe was known to hunt in the bayous near their Mississippi River basin home, catching small game such as opossum for his wife to prepare for hungry white travelers. In the case of Farner and his friend George, who had traveled South for a bear hunt, Clare sold them a full opossum dinner for what she decided was "'mos too much faw sich a poo meal," while Gabe informed the men of the best nearby places to hunt in exchange for "a generous quantity of flat sweet store terbacker." Such income was important, particularly to a pair of ostensibly poor bayou denizens such as Gabe and Clare.[89]

Narrative evidence indicates that African Americans marketed most fish and game locally, particularly to nearby whites with available hard cash. Describing South Carolina rice birds, or bobolinks (abundant in the Lowcountry during autumn), a writer calling himself Lawtonvillian noted that former slaves killed these birds in great quantity, taking them to town to sell for whatever they could get. Consumers and wholesalers at the South Carolina markets that absorbed such game paid, in 1876, 5 cents per pound for turkey, 20 cents per pair for quail, and individually negotiated prices for the scarcer, more coveted woodcock.[90] Frances Butler Leigh indicated that at war's end, in Georgia, it became difficult to find much meat other than that obtained locally, often through former slaves. "Yes-

A 1912 postcard, created by photographer F. Marchant of Hamlet, North Carolina, depicts an elderly African-American man proudly displaying his captured opossum. Images of this type illustrate the connection between people of color and hunting, and such scenes played a key role in white audiences' common assumptions about Southern black life. (Courtesy of Florida Photographic Collection, State Library and Archives of Florida)

terday one of the negroes shot and gave me a magnificent wild turkey, which we roasted on one stick set up between two others before the fire, and capital it was," Leigh recalled. "Our food consists of corn and rice bread, rice, and fish caught fresh every morning out of the river, oysters, turtle soup, and occasionally a wild turkey or duck. Other meat, as yet, it is impossible to get."[91]

Touring the Norfolk, Virginia, waterfront in 1874, Edward King witnessed the work of "barelegged negro boys sculling in the skiffs which they had half-filled with oysters, and passed through streets entirely devoted to the establishments where the bivalve, torn from his shell, was packed in cans and stored to await his journey to the far West."[92] James Henry Rice Jr. claimed that African-American children dominated the trade at the Georgetown, South Carolina, rail terminus where fish and game were shipped north and west. Near harvest season, local children descended on rice fields in the early morning, when birds that had gorged themselves overnight were sluggish to the point of immobility, collected large quantities of the birds, and took them to town for sale. "They received two cents a dozen for this and made money at it," Rice noted. "To give an idea of the enormous number shipped, one firm in Georgetown shipped sixty thousand dozen or better in a single season."[93]

African Americans also marketed other animal products acquired through hunting and fishing, besides meat. Elizabeth Allston Pringle of South Carolina (writing under the pen name Patience Pennington) recalled that two tenants, Mr. and Mrs. Z, obtained food and money by catching and selling fish, often to Pringle herself. Mrs. Z also made "flowers" out of the fish scales, and strung them and sold them as necklaces to local whites, charging 50 cents per necklace.[94] Descriptions of such practices even pervaded sporting poetry. M. L. Murdock contributed a poem to *Recreation* in which he recalled the fine hunting dogs sold by African-American Pop Peters:

> Pop Peters kep' a beagle hound,
> Bow-legged as a Turk,
> Fer runnin' rabbits, I'll be bound,
> She done jes fancy work.
> Pop held her pups fer 5 apiece,
> And fast as they wud wean,
> He sold 'em off as slick as grease,
> Though they looked mighty mean.[95]

With experience drawn from centuries of servitude, no one knew better than former slaves how to exploit hunting and fishing. African Americans sold meat and hunting dogs (by reputation, the best in the South if raised by former slaves) and also marketed animals' skins, teeth, bones, hooves, and products manufactured from them, such as Mrs. Z's necklaces. Alexander Hunter had employed an aged African American named Zeb West to lead him and a cousin on an eastern North Carolina raccoon hunt. Judging by what he saw in West's cabin, Hunter noted, "there certainly must be plenty of coons, for scores of their skins were nailed over wall and roof to dry." West later told him he sold skins for 25 cents each. In that hunt alone, they caught nine raccoons. If Hunter allowed West to keep them, a customary practice among elite white sportsmen (who typically thought the raccoon beneath them), that night's work could have yielded $2.25 for West.[96] *Forest and Stream* contributor Chasseur, writing in 1875, asserted that with the growing popularity of keeping fawns (baby deer) as pets, African Americans in the Nottoway region of Virginia "catch many of them to sell in the Petersburg markets."[97] Hunting and fishing under bondage had imparted the crucial lesson that no animal, or part of an animal, that could be sold or consumed should be squandered.

Freed people exploited fish and game to the fullest, and the cash from marketing became a larger part of their survival than during slavery. Alongside many extant references to African Americans supplementing their income through hunting or fishing, there are occasional examples of former slaves making all or nearly all of their living from these activities. Growing up on his South Carolina plantation, Hickory Grove, Henry Edwards Davis knew that African Americans would work there only when necessary, preferring to survive through more agreeable means. There was "old George, who spent practically all of his time when awake hunting and fishing and who had as much aversion to work as a goat had to rain," and who derived most of his living in that fashion. Of a "musket toter" named Old John, Davis recalled: "I saw him frequently for years and I never saw him without his musket and I never knew him to do any work, as that was reserved for his wife and children." Finally there was Stephen Brown, "the best hunter and fisherman among the plantation negroes of Hickory Grove," who "had considerable aversion to work but who made a good living for himself and his family out of Santee Swamp with his musket, fishing cane and a few cur coon dogs . . . He specialized in ducks, turkeys, fish and coon hides."[98] African Americans such as old George, Old John, and Stephen Brown struggled to avoid being forced to labor exclusively for whites. Hunting and fishing made a relatively independent subsistence, if rarely lucrative, at least much more likely. Each animal killed or captured, each carcass or hide marketed, each pup trained and sold, represented another step in the quest to cultivate that independence. Edward King noted that "if [the former slave] settles on a small tract of land on his own, as so many thousands do now-a-days, he becomes almost a cumberer of the ground, caring for nothing save to get a living, and raising only a bale of cotton or so wherewith to get 'supplies.'" This independent subsistence away from regular farm labor posed a problem for white employers. "For the rest he can fish and hunt," King concluded. "He doesn't care to become a scientific farmer."[99]

Few African Americans completely escaped laboring for whites, but it did happen. If lucky and hard working, some might transform hunting and fishing into lucrative economic enterprises that became the envy, and sometimes the bane, of white observers. Baltimore sportsman "Delmo," for example, writing to *Rod and Gun and American Sportsman* in 1875, noted that African Americans dominated local terrapin hunting, a dominance that led to moneymaking opportunities. "These men make very good wages during the early part of the season," Delmo noted, "as two men will sometimes capture as high as twenty terrapins in a day."[100] African Americans had reportedly dominated large-scale terrapin hunting, particularly in Maryland, Virginia, and the Carolinas, for well over a century. After

Emancipation, their hold on the market continued. Baltimore resident Edward A. Robinson, writing to *Forest and Stream* in 1899, described African Americans' terrapin hunting on Harris' Neck, a small strip of land near Barbour Island River, McIntosh County, Georgia. Noting that Harris' Neck is "owned and operated entirely by negroes" and that "many of the negroes follow catching [terrapin] for a living," Robinson went on to describe the market work of two African Americans, Grant, who ran the terrapin market, and his associate Pat. "Each terrapin as it is brought out is held against a notched measure, and Grant would call out the size to Pat, who would put it down in his book," Robinson noted. "These fellows in the height of the season make from $15 to $20 per week."[101] The traditional association between hunting or fishing and African-American labor, combined with the long-term material and financial products of such associations, provided rare openings for more formal business opportunities.

By the late nineteenth century, rice planter Elizabeth Allston Pringle, against the advice of family and friends, had managed to purchase her late husband's White House plantation near Georgetown, South Carolina, her own family's Cherokee plantation, also in Georgetown, and even a summer home in North Carolina's renowned "Sapphire Country," the popular resort area in the state's mountain west. At both Georgetown and her North Carolina "castle in the air," Pringle's farmhands did substantial fishing, including netting and seining in area waterways and establishing marketing networks to sell their shad. Problems began when a North Carolina employee named King, or King Stork, started an efficient fishing business in the rich area rivers and streams. Pringle, at the time planning to sell the mountain getaway, discovered that such constant fishing was lowering the value of her property.[102] Once she even agreed to an offer, "but the purchaser withdrew; it is so with everything—no one wants to buy anything. If our valiant, voracious, and vivacious King Stork would only desist from his activities while a few small creatures were left it would be a mercy; but I fear when he gets through, there will be none but sharks, devil-fish, and swordfish left." Some time later, King asked to be given a house on the South Carolina White House property, where he might expand his business. "He is absolutely worthless and unreliable," Pringle declared, "but he spoke of his large family and how necessary it was for him to get where he could pursue his business of shadding, and Casa Bianca [White House] was the very best pitch of tide for the shad fishing." Pringle saw in King's request a way to keep him happy and protect the resale value of the North Carolina getaway. "He gave me an idea, and I told him he could have the house if he would give me two shad a week during the shad season, two and a half months. This he most willingly agreed to do." Pringle hoped that through this accommodation she could sell her North Carolina property, obtain free fish, and draw more efficient labor from a contented King.

At the time King was still fishing in North Carolina, Pringle dealt with similar problems at the South Carolina White House and Cherokee plantations, where farmhands were taking shad and other fish without giving her anything in return. "I never have been able to get any tribute at all from the shad nets, which are set in front of my doors all winter," she declared. "Five or six men shad there regularly, but they elude all demands, and I rarely eat a shad, as they are too great a luxury for me to buy unless I have company; they are like the wild ducks which swarm in the rice fields at night in the winter, 'so near and yet so far.'" Worse still, her South Carolina farmhands had more interest in fishing than in working in the rice fields. "They planted five acres of rice-land apiece," she noted, "but did not work it at all, so they did not pay their rent, and I know they would do worse this year. It has proved a splendid crop year, and they could get $1.15 a bushel for their rice, but they have none, because they were too lazy to work at it." Feeling desperate, Pringle promoted one of the farmhands, Nat, to overseer and charged him with stamping out the intractability. When that failed, Pringle discharged the most uncooperative of the crew. "I told Nat to do the best he could with the few left," she recalled, "and to extract a shad a week from the fishermen who are now spreading their nets in the river just in front of the house."[103]

Probably few former slaves turned hunting or fishing into such lucrative, semipermanent enterprises, but examples can be found—demonstrating that African Americans tried to expand customary activities to their limit. The Reverend Irving E. Lowery, once a slave in Sumter County, South Carolina, recalled that former slaves in Charleston seized every opportunity: "in Charleston, the butcher's business is largely controlled by colored men. This is true both in the down-town market and also in the green grocery business, as it is called, throughout the city." He recalled that one person in particular, "C. C. Leslie, the colored fish merchant, did a fine business for nearly thirty years. He did a heavy business in supplying the local market, and shipped large quantities of fish to all parts of the State to both white and colored customers."[104] Cities such as Charleston, blessed with plentiful nearby wildlife, accessible rivers, and a thriving port, became key markets for African Americans' fish and game. Leslie was not alone in his success there.

In a lawsuit in the 1890s, Charles Pringle Alston, a planter of Georgetown, South Carolina, tried to make an example of African Americans who worked to secure their livings in such a fashion. He was trying to stop trespassing on his lands between the Waccamaw River and the Atlantic Ocean by people who "have undertaken to trespass and invade upon plaintiff's said marsh land and creeks, and to take and remove the clams and other shell fish from the beds of the creeks and also fish and seine and remove the fish from the said creeks and in addition to habitually trespass upon, shoot, frighten and scare off the game upon the said described property." Alston initially accused two area residents, Edmund Cain and Isam Miller, both white, of the trespassing. Cain and Miller informed him that African Americans were responsible. Alston eventually sued a white man named J. F. Limehouse, whom the court found to have "a large number of flat bottom boats to lend to negroes to depredate all the surrounding creeks, & he continues to send up to the cannery every week oysters & clams by the flat load." In addition to Limehouse, Alston sued other men, both black and white, "fishermen who fish and gather oysters, clams and other shell fish for a living," eventually securing an injunction to stop the defendants' hunting, fishing, and oystering on his lands. For Alston and other landowners, trespassing by hunters and fishermen, prompted by marketing opportunities, created both an annoyance and a serious financial burden.[105]

Other white observers also noted the ubiquity of these hunting, fishing, and marketing activities by African Americans. According to Robert Barnwell Roosevelt, naturalist, U.S. Fisheries Commission founder, and uncle of Theodore Roosevelt, "all around Charleston the Negroes seem to be in possession of the country . . . It is they who supply the Charleston market, it is they who do the fishing and the work." He also commented on similar activities across the South, indicating that wherever there was money to be made through hunting or fishing, former slaves waited to take advantage. Traveling through Fernandino, Florida, R. B. Roosevelt noted, "we found the colored population, which takes to fishing as naturally as the bee is nautically supposed to take to a tar bucket, everywhere, pursuing the finny tribes through the numerous creeks and arms of the sea." He also claimed that by the 1880s, African Americans' market activities also threatened the once plentiful supply of rail (a wetland game bird found in many parts of the South). "It is only of late years that many of the rail were killed at the South," Roosevelt opined. "The old-time battue [beating of vegetation to flush game] of the Negroes at night time, with paddles and torches, did not amount to much, but now hundreds [of rail] are killed daily through the season in the rivers below Washington, although the weather is usually so hot that half of them spoil."[106] For Roosevelt and other white observers, it was obvious that African Americans had stepped up their sporting activities since liberation. For many, particularly landowners and sportsmen, that fact would become a source of consternation.

Black Southerners, then, hunted and fished all across the region and, when

In a 1903 photograph, an African-American fish vendor sells his wares in the street, probably in Augusta, Georgia. This was a common sight in Southern cities and towns in coastal and riparian parts of the region. Selling fish and game provided African Americans not only with food but also with an entry into valuable market activities, which they expanded as best they could. (Courtesy of the Library of Congress)

able, used those activities in the richer fish and game areas—particularly in the coastal and riparian South—to create market opportunities that sometimes allowed them to break free from dependence on white employers. Independence became the greatest benefit of such marketing opportunities. African Americans cultivated independence from the poor nutrition that plagued so many lower-class Southerners, particularly former slaves; independence from white-imposed definitions of acceptable means of earning a living; and, perhaps most valuable, independence from whites' efforts to restrict their subsistence options. That independence gave many African Americans greater opportunity to improve their financial and material condition and greater experience with a more unrestricted, autonomous subsistence than they had ever known. Both outcomes carried the potential for increasing the distance between former slaves and their former masters.

HUNTING AND FISHING AND THE "LABOR QUESTION"

In her reminiscence of nineteenth-century Fayetteville, North Carolina, Sally Hawthorne wrote of the role of the swamps as safe havens for plebian populations. She noted that the tradition began with Native Americans, who "were at home in the swamps, hunting and fishing," eventually making the swamps a retreat for "a motley crew of free negroes who were no credit to their race, some runaway slaves, as well as . . . a few white men, who for one reason or another, were in hiding," all of whom used the wildlife of the swamp to eke out a living.[107]

The existence of such a refuge annoyed planters but, according to Hawthorne, none felt compelled to act. That changed after Emancipation, when planters began having trouble finding "workers from among those who had always lived on the plantation." Apparently, too many former slaves had taken to area swamps, drawing on customary practices such as hunting and fishing to guarantee subsistence. "One and all, when they had no money to buy what the islands did not produce," Hawthorne noted, "just paddled along the stream to the most likely place and helped themselves to anything that came in sight." This led to an even greater nuisance when the swamps became a base for depredations against local plantations, through the theft of livestock, food, and goods from stores and smokehouses. According to Hawthorne, the military eventually stepped in to deal with the crime originating from this swamp community. Over time, as development intruded on the swamps, civilization and capitalization spoiled them as a potential escape from plantation labor. Within a few decades of the Civil War, according to Hawthorne, the African-American population that had made the swamps its home had been all but driven out.[108]

Buried in Hawthorne's dubious yet highly intriguing account are significant truths about African-American economic life and subsistence in the rural South before and after Emancipation. First, the use of hunting and fishing to resist attempts to force former slaves into employment that limited their freedom was deeply rooted in black culture. As the similarities between hunting and fishing before and after liberation suggest, the desire to exploit fish and game to its fullest reflected African Americans' willingness to employ cherished survival mechanisms carried over from bondage. Second, the nutritional and financial rewards of hunting and fishing, if utilized to their fullest, could greatly improve former slaves' material circumstances. Those such as King Stork, who turned shad fishing into lucrative businesses in North and South Carolina, and C. C. Leslie, who became one of the best-known fish merchants in the Deep South, seized the opportunity to take control of their own livelihoods.

Many white Southerners, as evidenced by the reaction of Fayetteville residents to the swamp community, did not respond favorably to blacks' long-term exploitation of Southern environs. Planters and employers often thought of African Americans' hunting and fishing as strictly sources of money and provisions. But as independent actions that pulled former slaves away from regular labor, or as market endeavors that gave African Americans a chance to live apart from whites' control, hunting and fishing threatened the South's labor discipline and its racial hierarchy. Employers and landlords had always been anxious about labor tractability and would, as the postwar period wore on, become increasingly alarmed by this perceived erosion of white supremacy.

The natural bounty of the South was frequently heralded by white elites as one of the greatest attractions of the region, but they described its enabling former slaves to survive apart from agricultural labor in decidedly negative terms. As noted in an 1868 editorial in the Charlotte, North Carolina, monthly *The Land We Love*, "we might attribute the negro's indolence to nature's bounty which . . . often gave food in return for the mere stretching forth the hand."[109] R. L. Dabney noted that in a region as naturally blessed as the South, "the last freedman multiplies, unstinted by his poverty," allowing former slaves to survive without an obligation to hard work. Living in a region with a mild climate, short winter, and bountiful fish, game, and forage, former slaves could work less diligently and, "between these various resources, country Negroes [could] manage to sustain those low conditions of existence, which enable so low a race to multiply; and they multiply on, as yet, very much as in old times."[110] As Southern whites had long been aware, customary practices such as hunting and fishing were common ways in which former slaves exploited such bounty.

Frances Butler Leigh described that connection between the natural bounty and former slaves' unwillingness to labor for whites. Like other planters, her father had tried a variety of means to get his laborers to work, but "as for starving them into this, that is impossible too, for it is a well-known fact that you can't starve a negro." There were "about a dozen" African-American laborers on the Leigh family's Butler's Island, Georgia, plantation "who do no work, consequently get no wages and no food, and I see no difference whatever in their condition and those who get twelve dollars a month and full rations." The situation was explained by blacks' ability to feed themselves by means other than exclusive labor in the service of whites. "They all raise a little corn and sweet potatoes," Leigh noted, "and with their facilities for catching fish and oysters, and shooting wild game, they have as much to eat as they want . . . not yet having learned to want things that money alone can give."[111] The quest for "things that money alone can give" was, in the opinion of Southern landowners, incompatible with the freedom from controlled labor that customary rights could provide.

The almost constant complaints about African Americans' hunting and fishing made by frustrated Southern landowners, sportsmen, and lawmakers, from Emancipation through the 1920s, demonstrate the vital link between the "labor question" and African Americans' customary rights. Almost as soon as the Civil War ended, planters began to lodge complaints about labor irregularity that cited hunting and fishing as a contributing cause. Susan Dabney Smedes, daughter of Virginia and Mississippi planter Thomas S. Dabney, wrote that her father "had small patience for the shiftless, lazy ways of the negro race after they were set free . . . Tenants were brought in from other plantations, but they were more fond of barbecues and big meetings and hunting and fishing than of keeping the grass out of the fields."[112] Indeed, almost as soon as slaves became freed people, complaints linking hunting and fishing with labor evasion became commonplace. "The most of the former laborers are here, but won't *labor*," one South Carolinian complained. "The negroes . . . can do with very little bread—live on fish and oysters, coons, &c., &c. There being therefore but little necessity for labor, very little work is done by the negroes . . . I am fully satisfied the negro now . . . is not able to do more than one fourth of the hard work he could easily have done when a slave."[113] The editor of *Southern Planter and Farmer* put the matter even more bluntly in July 1877: "There are portions of the state where it is almost next to impossible to procure any reliable labor. In the ability on the part of the idle Negroes there to hunt and fish at will is to be found the cause; and the sooner that is corrected the better."[114]

In some cases, African Americans could use hunting and fishing to avoid working for white planters entirely, as in the case of William Carter, who disappeared with his hunting dog Jack. In other cases they might work for whites only when absolutely necessary. For decades after Emancipation, agricultural employers were burdened with the knowledge that laborers could subsist on hunting and fishing. "In Tidewater Virginia there is frequently difficulty in getting sufficient supply of labor during the fishing season," wrote Thomas Pollard, former Virginia Commissioner of Agriculture, in 1883.[115] Another observer noted that "we try to treat [black laborers] fairly, and to impress them with the idea that we take an interest in them, which we really do. Yet with all this, when fish bite, they will go fishing, no matter how important their labor may be."[116] Likewise, Mississippian Andrews Wilkinson described former slave Ebenezer—whose name he shortened to "Ebony for the convenience of brevity, and for cause"—as a devoted hunter and fisherman. "He was born with a passion for hunting and fishing which far exceeded even his fondness for shirking his alleged work most of the day or loitering with idle companions of his own race half the night on the back streets of the little Mississippi town."[117]

White commentators believed these occurrences to be symptomatic of African Americans' idleness and used such examples as the basis of many of the late nineteenth century's most enduring negative characterizations of people of color. But these accounts reflected much more than racial stereotypes. They also reflected rural African Americans' ability for using hunting and fishing to minimize whites' control of their labor, to avoid work relationships that smacked of quasi-slavery, and to reject elite-espoused values of a "free" labor system, if that meant reduced freedom and the loss of cherished customary rights. "In the mind of the negro a great deal of idle time is the *sine qua non* of happiness," wrote Jas. H. Oliphant of Stellaville, Georgia, in 1875. "Since he has been set free, he has taxed his limited intellect to the utmost to discover some plan by which he can give a large portion of his time to fishing, hunting, meetings, visiting, politics, and general idleness; but how to make money, accumulate property, and secure the solid foundations of life, are questions with him of minor importance."[118] Such comments are often dismissed as simply landowners' racist frustrations. I would suggest, however, that for former slaves, such ways of accumulating the "solid foundations of life," if that meant abandoning traditions that served them so well under bondage, might very well have been "questions of minor importance."

More important to African Americans was the role of hunting and fishing in helping them make the most of their freedom. Frances Butler Leigh noted that freed people in Georgia "were encouraged in the idea that freedom meant no work, twenty acres of land, a mule, a gun, a watch, and an umbrella," things largely denied them as slaves and symbolic of both material improvement and independence.[119] Philip A. Bruce hinted that this desire to avoid whites' control and achieve independent subsistence had strong links to both the acts and products of hunting and fishing. He described the living conditions of freed people in Southside Virginia who managed to live, away from whites' oversight, "on a few acres that lie on the backbone of a vast ridge, far removed from every stream and apparently from all trace of civilization." In these harsh conditions, with their few crops, vegetables from their small gardens, and "the animals that they trap or shoot in the neighboring woods, they keep their families alive, but the struggle to do so is continuous, and barely successful." Yet to Bruce's surprise, "they prefer to live as they do . . . where they are at liberty to act as they choose, to working on the most extensive and prosperous of the adjacent plantations."[120]

For employers, blacks' subsistence activities became sources of idleness and inefficiency; but for African Americans, they brought a measure of economic and physical independence. Over time, their ability to obtain fish and game, which for landlords might otherwise be merely an annoyance, could evolve into activities that presented an overt threat to whites' economic world. Robert Henderson Allen, a planter of Lunenburg County, Virginia, outlined the harmful effects of such activities. "No work done today," he wrote in his diary on December 13, 1867. "All our Freedman laborers went hair [*sic*] hunting. Indeed they are perfectly worthless. Have not made expenses generally since the war, and there is no remedy . . . and the labor system grows worse and less effective every day."[121]

Constant complaints about hunting and fishing as the cause of lost work time on farms and plantations mounted in the postwar South. Elizabeth Allston Pringle, whose problems with laborer and fishing entrepreneur King Stork left her in no doubt as to former slaves' attachment to such customary activities, frequently lamented blacks' penchant for abandoning work for field, forest, and stream. A farmhand named Gibbie had to be scolded several times for bad work habits. "Yesterday I gave Gibbie a severe talk because of his total neglect of work," she wrote, "the stables not cleaned, no pine straw hauled for bedding, the calves starved, yet the cows only half milked." She suggested that he failed to complete certain tasks "because he is in such haste to go out hunting." Gibbie was working less and hunting more, which alarmed Pringle both for its impact on her labor supply and its apparent influence on Gibbie's interactions with his employers. Describing the chiding she gave him, she noted that "he is intoxicated with the rice bird and coot fever and spends every night out hunting, and of course in the day he is too sleepy to do anything. He answered almost insolently for the first time, for usually he has the grace of civility." Gibbie's excursions did not cease after the scolding. Later in the memoir Pringle recounted a daily inspection in which she "got down to the plantation early, expecting to send Gibbie out with the ox wagon to move the heavy things." There she "found he had sent a message to say he was sick . . . I went to see Gibbie to see if he were really sick or only resting after his month's night hunting." Much to Pringle's surprise, Gibbie was sick with pneumonia—no doubt a result, she believed, of his frequent hunting at night when he should have been resting for work.[122]

Although agricultural employers such as Pringle were often the most vocal about unregulated African-American customary rights, others also joined the chorus. Throughout the post-Emancipation period, other groups, especially sportsmen, came to realize that coping with threats to the Southern labor system dovetailed with their own interests. In 1881, a contributor to *Forest and Stream* hinted at a link between the unsettled state of affairs since Emancipation, Southern economic inefficiency, and sporting interests. "There is hardly a place in North Carolina where a true sportsman may not enjoy himself . . . Altogether we offer both a field of sport and interest," he wrote. But there was still work to be done, particularly in relation to the unsettled nature of Southern hunting and fishing since liberation. "We are a peculiar people with our 'peculiar institution' gone, and although we have gotten used to the loss, we have not all learned the most profitable ways of the 'new departure,'" the writer warned. "The saying that it is hard to teach an old dog new tricks is as applicable to men as dogs, and I am inclined to think it especially so of men who live under a southern sun."[123]

There is little doubt that Southern sportsmen, many of them also agricultural employers or landowners, believed former slaves' hunting and fishing activities were threats on several fronts, and they merged their grievances over labor with calls for proper sporting behavior. A contributor writing under the name N.A.T., of Palestine, Texas, mixed former slaves' independence from labor with concern over their sporting excesses. "When they were 'turned loose' . . . they became at once a race of sportsmen," he wrote. "Every man and boy was eager to be the owner of a gun, and as old muskets and Enfield rifles were very cheap in those days, they had not much difficulty in supplying their wants"—an ease of subsistence that threatened employers' control. "It may also be so, that they looked upon possession of firearms and gunning as the highest privileges of freedom." This feeling of freedom might indeed have unintended consequences. "Those were the halcyon days of the negro race in America," N.A.T. wrote. "I must say that if the freedman ever put on provoking airs toward the white people, it was when he was met by the latter in those hunting expeditions of his early freedom."[124]

Thus, although originating with Southern farmers and landlords, complaints about African Americans' unrestrained pursuit of fish and game would not end there. Elite sportsmen, who increasingly turned their gaze southward in the decades following Emancipation, also took up the cause of linking former slaves' exploitation of the Southern natural environment with a general lack of control over people of color. Over time, the cacophony of angry white voices raised against blacks' customary rights would lead to the adoption of widespread and comprehensive legislative measures that left African Americans increasingly restricted in their use of such cultural traditions as a way of subsisting, or even prospering, apart from agricultural labor in the service of whites.

"The Pot-Hunting Son of Ham"

*White Sportsmen's Objections to African Americans'
Hunting and Fishing*

The fact is the *esprit* has been destroyed since these
hordes of negroes have taken to the pursuit of game as
their principal occupation.

— *Doctor Macklin*, Richmond Whig, 1872

Agricultural employers and landowners had allies in their campaign to represent black independence as the biggest problem facing the post-Emancipation South. These other groups, although not tied as directly by economics to the need to circumscribe blacks' subsistence activities as a way of cultivating labor tractability, nonetheless detested former slaves' ability to freely exploit the natural environment. Led by the growing ranks of Southern and visiting sportsmen, these groups identified former slaves' hunting and fishing excesses as leading contributors to their own postwar difficulties. While seeking solace in the South's seemingly endless supply of fish and game—which made Dixie, particularly its black belt, a leading sporting destination for visitors from the North and around the world—white sportsmen were increasingly alarmed by the depletion of wildlife since the late nineteenth century.

The sportsmen and the landowners and employers had different objections to African Americans' hunting and fishing. Landowners and employers decried these activities because of the supposed dangers posed by subsistence or semi-subsistence garnered independent of whites' control. Sportsmen mostly took issue with the basic acts of hunting and fishing by former slaves. White agricultural interests feared unrestricted black customary rights as threats to the South's labor system and future economic prosperity; sportsmen feared them because they believed that, if left unchecked, African Americans would deplete Southern wildlife and ruin elite whites' cherished sporting privileges.

In March 1888, an unidentified Louisiana sportsman wrote an editorial for *Outing* magazine, angrily outlining the most serious barriers to wildlife preservation in Louisiana. "Even as late as twenty years ago, there was no lack of game . . . the emancipation of the negro changed all this," he began, echoing a common sentiment among the many Southern sportsmen who equated black liberation with a precipitous decline in the quality of field sports in Dixie. "The first idea of the free negro was to become possessed of an old shot gun of some kind, a rejected army musket or rifle," the writer continued. "This was proof positive of freedom since no slave was allowed to keep a weapon of any kind." This development brought great misfortune to Louisiana. "The effect of arming some hundred thousand negro men and boys with shot guns can be imagined. When it is further stated that each negro possessed at least a half dozen worthless curs of the breed known in the South as 'yaller, nigger dogs' . . . it can be readily understood that it did not take them long to exterminate the deer and rabbits." To make matters worse, the editorial concluded, African Americans, unlike white sportsmen, "killed anything they encountered, whatever its age or species." The writer's solution to this problem was to strengthen fish and game laws "in order to prevent the complete annihilation, by the negroes and their dogs, of everything that can be styled game."[1]

Complaints such as these illustrate several key components of whites' attitudes toward hunting and fishing by freed persons. First, elite Southerners, looking to the antebellum South as their model of social and sporting relationships, constantly harked back to the Old South as the halcyon age of Southern sport. Blaming Emancipation for both labor problems and wildlife shortages, they longed to return to that bygone era of racial control. Second, white sportsmen, believing that African Americans challenged their sporting mastery, worked to create a public perception of former slaves as immoderate, unsportsmanlike, and dangerous. Ultimately, these ideas—that freedom transformed the Southern sporting field, that unrestrained former slaves depleted wildlife, and that African Americans made poor sportsmen who did not live up to the standards of their white betters—culminated in attacks on African Americans' right to hunt and fish. The attacks intensified in the late nineteenth century and peaked in the early twentieth century, when sportsmen, landowners, labor lords, and lawmakers exploited perceived connections between hunting and fishing and the race problem to establish effective state-level fish and game regulation.

White sportsmen offered loud and frequent objections to African Americans' sporting behavior in the South between Emancipation and the 1920s, a period that began with former slaves enjoying more ready access to the South's natural environment and ended with a coalition of white interests employing fears about lost racial control and negative characterizations of blacks' sporting behavior to impose greater regulation of hunting and fishing. Southern sportsmen held up African Americans as archetypes of poor sporting behavior and blamed them for both destroying Southern natural environments and besmirching the good name of "legitimate" (meaning elite and white) sporting enthusiasts. Their complaints, dependent on the creation of disapproving representations of blacks' sporting behavior, skill, and intelligence, reflected elite whites' frustrations and served as another, and for historians largely overlooked, cultural space in which white supremacy could be cultivated. In their sporting narratives and in the pages of sporting periodicals, whites sought to embed in the Southern (indeed, American) mind that African Americans were bad, even dangerous, sportsmen and that the South's biggest problem — its lack of control over the black population — could be seen in miniature in the struggle over hunting and fishing. "The negro is deteriorating from the civilization he possessed as a slave, and relapsing into his natural barbarism," an editor of the *Southern Review* declared in 1869. "Will this process of deterioration tend to break down the characteristics of the white men?"[2] In voicing such fears, the editor also spoke for white sportsmen who experienced and exploited the same sentiments.

Between the 1870s and the 1920s, sportsmen and conservationists made some gains in the South. After decades of resisting restrictions on hunting and fishing, due to a general public distrust of such actions, lawmakers finally took lasting steps to regulate Southerners' pursuit of wildlife.[3] As observers of this legislation noted, fish and game protection had long been inadequate to address the concerns of sportsmen and nature enthusiasts.[4] The noted conservationist William Temple Hornaday, for example, acknowledged the gains made in Southern fish and game protection by the 1920s but remained critical of Southern lawmakers, noting sarcastically that "the Southern States have done less actual [game] extermination than our heroes of the North; but they are getting into shape to show more results."[5] Clearly, even in an age when fish and game law was becoming more comprehensive nationally, more work had to be done.

For long-suffering proponents of such legislation, this problem stretched back more than half a century. Both the push for legal restrictions and the perceived shortages that brought them about had been debated in the South before the Civil War. Sportsmen's concerns about the proper use of wildlife originated in early colonial history, as agricultural elites worked to make field sports a strictly aristocratic affair, and its most vocal expression developed in the 1830s when changes in firearms and transportation technology greatly increased the amount of fish and game consumed.[6] By the 1850s, the smoothbore musket had become all but obsolete, replaced by the rifled musket and, later, the breech-loading rifle, both of which allowed for greater accuracy, longer range of fire, and shorter loading intervals.[7] This development, coupled with the spread of steamboats and railroads that much reduced the distance between urban populations and the fish and game they craved, greatly increased the amount of wildlife killed for food and sport. Through the balance of the antebellum period, as firearms and fishing technology evolved and as transportation advances made Southern wildlife more easily accessible, the slaughter of fish and game continued apace.

Thus, between the Civil War and the turn of the century,[8] Southern sporting enthusiasts (including many in the former plantation elite) who had long sought exclusive hunting and fishing rights, and sporting tourists from around the United States, grew increasingly alarmed about the unrestrained slaughter of wildlife that seemed to characterize the region.[9] "Game is disappearing from our home country," Robert Barnwell Roosevelt wrote in 1884, "and if we are to obtain satisfactory shooting, we must go some distance for it."[10] Likewise, Henry B. Ansell, in his history of Knotts Island and Currituck County, North Carolina, lamented the decline of that once celebrated fowling region, noting "seventy years ago our country was thinly-populated; our gunners used the old flint and steel muskets to kill ducks . . . The ducks in those days had only to watch the margins of coves, creeks, ponds, bays and other shore lines for the shooters." But between the Civil War and the early twentieth century, "the millions of wild fowl that once swarmed our waters have wonderfully decreased—all but disappeared."[11]

Sportsmen offered many explanations for this decline. Some pointed to the advances in transportation that brought more sportsmen to the South. "There are fast lines of steamers and rail-roads that care little for distance," Ansell wrote. "These and most all commercial houses have refrigerators to keep ducks from taint; with the product of the ice plant ducks can now, if needed, be kept for months."[12] Others blamed the scores of Northerners who came South after the war. Virginian James Booth Walters noted that it was "not an uncommon thing for hunting parties from a distance to visit here at any time during the shooting season." Such visitors "sojurn [sic] for a season of one or two weeks and wage dreadful warfare upon the wild tribes of the surrounding county."[13] An anonymous sportsman, writing to *Forest and Stream* in 1885, described the multitude of visitors from the North who "are spending the entire winter in the South, and are making quail shooting a duty rather than a pastime. Many of these gentlemen can boast of records of from none to twenty birds daily for the season, and will proudly produce their diaries showing their score."[14]

Still others blamed increasing firearms availability for the South's wildlife woes.[15] The Civil War had made guns more attainable than ever before. In the years after the war, hundreds of thousands of surplus military weapons, taken home by returning soldiers or sold cheaply by the federal government, made their way into the hands of people who previously could not afford them. Echoing a common sentiment among wealthier Southerners angry at the wider availability of firearms, one Louisiana sportsman noted that "in the ancient antebellum era the hunting grounds of this State were famous throughout the South. All over the State they were preserved and worked in the shooting season, principally, by gentlemen sportsmen." But with saturation of the region with surplus weapons, as Virginian Alexander Hunter lamented, "every kind of gun, from the old Springfield musket to the modern-loader, is used relentlessly, and in the settled neighborhood, the deer are simply gunned to death."[16]

Inadequate fish and game legislation was another culprit. North Carolina Commissioner of Agriculture L. L. Polk opined in 1879 that restrictions, though unpopular, had become necessary. "While I am aware that no general game law can be enforced effectually unless supported by an intelligent public opinion," Polk wrote, somewhat optimistically, "yet I feel warranted in saying that . . . a law to prevent the indiscriminate slaughter which so seriously threatens extermination to many of our most valuable species of game, would be warmly received and endorsed."[17] Yet as late as 1894, according to North Carolina's Shocco Game Association, "owing to the want of better game laws and lack of enforcement of existing laws for the protection of game, the quantity of game is rapidly diminishing in all parts of the country." Many came to believe that only extreme measures could repair such a dire situation. "In order to remedy this evil, men of wealth who hunt for sport have in different places combined for the purpose of establishing game preserves similar to those of England and other parts of Europe."[18] Land and lumber speculator Robert Pinckney Tucker of South Carolina, who grew wealthy by purchasing abandoned lands and reselling lumber and sporting rights, agreed: "any sportsman not making provision for the future will find it increasingly difficult in a few years to obtain a days sport. The country everywhere is being shot out, taken up by the clubs, or posted by individual owners."[19] Put succinctly,

Southern sportsmen, increasingly alarmed about dwindling fish and game, moved to make it more difficult to duplicate the wildlife slaughter that characterized the period from the end of the Civil War to the early twentieth century.

AFRICAN AMERICANS AND THE WHITE SPORTING IDEAL

Despite the frequency with which sportsmen commented on advances in transportation, increasing numbers of sporting tourists, surplus firearms, and a lack of fish and game law as causes of wildlife depletion, many others argued that freed African Americans provided a better explanation. Almost from the moment of Emancipation, many Northern and Southern sportsmen identified former slaves as one of the deadliest causes of fish and game slaughter. One cannot read a late-nineteenth-century sporting periodical without being struck by the frequency with which contributors pointed to black sportsmen as one of the forces most destructive to Southern field sports and characterized them as the epitome of the poor sporting behavior that would destroy the region's wildlife. Frequent *Forest and Stream* contributor "Chasseur" blamed freed slaves for the Old Dominion's lack of deer. "Where there were a dozen [deer shot each week] just after the war there is one now, and the ubiquitous darkey is the cause . . . Each African is the possessor of an old army musket and two or three mongrels, who will chase anything from a squirrel to an antlered buck."[20] "G.T.N.," a Clarksville, Tennessee, contributor to the *Rod and Gun and American Sportsman* in 1875, describing the condition of his favorite South Carolina hunting grounds, wrote of "the terrible incubus of *blackness* which hangs over that commonwealth" due to "the constant stream of loafing Africans, each one with a musket on his shoulder." He noted that although "ten or fifteen years ago, I was accustomed to flush from twenty to thirty coveys [of quail] in a day, not more than six or eight can be found now. Duck shooting has been spoiled in the same way."[21] English sportsman J. Turner-Turner, in an 1888 memoir of his North American hunts, recalled the scant game in Liberty, Virginia, noting that partridge and rabbits were by no means plentiful, nor "was this to be wondered at in a place where every nigger carried a gun."[22]

According to alarmed white observers, then, African Americans' hunting and fishing, unrestrained since the end of slavery, was the principal cause for the decline of good sport. James Henry Rice Jr., describing hunting on St. Helena Island, South Carolina, recalled that "several years ago, during the reign of crime around here, the negro played havoc with the fox squirrels, killing over two hundred in all. They have never recovered their numbers."[23] South Carolina planter and sportsman J. Motte Alston wrote that "the game, once so bountiful, is fast disappearing for various causes. The negroes previous to the war were not permitted to kill the same for market, and so there was no visible decrease. But even the sea birds . . . that used to be so abundant have dwindled away in Carolina."[24] Referring to the African-American sportsman as "The Pot-Hunting Son of Ham," a writer from Hearns, Texas, calling himself B.C.H. asserted that "he is very numerous in Texas, and especially so in the vicinity of the Brazos river."[25] Linking game slaughter to blacks' immoderate sporting habits, B.C.H. insisted that the black hunter "carries his old relic of war times wherever he goes, and no matter in season or out of it, he bangs away at some nice pond or some place on the river where you have been preparing to go for a week." In the end, the angry Texan concluded, African Americans had taken over much of the region's prime sporting ground. "You go there at first peep of day—and there you find one of those animated black walnut statues, who has been there for two hours."[26] Such complaints sounded across the South in the late nineteenth century as sportsmen and landowners worked to persuade the public of the link between black liberation and the depletion of wildlife.

Southern sportsmen were disgusted at the destruction of the old order, a time when most wildlife had been reserved for men of means: "The old time gentlemen hunter of Virginia is becoming a thing of the past," Doctor Macklin declared in 1872. "The fact is the *esprit* has been destroyed since these hordes of negroes have taken to the pursuit of game as their principal occupation."[27] Free of the slave-era restrictions on their long-cherished hunting and fishing, liberated African Americans took to the Southern sporting field with vigor. For white observers, this signaled numerous dangers. African-American huntsmen carried weapons. They did not respect fish and game laws. And they did not follow whites' sporting codes. At the heart of these complaints lay a trope of lost control and a sense that a glorious epoch in Southern history had passed. This confluence between anger over perceived hunting and fishing abuses by African Americans and lamentations about lost racial subordination stands as one of the most striking features of late-nineteenth-century Southern sporting literature. Romantic longings for the slave South permeate this literature. According to Harrisonburg, Virginia, attorney John Edwin Roller, "to those who lived any part of their lives amid the surroundings of Southern slavery, in its better aspects, there comeback [*sic*] from those days the sweetest memory possible." For Roller, hunting stood at the center of that memory. "Who can forget the glorious hunts at night . . . the shouts of merriment and triumph at the success when the toothsome game was secured; and then the long and wearied tramp back home to be followed by the sweetest slumbers that mortal man ever knew?"[28]

Sportsmen often coupled the heyday of the Southern racial hierarchy with the glory days of Southern field sports. Describing his former plantation, Tower Hill, in Sussex County, Virginia, Chasseur recalled an age when "a rich Virginian counted his broad acres by the thousands, his sable servitors by the hundreds, his horses by the score, and he lived his life like a baron of the good old age of the squire."[29] In that golden age, whites stood as the unquestioned masters of the black population and thoroughly controlled Southern hunting and fishing. "The typical Virginian of those days was a thorough sportsman," but "the slaves, of course, were forbidden to carry or possess any firearm, and confined their hunting operations to the legitimate darkey game — the 'coon, the rabbit, and the 'possum."[30]

Anger over African Americans abandoning stereotypically "black" sporting patterns was another point of contention that pervaded Southern sporting narratives. *Forest and Stream* contributor "N.A.T." argued that with Emancipation, "the ancestral instinct to go a-hunting broke out within [former slaves] in an ungovernable manner and hurried them forth into the road and briar patches." The writer pined for the days "before the unpleasantness," when "the only hunting enjoyed by the negroes was rabbit hunting on Sundays and 'possum and 'coon hunting o' nights. They had no firearms in those days, and had to depend exclusively on the dog for their rabbits, and on the dog and ax for their 'coons and 'possums." N.A.T. lamented the loss of an age when African Americans confined themselves to certain kinds of game. "The negroes pursued these sports . . . with a wonderful enthusiasm and enjoyment . . . And yet since they have become free they have totally abandoned the 'possum and the 'coon as far as I can learn . . . He seems to consider that he has entirely outgrown the 'possum, got far above him in the social scale, and to look upon any reference to that animal in his presence as an intentional and heartless reminder of his previous condition of servitude."[31]

Increased gun ownership by blacks created another concern embedded in such complaints. Free from antebellum restrictions on firearms, at least after most states repealed their "black codes," freed slaves made firearms both a powerful symbol and an immediate priority of liberation, a fact not lost on white observers. "The negroes certainly rejoice in the possession of weapons to a large extent," Edward King noted in 1875. "Since the war every black man has felt himself called upon to own a shot-gun."[32] Likewise, writer "M" of Northside, Virginia, noted that "having been previously prevented by law from carrying fire arms, [former slaves] naturally exhibited a childish delight in exercising their constitutional privilege."[33] N.A.T. asserted that when African Americans were "'turned loose,' as they generally express it . . . every man and boy was eager to be the owner of a gun, and as old muskets and Enfield rifles were very cheap in those days, they had not much difficulty in supplying their wants."[34] This increased gun ownership provided a way for African Americans to resist whites' domination and became both a powerful emblem of liberation and, as some Southerners feared, a possible source of open violence against whites.

Blacks' ownership of guns, whites believed, also endangered Southern wildlife. After Emancipation, the ease of obtaining a gun made hunting more efficient for the average African-American sportsman. Alexander Hunter, musing that it was not just firearms but the users of firearms that led to the destruction of game, argued that "even worse than the breech-loader [a relatively new innovation in the 1880s], was the old army musket, loaded with a handful of shot, with a lately enfranchised freedman behind the big end of it." For Hunter, when freed persons took to the field with firearms, they became a threat to all Southern game. "It is then that the old army musket is converted into a terror, . . . and [if] its contents are turned loose, every bird will be either killed or crippled."[35]

Others tied such slaughter not only to guns but to the ability of freed people to hunt at will. "I have often meditated over the sudden conversion of the colored race into sportsmen, which we witnessed at the close of the civil war," N.A.T. wrote. "What was it due to? Perhaps to their wild ancestral instinct, which, suppressed so long in slavery, broke out beyond all reason when their freedom came . . . It may also be so, that they looked upon possession of firearms and gunning as the highest privilege of freedom and manhood." Gunning without restraint became the best way African Americans could testify to their freedom. "How often I have met these ebony sportsmen in their rounds, and how keen was their enjoyment of the fun!" N.A.T. recalled. "Sometimes I have met paterfamilias in the woods, musket on shoulder, attended by his wife and all his young. Oh, it was enjoyment keen, intense! Those were the halcyon days of the negro race in America."[36]

When sportsmen complained about blacks' gun ownership, they were expressing fear and frustration about several separate yet, within the context of the sporting field, interrelated developments. Newly freed and newly armed, African Americans exploited freedom to the utmost, traversing the Southern landscape and competing with white sportsmen for the region's best fish and game. When blacks took to the field they did so out of necessity, with little regard for the practices espoused by their white "betters." Sportsmen cried foul when African Americans engaged in activities considered either beyond the pale of acceptable black behavior or as best reserved exclusively for whites. Guided by nostalgic longings for antebellum aristocracy and deep uncertainties over fish and game scarcity, white sportsmen purposefully tied African Americans' sporting behavior to larger anxieties about Southern race relations. Sportsmen once celebrated a hard-working and mostly unarmed black population, but with Emancipation, "nearly every negro owns a pot-metal shotgun or old musket, and he spends much of his time wandering about . . . in search of 'Br'er Rabbit' or 'Br'er Squirrel.'" Unfortunately, this *Forest and Stream* contributor continued, the former slave "eschews possum hunting at night, of which we, who were the sons of slave owners in the old times, cherish fond recollections, as the youthful romances of old plantation life."[37]

Aside from abandoning "black game," arming themselves, and simply taking to the field, African-American hunters and fishermen angered whites by ignoring the code of fair sporting behavior that supposedly guided middle- and upper-class sportsmen's actions in the field. For late-nineteenth-century Southern sportsmen, particularly those who aspired to a fictionalized aristocratic antebellum plantocracy, pursuing fish and game carried certain obligations. Elites used this code of sportsmanship, always more idealized than actual, to separate true gentlemen from men who hunted and fished for need or financial reward, drawing clear lines of demarcation between aristocrats and the masses.

The amorphous codes binding the nineteenth-century American sporting fraternity contained certain key and constant components. Whether a huntsman or fisherman could be counted a "true sportsman," as sporting publications used the term, depended on a variety of factors, including his reasons for hunting and fishing, his methods of capturing prey, and his behavior in the field. A Delaware, Ohio, sportsman, "H.P.U.," succinctly summarized these key components in an 1881 *Forest and Stream* editorial. First, a true sportsman should be "a thorough-going business man . . . and not a loafer, dead-beat, nor bummer." Second, he should be a "votary of art and science" and have "a love for the true and beautiful, wherever found." Third, and perhaps most important, he must follow a code of restraint in the field and pursue sport purely for its own sake. "He is a gentleman, not a butcher, and makes of hunting and fishing a noble pastime, and not a money-getting trade. He takes to the field not because he loves the kill, but because of the healthful influences with which a hunter's life surrounds him."[38] As fish and game seemed to disappear at an increasing rate, sportsmen became more eager to separate themselves from those who did not conform to such codes.[39]

Although rarely stated so bluntly in contemporary periodical literature, it is clear that only men of means could be ideal sportsmen. A true sportsman had to be many things, including, in the words of H.P.U., "a thorough-going business man," "a votary of art and science," possessed of "a love for the true and beautiful," a "lover of fair play," and a "gentleman." Sporting literature constantly referenced such qualities, making plain that worthy devotees of fur, fin, and feather possessed manhood, refinement, education, and wealth. In other words, true sports-men came only from the middle and upper classes. As many scholars have demon-strated, the sporting codes transmitted in print in the late nineteenth century —created by and for and upheld by those who could afford to uphold them—became inherently and intentionally exclusionary.[40] Elite sportsmen thus worked to completely exclude lesser persons such as immigrants, poor whites, Native Americans, and African Americans.

In short, true lovers of the chase hunted purely for sport, not for food or profit. According to Eugene P. Odom, in the biography of his mentor, North Carolina naturalist Herbert Hutchinson Brimley, real sportsmen cared neither for killing nor for material or financial reward. In fact, "when the methods are fair and 'sport-ing,' comparatively few animals or fish are actually bagged, the ones that get away being both numerous and large! This is as it should be." For Odom and Brimley, the goal of hunting or fishing was something higher: "the long hikes through country unspoiled by man, the chance to get away from petty troubles of complex modern civilization, the matching of wits with cunning wild kindred, the hearty meal cooked in the open, and the companionship around the campfire." In fact, "even the unsuccessful trip is a success to the true sportsman if he is also a nature lover."[41] For these individuals, the hunting and fishing ideal was sport for sport's sake; such activities should remain ever unencumbered by less pure motives.

Standing in marked contrast to this ideal were the true sportsman's nemeses, the "game hog" and the "pot hunter," who angered sporting gentlemen primarily because they rejected such elite ideals. The proper sportsman hunted or fished for the love of pure sport or for the love of nature. Those who hunted or fished for money, dubbed "game hogs," and those who did so for survival, dubbed "pot hunters," did not deserve the appellation "sportsman." "This is to say that the game must be saved for the enjoyment and benefit of those who pursue it for the sake of pursuit," a *Forest and Stream* contributor argued in 1894. "A grouse which gives a man a holiday afield is worth more to the community than a grouse snared or shot for the market stalls."[42] Lovers of nature and sport valued hunting and fish-ing for the pursuit, not merely the kill. The sportsman who, according to A. M. Scudder, was "heavily loaded with the 'instinct' to kill for the price, with an elas-tic conscience regarding the manner of capture, to say nothing of his faculty for not discerning between open and closed seasons," threatened supplies of fish and game better reserved for those who showed the proper deference.[43] "I do not be-lieve any man has the right to kill more game than he can conveniently consume," wrote "J.D.H." of Savannah, Georgia, in 1899, laying bare the requirement that hunting and fishing be neither immoderate nor commercialized.[44] Unrestrained slaughter was the purview of the game hog, the man who both loved the kill and depended on its profits. "F.P.W." left little doubt of his estimation of game hogs in his poem "The Hog behind the Gun":

> He kills whatever comes to hand,
> Quails, grouse or rabbits, while they stand,
> Death to the game till the game is done,
> Death to the hog behind the gun[45]

Well-to-do sportsmen throughout the country shared this opinion and despised those who depleted fish and game without restraint or respect.

The "pot hunter" became the other great violator of sporting codes and the other great enemy of sporting gentlemen. Pot hunters were those poor and lower-class folk who depended on hunting and fishing for part or all of their living. Unlike game hogs, who flouted sportsmanship for commercial reasons, the pot hunter did so simply because he could not afford to do otherwise. According to the *Rod and Gun and American Sportsman,* pot hunters tended to be men "who break the laws, slaughter the game, and reckon up their trophies by the count of the bag and not by the skill shown in their day's work." Skill, moderation, and love of nature meant little to this hunter, because he "notoriously labors under the imputation of being obliged to bring home a bag which must be made, honestly if possible, but if not it must still be made." Most granted that pot hunters performed their evil acts out of the necessity to make their catch by any means, and that some may even have preferred a restrained and respectful sport. "There are doubtless some pot-hunters of a good sort," the editorial concluded, "but we are afraid there are more of the other stripe."[46]

Most Southern sportsmen shared this hatred of those who hunted and fished for pot or market. According to A. S. Salley Jr. of Orangeburg County, South Carolina, "a pot hunter . . . always tries to kill as much as he can and as many at a shot as he can. He has no appreciation of sportsmanship; no respect for the ethics of the field and forest and only regards the game laws when there is grave danger of his getting entangled therewith."[47] Sportsmen agreed that such destructive agents had to be eliminated one way or another. The hunter and fisherman "who kills brooding birds and their half-grown young for market or the tickling of his wolfish palate; and catches fish any way he can, the fish that are spawning or guarding their fry" was described by one angry sportsman as "a nuisance, that should be abated by any means within the law, or even by straining the law a little."[48] For the South, such complaints take on added significance: when sportsmen voiced anger over such abuses, they often simultaneously complained about a loss of control over the black population.

Because of Southern sportsmen's direct links to long-standing traditions of European aristocracy,[49] because elite sport became intertwined with the genteel life of leisure of the Southern plantocracy, and, not least important, because the hierarchical sporting structure of the South mirrored the region's racial and class structure, elite Southern sportsmen became perhaps the most zealous defenders of the sportsman's ethos. "Taken as a class, no finer sportsmen or better game shots ever lived in America than the landowners of the South Carolina Lowcountry during the latter two-thirds of the nineteenth century," Henry Edwards Davis wrote. "I grew to manhood under the tutelage of men of this class, and know from experience what they could do with either a shotgun or a rifle; and I had from them accounts of their predecessors with weapons of the same type."[50] Many Northern sportsmen agreed. "Therefore I say that the South is the seat of the truest sportsmanship of America to-day," Chicagoan Emerson Hough declared in 1895, "because there neither game nor sport is held generally as matter for barter or sale. Both are held as the privileges of gentlemen, and this is the right way to look at it, too." Openly hostile to hunting or fishing for any reason other than sport, Hough noted that "the wild animal should belong of right to the man who is enough master of the chase to reduce it to possession, and it should belong to no one else." He concluded that "I would not change the old conservative ways of the South if I could and hope they never will change."[51]

Like much of postwar Southern culture, the drive for exclusivity in hunting and fishing came in part from a longing for the mythologized antebellum plantation South. An unnamed 1880 *Forest and Stream* contributor argued that the best sportsmen in the United States—usually lawmakers—came from Dixie. "Before the war the sporting gentlemen in Congress almost invariably came from the South. Such men preserved the ancient sporting traditions. His kennels were filled with fox and deer hounds, and his stables contained hunters which would do credit to the fields of England and Scotland."[52] Alexander Hunter also lamented the passing of such sport, noting that the fine Southern deer hound, once something of an art form as a hunting dog, had disappeared for good. "Now all this is changed," he concluded. "The two or three hounds that are found on the farm—plantation no longer—are all 'round dogs, and will follow anything which leaves a scent . . . The sleek, well-kept dog of the Southern plantation is a thing of the past."[53]

An almost palpable sense that the best days of Southern hunting and fishing had slipped away gave postwar sporting literature a decidedly nostalgic tenor, thoroughly romanticized and inherently linking antebellum field sports and race relations. Indeed, recollections of antebellum Southern sport invariably included slave subordinates. "Many a dark, drizzling night . . . when I was a small boy," a sportsman writing as Coahoma recalled in 1891, "have I gone forth with my favorite negro 'possum hunter' Ellis, one of the plantation hands, and his two faithful 'possum dogs' in the old antebellum times; and with great exhultation [sic] have I gone back to the house at 2 or 3 o'clock in the morning and waked up my parents to show the fine live possum I had in a bag."[54] *Forest and Stream* contributor "P" made the connection between the hunting and fishing and race relations of the Old South even clearer, noting that an opossum hunt "seems to get into the very air and become infectious, and by some sort of freemasonry is at once known to all male kind on the plantation, from the austere master and the young gentlemen of the 'great house' to the white-wooled old 'uncle' and monkey-like pickaninnies of the 'quarters.'" At such times, "I have often snatched one of those whimpering and dusky nimrods from the grasp and wrath of his irate 'mammy' and borne him in triumph to the woods, he feeling that the luxury was cheaply purchased even at the expense of the severe paddling he was sure to get on the morrow."[55]

An idealized version of antebellum social relationships and, later, the drive to reproduce them became important components of the Southern sporting code. John Fox Jr., in his *Blue-Grass and Rhododendron: Out-Doors in Old Kentucky*, made this point clear. Describing a hunting excursion he once witnessed that involved the former slave Old Ash, a poor white man named Tray, and a well-to-do white man known simply as "young Captain," Fox noted how the scene resurrected the Old South. "And there the three stood, the pillars of the old social structure that the war brought down — the slave, the poor white, the master of one and the lord of both. Between one and the other the chasm was still deep, but they would stand shoulder to shoulder to shoulder in the hunt that night."[56]

That so many sportsmen made slaves a centerpiece of a romanticized Southern sporting field presents an apparent contradiction, when examined in conjunction with the venomous attacks on African Americans' hunting and fishing after Emancipation. Yet this makes sense. Both the fond memories about slave companions found in antebellum narratives and the harsh postwar criticisms of the "Pot-Hunting Son of Ham" spring from a common belief in blacks' subordination. For Southern sportsmen, this subordination was best exemplified by the antebellum sportsman-servant relationship, the loss of which explained blacks' destructive sporting practices after Emancipation. Ultimately, criticism of African-

American huntsmen and fishermen did not just reflect contemporary concern over wildlife. It simultaneously expressed fear for the future of both Southern wildlife and white supremacy and lamented the loss of the racial subordination and labor control that anchored elite whites' vision of the Old South.

CRITICISM OF AFRICAN AMERICANS' SPORTING HABITS

Several key components comprised whites' characterizations of blacks' sporting behavior, each revolving around the core idea that class position and racial makeup made African Americans poor sportsmen who would not adhere to proper sporting codes. Like all who depended on hunting and fishing for subsistence, African Americans privileged the quantity of their catch over the quality of their sportsmanship. In the opinion of well-to-do white sportsmen, blacks killed fish and game at an alarming rate,[57] and because of character traits peculiar to their race, black sportsmen lacked the basic competency, technological prowess, and concern for rules possessed by their white counterparts. African Americans who hunted and fished independent of whites' oversight inevitably made poor, even dangerous, hunters and fishermen. Whites relied on these assumptions to convince the sporting public that former slaves threatened Southern wildlife and to exalt their own status as restrained, refined, and intelligent sportsmen.

Upper-class sportsmen typically asserted that African Americans did not care for sport and merely used hunting and fishing as sources of food and income.[58] This characterization associated African Americans with inferior sporting practices and furthered the notion that black sportsmen concerned themselves only with animals deemed "black game" or "negro game." Indeed, an enduring stereotype of rural African-American life, frequently and energetically reinforced in nineteenth-century sporting magazines and narratives, portrayed blacks as driven (apparently by more than mere habit) to seek out the opossum and raccoon as their favorite quarry. The association between African Americans and small game, taking root under slavery as masters sought to separate aristocratic sport from the subsistence-oriented hunting of their slave property, became a standard trope of Southern sporting narratives. On one level, such an association reflects the reality of slaves' hunting habits. Small game was widely available and the easiest to trap or catch at night, and this activity was the least likely to draw the ire of white observers. Yet constantly linking African Americans with small game also reflected the wishful thinking of elites eager to believe that large game and fowl were safe from their sporting inferiors. This assumed division between "black game" and "white game" was so well recognized, as Archibald Hamilton Rutledge

A group of African-American men and children eagerly await the capture of a treed raccoon. Like many other images of black Southerners made for a national audience, this 1902 stereograph was probably posed, driving home the widely broadcast link between former slaves and such small game. Stereotypical though it may have been, the image also reflects a material reality for many African Americans across the South. (Courtesy of the Library of Congress)

joked, that even animals were aware of it. Writing about blacks' sporting habits, Rutledge asserted that "I have frequently been persuaded that deer pay less attention to Negro rovers of the woods than they do to white men. Nor would this be unnatural; for it is a law of the caste system of the South that Negroes shall not kill deer."[59]

Assertions linking African Americans with the hunting of stereotypical "black game" abound. H.P.U. claimed to have consulted an African-American acquaintance on the topic. "Thinking I might possibly be able to throw some light on the vexed question of 'How to cook dat 'possum,' I interviewed my ancient colored friend, Uncle Dan'l, with the following result":

Uncle Dan'l speaks:
Iz I ebber cooked a possum?
Yah! Yah! Yah! You'z shoutin' now!
Wan 'ter know the way to boss 'im?
Sho! Any fool nigga tell yo' how.[60]

White sportsmen, desperate to believe that African Americans confined themselves to certain game and eager to saddle people of color with badges of inferiority, advanced such stereotypical ideas throughout the nineteenth century.[61]

A Denver, South Carolina, sportsman writing under the name Blue Ridge helped keep such associations alive. Commenting on South Carolina's small game, he noted that "a few opossums are still left to entice the night hunter to forego the pleasures of sleep for a time and ramble around in search of them." Moreover, marveling at "how so sluggish an animal as a possum survives the nightly attacks made on them by the proverbial darkey and his dogs," he assured readers that the animals had reasonable prospects for survival.[62] Sportsman F. A. Olds, describing the popularity of the opossum in North Carolina, similarly noted that "there is no sport which possesses a tenth of the fascination for the negro, certainly for the North Carolina negro, that 'possum huntin'" does." Moreover, Olds claimed, "the 'possum is something which brings to the surface all the unctuousness of the darkey, and the darkey does not live who can stop a smile at the sight of one of these queer animals."[63]

Such assumptions penetrated into late-nineteenth-century sporting poetry, a common staple of sporting periodicals. The anonymous poem "Coon," for example, makes the point with a rhetorical question:

Dar's a coon on de groun'
An' a coon in de tree;
Now what do you think
De end will be?

Endorsing the stereotype that former slaves would do virtually anything to catch a raccoon, the poem leaves little doubt as to the confrontation's resolution. The African-American subject of the poem is driven, almost pathologically, to retrieve the raccoon from the tree:

An' soon he will land
On dat coon in de tree,

With a club dat will end
Mr. Coon; you see.
For with a coon on de groun'
An' a coon in de tree,
It is easy to guess
What de end will be.[64]

So strongly did white sportsmen connect African Americans with small game, unfit for proper sportsmen, that the discussion found its way into the debate over fish and game law. Noted conservationist T. S. Palmer, long-time secretary of the American Ornithological Union, speculated in a 1904 address before the North Carolina Audubon Society in Greensboro—probably for humorous effect—about the legal status of the raccoon. "An Iowa court decides that a coon is not the subject of larceny, but an Arkansas case criticizes this decision and takes issue with it, on the grounds that in some localities these animals are regarded as proper food and under such circumstances would be the subject of larceny . . . The Arkansas decision was doubtless deference to the tastes of our colored friends for that animal."[65]

As eagerly as white commentators linked black sportsmen with certain game, they just as quickly pointed out times when, regrettably, African Americans strayed from such associations. Their reactions demonstrate both how jealously white sportsmen guarded their assumed dominion over larger and more valuable game and how commonplace the notion of "black game" had become. White sportsmen preferred to believe that former slaves rarely moved beyond their love for small game, but not all remained so unrealistic. "Rallywood," for example, in response to assertions that African-American sportsmen did not stray from traditional "black game," asked simply, "Is there a white man in the world so green as to believe that they [former slaves] refrain from shooting partridges whenever they come upon them, the game law to the contrary notwithstanding?"[66] N.A.T. perceived former slaves' stepping out of place as both threatening Texas's fish and game supplies and reflecting whites' loss of control. "The negro now seems to regard it as almost an insult to talk to him about a 'possum. I have noticed this so frequently among our colored people that I am now very careful to abstain from all allusion to the 'possum when in their hearing." He concluded by wondering if this problem had become widespread. "Have the negroes in the other Southern states grown so proud as this? I hear that they have, but could not personally say so."[67] For former slaves, rejecting "black game" continued the age-old struggle to maximize their customary activities. For former masters, it represented a sea change in Southern field sports that held dire implications.

The manner in which African Americans caught their quarry may have irritated white sportsmen more than their tendency to progress beyond stereotypically "black game." According to the sporting press, former slaves slaughtered fish and game and lacked the decent restraint that supposedly characterized the refined white sportsman. Free from both the Old South's racial hierarchy and a code of proper sportsmanship, African Americans took as much fish and game as they could. Farmers in the South Carolina Lowcountry, for example, complained bitterly about such nuisances. Summerville resident F. C. Ford expressed his outrage in a letter to James Henry Rice Jr. in November 1909. He recounted a morning run-in with a black huntsman on a train. Ford noticed the man carried an unusually large quantity of wild fowl. "On the rear of the street car I questioned him, but did not learn his name. However he advised me that he had killed some sixty odd coots, ducks, etc., last evening in Goose Creek." The huntsman informed Ford that another African American, a Frank Sharper, kept boats in the nearby marshes to rent to black hunters and fishermen. "This negro said that he had sold most of his game before reaching the City, and I judge his purpose in going to market was to sell the balance," Ford continued. "It seems that he and others are making a practice of this thing."[68] For Ford, concerned about area wildlife and the violation of sporting rights purchased by fish and game clubs, such behavior was unacceptable. He hoped that Rice, as secretary of the Audubon Society, which at the time was charged with limited power to enforce state fish and game laws, could instruct one of his agents to detain such offenders as Sharper.[69] "It is certainly distressing," Ford concluded, "to feel that these negroes should be destroying the birds and other game which the Otranto Club, the Goose-Creek Club, the Liberty Hall Club and others in that section are trying hard to preserve by protection — in fact are spending money to feed them, etc., to encourage their increase. We hope that you will take quick action in this matter."[70]

While most hunting for market by African Americans did not assume so large a scale, it nonetheless distressed white observers. "If our lands were not posted we would not have anything to hunt," H. P. Wilder of South Boston, Virginia, declared in 1898, "nor would we be able to get any work done here in the open season, for the negro is a very persistent market hunter, and will kill more birds in one day than will one of our Northern friends in three." The reason, according to Wilder, was the different intent of black huntsmen. "I do not mean to reflect on the ability of our visitors, but as they are out for sport and not for slaughter they do not exterminate the game like our own pot-hunters."[71] Portraying black hunters along Texas's Brazos River as unskilled and immoderate, B.C.H. noted that "when he [the black hunter] finds where a covey of quail 'use,' he takes his gun . . . and watches for them. As soon as he gets them nearly in a bunch as possible, he 'turns loose' his old cannon. When he 'come too' and finds his gun hasn't 'busted,' he takes what he has killed, never getting what have only been crippled and hobbled off to die, and goes to town to sell his booty."[72] According to N.A.T., that slaughter began as soon as freed persons obtained weapons: "they made a rush for the fields and woods, and for a long time, summer and winter there was a perpetual fusillade. They slaughtered indiscriminately, shooting everything above the bluebird in size. Even the mocking bird, for all his songs, was not safe."[73]

An excellent illustration of the perceived and actual differences between elite white and African-American conceptions of proper hunting and fishing comes from Fred Mather's account of a journey down the Red River from Shreveport to Alexandria, Louisiana, while collecting specimens for the United States Fish Commission in the mid-1870s.[74] To help him on the expedition, Mather employed Sam, an aging black laborer who supplemented his income by working as a guide. The two did not see eye to eye on matters of sport, and their many disagreements provide valuable insight into the differences between blacks' and whites' sporting habits. Their relationship became strained before the trip began, as Sam landed a large catfish that dwarfed Mather's personal best. "It was 3 ft. 4 in. long, and weighed 63½ lbs. It was a record catfish for me, for a 10-pounder . . . was my largest," Mather noted. Obviously irked by Sam's haul, and then by Sam's decision to sell the fish, Mather assumed he would use the money foolishly. "Uncle Sam, as [locals] called my lone fisherman, sold the fish for $2.50, about 4 cents per pound, and with so much wealth in his possession I expected he would blow it all on booze." Once the two got underway, Sam impressed Mather with his steering prowess. "I thought I knew a trick or two in running streams with a boat, but now I had learned from another poor darky, and might truthfully say that I knew a trick or three." Grateful for what he had learned, Mather began to regret his previous hard feelings. "I wanted to apologize," he noted, "but that would never do." Note that although it was not acceptable for Sam to upstage Mather in sporting prowess, in the subordinate role of paddler and guide, Sam could teach his employer new steering methods.

Needing samples for his study, Mather promised Sam new fishing hooks if the guide landed an alligator snapping turtle larger than 60 pounds, and the two began fishing in earnest. A running philosophical discussion of proper fishing began when they caught a number of turtles that, according to Mather, were too big to taste good. He wanted to throw them back, while Sam wanted to keep them. Mather eventually compromised, letting Sam keep one, but not before a dialogue on sportsmanship. "Sam and I discussed the snapper question for a while with no prospect of agreement, and then he said: 'Yo ain' gwine let all dese snappahs go 'case dey ain' de kin' yo' want an' I want de big one to cook fo yo', an' yo'll say he's de bes'es tuttle yo' eveh stuck a toof in.'" Mather gave in, but imparted a lecture on proper sport, warning his guide that "what we catch is for our own use, if we want it, but I don't want to kill any animal, fish, bird or turtle unless it is needed for food or it is my enemy, as a rattlesnake is." Mather was uncertain of the extent to which "this new religion penetrated Sam's brain," but he was gratified several days later when Sam "carefully unhooked a big sunfish and let it go, when on previous trips he might have dropped it in the boat to die, and then have thrown it away."[75]

For Mather, releasing extra animals showed proper sportsmanship; for Sam it was wasteful. "Sam did not accord with my views of killing only for our needs," Mather explained; "there was a market for food of all kinds in Alexandria, and now that we were capturing fish and turtles in greater number than we could use, he naturally desired to utilize them for that market." Here lay the essential difference between elite whites' and poor blacks' sporting habits: "From [Sam's] point of view it was the height of idiocy to turn loose catfish and turtles which had a considerable market value; he could not understand it. As for me, I had not journeyed to the lake on a commercial venture." Noting that Sam "interpreted the law of 'dominion' of man over 'the beasts of the field' in a different manner from my interpretation," Mather described the biggest divide between black and white sportsmen. "They think that a day which sends them an extra lot of birds or fish is to be credited to them as a great sportsman, and don't know that they are men of that abominable class called hogs; I have a vocabulary of words to describe them, but the editor would blue-pencil them all."[76]

Embedded in Mather's account are essential features of white sportsmen's attitudes toward blacks' hunting and fishing. African Americans had long relied on the Southern environment to guarantee subsistence and provide a degree of material comfort and independence otherwise denied them. Slaves and freed persons could not adhere to sporting codes proffered by white sportsmen who, as an emblem of personal and class status, eschewed the drive for food or profit. White sportsmen, eager to improve their sport and their standing in the sporting fraternity, cultivated images of racial subordination and blacks' sporting inferiority both to portray African Americans as archetypes of poor sportsmanship and to stamp them as inherently inferior.

Mather and other white sportsmen believed African Americans were incurable fish and game slaughterers, but they moved beyond this to also condemn African Americans' supposed lack of concern for fair sporting methods. For whites, such behavior was more than a marker of bad sport; it was a vibrant symbol of both racial identity and racial inferiority.[77] Well aware that African Americans hunted and fished out of necessity, white sportsmen nevertheless decried the methods used to maximize the catch. N.A.T. wrote in 1883: "We have many negroes who follow gunning as a means of livelihood in ducking season." Noting that the black hunter "returns with just as many ducks as the white man, and even more if the latter not be a very good hunter," he explained this success by pointing out the frequent violation of codes of moderation. "The way he does it is this: he finds a good place for ducks; to that place he repairs early in the morning, and on that spot he stays all day long." Once there, the African-American gunner worked to maximize not his enjoyment, but his kills, for even though "his weapon may be an old musket, or an old rickety double-barreled muzzle-loader, he often kills as many birds at a fire, and indeed generally does . . . In this way they often make large bags in a day."[78] The method described here, it should be noted, is nearly identical to that employed by poor white hunters across the South, particularly in such rich ducking areas as the Chesapeake Bay, the North Carolina sounds, the South Carolina Lowcountry, the Louisiana lowlands, and the Mississippi flyway. Yet whites reserved special anger for African-American gunners who killed as many ducks as possible with each shot.

Disgruntled observers also complained that African Americans killed any animal that crossed their path, whatever the species or the time of year.[79] One writer described such unlimited hunting in Louisiana, noting that it took a heavy toll. "It is no unusual thing to see a negro tramping over some back plantation road with a bag of that exquisite singer, the Southern nightingale or mocking bird, at his side . . . and were he to encounter the European nightingale itself, carrier pigeons, or any other fancy bird, it would make no difference to him, he would bang away at anything that looked as if it might be edible." The frustrated sportsman also noted that Louisiana fowling enthusiasts had "to adopt some sort of system in hunting to protect themselves from the thousands of amateurs, boys and negroes, who go duck hunting during the season."[80] Another perturbed sportsman, writing as E. Wanders On, expressed his outrage over freed persons' tendency to shamelessly slaughter Southern wildfowl: "the field is open to, and occupied by *heartless Senegambians*, who ruthlessly hunt and destroy our birds. All true sportsmen deprecate such conduct, and would be a unit in the effort to prevent it, if the law provided any remedy."[81]

Some writers simultaneously criticized blacks' hunting methods while lauding those of white sportsmen, accusing blacks of both unfairness and cowardice. Contributor M, stating that his preferred sport of turkey hunting "requires skill, patience and knowledge of the habits of the bird that few sportsmen indulge in it," complained that poor sportsmen resorted to unfair methods such as trapping to overcome skill deficiencies. "It is considered as decidedly unsportsmanlike to 'belt' or trap turkeys, and no one but 'cuffee' or a white pot-hunter ever does anything of the kind."[82] David Brainard Whiting recalled from his North Carolina youth what he saw as an example of African Americans' cowardice. He described a winter when a wild cat was in the area: "the few colored people there were too afraid to go out after sun set and the white people kept close at home too. Some of us took out guns and went where we heard him [the wild cat] the night before but we only found his tracks." Whiting concluded that they could have taken the wild cat with enough stout sportsmen to brave the danger.[83] Both contributor M and Whiting relay the same basic idea that African Americans, lacking fairness and courage, did not have the stuff to be proper sportsmen.

FROM SPORTING INFERIORITY TO RACIAL INFERIORITY

For some observers, African Americans' lack of skill and technical adeptness, rather than lack of courage or fairness, made them bad sportsmen. White sportsmen set themselves apart from their African-American counterparts by criticizing or poking fun at their seeming lack of skill, use of outdated technology, or unfamiliarity with modern sporting methods. White sportsmen's recollections routinely compared blacks' sporting methods unfavorably with their own. While on one of his Southern excursions, English sportsman J. Turner-Turner found great amusement in "an old nigger fishing with an enormous hook on the end of a piece of cord, and a stone for a sinker, the bait being a scarcely perceptible bit of worm somewhere on the hook; he told me he had never caught a fish there; and I was not much surprised."[84] A sportsman writing as J.E.W., who took to the field with an African-American laborer named Sparks, described the laborer's astonishment at his employer's breech-loading shotgun.[85] Noting that the "breech loading gun was a little too much for Sparks," he let the farmhand examine it. Unfamiliar with a breech-loader, Sparks was stunned when the weapon seemed to break in half in his hands. "Astonishment was depleted upon every feature of his face," J.E.W. recalled, "while his language deserves a place in 'the archives of gravity,' as one of our colored members of the Legislature said in 1868."[86]

Whites also interpreted African Americans' customary reliance on small game—a stereotypical association whites worked hard to propagate—as emblematic of backwardness. In his collection of dialect stories, William H. Frazer, president of Queens College, Charlotte, North Carolina, drew on the assumed connection between people of color and small game.[87] "The Possumist," for example, presents rural African Americans as unintelligent and concerned only with their obligatory quest for the opossum. In this story, set at the end of Reconstruction, a meeting of black leaders convenes to discuss the ramifications of a recently enacted grandfather clause. The first speaker, "a pompous brother . . . arrayed in broadcloth and patent leathers," rises and declares that, given the forces arrayed against them, the situation is hopeless. "Yas sah, I'se er pessimist," he concedes. A second speaker stands up, "another very pompous brother," who asserts that given the relative equality in Northern states, there is reason to hope. "Brudder Cheerman," he declares, "I'se er optimist." Finally a third chimes in, "an old negro from the country" who "gives a loving description of catching a possum and his wife cooking it. 'I ain't none ob yo' optimist, en I ain't ob yo' pessimist, but I'se er possumist, I is, yas sah, I'se er possumist.'"[88] This story of how African Americans remained unprepared for the franchise hinges on the image of the "old negro from the country," reared under the racial and sporting relations of slavery. He cares not for politics, only for the comfort of "black game." The story confirms whites' basic assumptions and hopes about African Americans' sporting behavior.

Forest and Stream contributor "L.J.M." portrayed African-American sportsmen as both backward and in awe of whites' mastery over new weaponry. Recounting his first use of a new type of shell in his shotgun, L.J.M. recalled that "the darkies were amazed at the slight report and at the distance as well, and, as it is not etiquette in the South to enter, unbidden, into a conversation with a white 'gemman,' they followed . . . their usual custom of talking at him among themselves." Quoted in the barely decipherable, broken English with which African Americans were typically credited, "the darkies" discussed the strange new weapon. One man in particular, 'Ras, was most impressed by the lack of a loud report. "Wot gits me's dat lill snappy noise like w'en she shoots," he declared. "Now ef I'd cut loose heah wif my ole smokestack [his older, louder weapon] 'twud shake dis yer whawf off'n its laigs."[89] For L.J.M., black sportsmen such as 'Ras, while perhaps perfectly adept at performing the brute labor required of sporting excursions, lacked the intelligence and culture to understand the weaponry and equipment of modern field sports.

Except in the context of the relationship between white sportsman and black laborer, whites rarely credited African Americans with true skill or knowledge. In fact, some narratives seemed designed to dispel the notion that African Americans could possess such attributes at all. A. J. Lipton of Hobucken, North Carolina, in describing a hunting trip with "a colored man named Jim," illustrates this point well. Bears had been seen in that part of Pamlico County, "and Jim, who claimed

An 1885 Currier & Ives lithograph depicts the likely consequences of pairing African Americans with fox hunting, the long-time bastion and symbol of aristocratic sport. This pairing, to white audiences both incongruous and humorous, reinforced the notion that former slaves, by their basic makeup, were not advanced enough to become competent sportsmen. (Courtesy of the Library of Congress)

to be a great bear hunter, proposed we should go after them." The two set out one night for the tall corn and a chance to kill a bear, but Jim soon lost his nerve. "Hadn't we better be gwine home?" he asked. "I'se shibberin wid de cole." Lipton agreed, but as the two departed they ran into the bear. Despite his claim of being a skilled bear hunter, Jim ran for cover, leaving Lipton to shoot the bear. "I called Jim, and presently heard him coming through the canes," Lipton recalled. Jim stopped at a prudent distance and inquired, "'Has you shuah killed de bar?' I told him to come and see it."[90] In this narrative, Lipton brags about his own skill and bravery and attacks the notion that African-American sportsmen could equal their white counterparts. Jim made bold claims about hunting skill, even proposing that he and Lipton should set out in search of the bear. But his claims ultimately proved false; he proved to be both a poor sportsman and a coward, who relied on his more competent white companion to save the day. Lipton's message is clear. Any pretense at true skill that African Americans might make was invalidated by the inescapable vagaries of black character.

Accounts of such episodes stamped African Americans as bad sportsmen undeserving of praise. Henry Edwards Davis, whose descriptions of his experiences with Old John, noted above, included the assertion that "I never knew him to do any work, as that was reserved for his wife and large family of children," adds a new component to agricultural employers' typical complaints about blacks' working habits. Apparently Old John used not hunting itself but the illusion of hunting to avoid work. According to Davis, Old John could be found every Saturday "in the local village leaning on his musket and telling the assembled audience of negroes about the many rattlesnakes he had recently killed after finding them by scent." Ultimately, Old John's claims, like those of A. J. Lipton's Jim, proved false. "Despite all his boasting, however, about his prowess, Old John never produced any tangible evidence of it in the form of a dead rattlesnake or a dead wild turkey."[91] His claims invalidated, Old John remained just a poor sportsman who used hunting to avoid work. Whites eagerly consumed such stereotypes of African-American behavior and used the pages of sporting periodicals to strengthen them in the minds of readers. Moreover, like Davis and Lipton, they connected blacks' sporting practices and black character, using sporting narratives to further these stereotypes of African Americans as shiftless, unskilled, and unintelligent.

Whites' frustration over blacks' sporting behavior also grew from the concern that hunting and fishing might embolden African Americans to break down traditional patterns of deference. Touring a plantation near Natchez, Louisiana, in 1873, Edward King had an encounter that confirmed those fears of blacks' assertiveness. Traveling with the landowner, a planter identified only as "the Colonel," King encountered "a brown man mounted on a stout horse" and armed with guns, a long knife, and a hatchet, evidently prepared for a deer hunt. On seeing the would-be poacher, the Colonel tried to warn him off, saying "there will soon be no deer left." Undeterred, the hunter announced his intentions. "'Yas, Cunnel,' said the fellow, imprudently shifting his long rifle from his right to his left shoulder. 'I reckon ef I see any deer I's gwine to go fer 'em, sho;' then, putting spurs to his steed, he galloped off."[92] Thus white sportsmen, disturbed by the breakdown of the Old South's social structure and afraid of the effects of unrestricted hunting and fishing on African Americans' behavior, framed "black sport" to fit their insecurities about the emancipated freedman.

Yet, despite the regularity of assertions linking African Americans' hunting and fishing with their basic character traits, and despite the frequency with which white writers described black sportsmen as unskilled and ineffective, the image of the poor, untalented black sportsman was not the only portrait of blacks' hunting and fishing presented to the public. White contributors to the sporting literature sometimes lauded African Americans' behavior afield, often presenting them as quite skilled. Indeed, some of the same sportsmen who created images of blacks' inferiority could quickly change positions and compliment blacks' sporting prowess a few sentences later. The same African-American huntsman or fisherman initially depicted as lazy, improvident, and untalented one moment might be portrayed as shrewd and skilled the next. Here is another apparent contradiction of late-nineteenth-century Southern hunting and fishing narratives. In opining about black sportsmen, white contributors often took two seemingly incongruous positions, simultaneously presenting people of color as slow-witted yet astute, inexperienced yet well-worn, unfamiliar with firearms yet crack shots, ineffective yet flush with fish and game. This seeming contradiction can be explained if we decode the narrators' basic messages.

In the winter of 1882 and spring of 1883, a debate about black sportsmen raged in the pages of *Forest and Stream.* Motivated by the claim that freedmen bore the blame for the decline in numbers of Southern quail, the Virginia sportsman writing as M sparked a volley of responses by asserting that freedmen should not be so accused. M declared that "I dwell in one of the largest old slaveholding counties of Virginia, where the freedmen are in a large majority; that I am a 'bourbon democrat' . . . and that I have been all my life an ardent and active sportsman," but "it is a slander upon the freedman to charge him as the guilty party" in the quail decline. For M, the freedman, by habit and tradition, simply did not have the skill to hunt such wildfowl on the wing (that is, while in flight); nor did he own the proper guns and dogs for such challenging endeavors. "He is by no means the pest some believe him to be, but as a rule is useful, law-abiding, humble and contented, trusting implicitly those, who, by fair dealing, have won his confidence."[93]

Two months later Rallywood responded, arguing that believing that freedmen could not or did not destroy quail was wishful thinking. "Indeed his [M's] faith in their simplicity is childlike and bland, whereas the craftiest diplomat that ever wore a white skin is a novice in the art of concealment compared with the Virginia negro." For Rallywood, freedmen, far from being incapable sportsmen, skillfully hid their true abilities. "Does 'M' imagine that the colored brother never interviewed a henroost because he has never seen the trophies of the interview hanging on the outer walls of his log cabin?" Rallywood did not claim that African Americans were solely to blame for the problem, but did point out "the scores of negroes from the James [River] to the Mattaponi River, and east of the Richmond & Fredericksburg Railroad," constantly "skulking along the edge woods, swamps, and thickets, and keeping carefully out of sight of white folks," who would probably be drawn to such a target as the quail. Unlike M, who wished African Americans to remain poor sportsmen, Rallywood acknowledged their competence and threat to Southern game. "I have no apology to make to the good-natured, shrewd, shiftless freedman, since I know he will take no umbrage at my saying he pops Bob White every time he sees him, if he has a fuse in his hand."[94]

This disagreement soon flared into a broader debate. In March 1883, M responded to Rallywood, challenging the idea that freedmen possessed enough intelligence to hide their sport. "It would be instructive for him [Rallywood] to tell us whether his experience bears out the assertion . . . as to the skill of the freedman as a diplomat."[95] M did not stand alone. N.A.T., the writer from Texas, while acknowledging African Americans' destructive potential, did not blame them for the quail depletion. "My candid opinion is that while he is still entitled to high rank as a game destroyer, he is not quite as bad as he used to be." He believed that although freedmen took to the field in large numbers after liberation, they gave up such sporting mania within a few years. "My judgment is that there is not one bird now killed by the freedmen where there were ten killed by him in the early days of his freedom." Unfortunately, N.A.T. argued, African-American sportsmen accounted for a great deal of quail slaughter through trapping. "Bob White is the principal sufferer by these implements, and I believe his destiny is to be destroyed by the negro . . . The only way to stop him [the black hunter] is to educate him into the conviction that he is behaving badly, and this, I fear, can never be done as long as Bob White exists."[96] Although freedmen lacked the will to assail the stately quail with guns, their poor sporting methods made them dangerous.

By April, sportsman "A.F.R." of Belvidere, North Carolina, had entered the debate, suggesting a third possibility. Freedmen, he argued "in defense of the darkey," could be perfectly fine sportsmen, at least for traditional "black game." But they had neither an abiding interest in nor the talent required for quail hunting. As evidence, he found a large covey of quail near a freedman's cabin. "The head of the family owned a gun, and was fond of hunting, but, like most darkies, he didn't hunt quail, because he didn't feel sure of killing on the wing, and didn't look for them on the ground. Nor is this an isolated instance. I can today, with my setter, find at least a dozen coveys of quail within 100 rods of negro cabins." According to A.F.R., freedmen might desire more "white game," but they simply lacked the skill. They also lacked the drive. Like other contributors who linked African Americans' hunting and fishing with their shiftlessness, the writer remained confident of Southern fish and game security because freedmen "are too lazy and worthless to hunt for a living. We have lots of negroes and plenty of quail, showing that the supply of quail is not cut off in this section by the freedman." For A.F.R., the freedman was competent enough to catch raccoons, opossums, squirrels, and rabbits, but lacked the ability and ambition to threaten white sportsmen's best interests.[97]

This debate, which began in *Forest and Stream* in 1882 and 1883, reappeared from time to time through the 1880s, with contributors split over the basic question of precisely what threat African Americans posed to Southern game. Some sided with M, believing that freedmen were too attached to smaller game and too unskilled to seriously threaten more advanced quarry. Moreover, for such observers, freedmen generally behaved properly when kept in line by the white community, and thus threatened only "black game." Another group agreed with Rallywood and asserted that freedmen would, and did, kill whatever they could, often without white observers taking notice. Too free from decent restraint, these freedmen posed a serious danger. A third group, as represented by A.F.R., believed freedmen showed competence as sportsmen, but only for traditional "black game." Blacks did not step out of place, because they were content with small game and feared turning hunting into work. These three competing ideas formed the core of the discussions of African Americans' hunting and fishing that littered sporting periodicals in the late nineteenth century. They also account for the often contradictory assessments of blacks' sporting habits and behavior.

This tendency to mix messages about black sportsmen is reflected in the writings of South Carolina's Archibald Hamilton Rutledge, a distinguished source on Southern culture who was raised on field sports and set many of his writings in and around the sporting field. Rutledge, through his many books of verse and prose, and his poems and stories for *Field and Stream*, *Harper's*, and the *Saturday Evening Post*, became the most important voice in spreading stories of the South Carolina sporting field to the wider American audience, helping to frame a particular vision of Southern hunting and fishing. His vision drew heavily on representations of African Americans.

Reared on his family's Hampton Plantation in the Santee River region near McClellanville, South Carolina, Rutledge learned to hunt and fish from family tenants and other local African Americans. In *Hunter's Choice*, he described his early sporting influences, including "an old African named Galboa," a slave huntsman and fisherman before liberation, who "could always get what he was sent after; and he could get it with an ease and nonchalance that were impressive, and were likewise suggestive of a kind of eerie skill instinctive to him and a few others of his race but denied the white man." Rutledge never took to the field with Galboa, who preferred to work alone. Another black huntsman, "Phineas McConnor, a slight, stooping, yellow Negro, who speaks with a lisping drawl," played a more direct role. Rutledge learned much from McConnor, who "appears to have an especial insight into the ways of wild creatures; he seems to think their thoughts along with them (or a little ahead of them). And he knows his woods." Rutledge, in his learning about the Southern sporting field, had no greater influence. "Whenever I want to know definitely about game, whether of the moldering delta or of the swamps or of the pine-lands, I consult Phineas. Among the Negro woodsmen of my acquaintance, he is the authority."[98]

Yet as often as Rutledge praised sportsmen such as Galboa and Phineas Mc-Connor, he refused to consistently credit African Americans with true skill. One moment he praised them as the finest sportsmen, and then he derided their performance in the field. Rutledge distinguished between two kinds of black sportsmen. The most common was the "tattered Negro with a battered gun under his arm . . . If he brings home a rabbit or a squirrel or a 'possum, he will be both lucky and happy." The other is "an entirely different kind of Negro hunter," who is "found only in the more remote wilds of the Deep South." This sportsman, ostensibly because of his purer African heritage, "comes by his genius naturally." According to Rutledge, the former outnumbered the latter by a wide margin: "I personally know about a thousand Negroes who live in good hunting country. Few of them hunt at all; and only two or three are really gifted in the lore."[99] Notice again an apparent contradiction—Rutledge makes clear that African Americans made the best hunters and fishermen, but only a rare few could be counted as truly skilled sportsmen.

Rutledge would move back and forth between these positions in his writings. In *Home by the River,* he presented African-American sportsmen in one instance as more skilled than white sportsmen, then in the next as decidedly inferior.[100] This tension between positive characterizations of blacks' sporting abilities and negative characterizations of their behavior, work habits, and intellectual capacity underlay writings by Rutledge and other narrators of Southern field sport. Recalling a standing offer he once made to local African Americans of a 10 cent reward for each report of a game sighting, Rutledge remarked that no one had more skill at locating game. A "Negro invariably sees more wild creatures than a white man," since the "Negro's quiet way of walking, his lack of stealth and purposeful intent, his happy blending with the plantation landscape—these things and perhaps others beyond my ken enable him to see much wild game that would be frightened by a plantation owner" (112).

Despite that skill, so Rutledge believed, African Americans usually lacked the intelligence to use it. One day a black man named Isiah came to Rutledge to report a flock of wild turkeys and collect his dime. Rutledge asked when he spotted them. "Well, sah," answered Isiah, "it would be about last Friday a week ago" (112).

Rutledge explained this tendency, what he called "a Negro's lack of a sense of time," as an African-American character trait. "So accustomed is the Negro to having the white man set things straight that usually, instead of acting in an emergency, he will feel his duty done if he merely reports the trouble." He recalled a specific time when "I sent one of them to find a wild gobbler that I had badly wounded. The Negro found the great bird; it was unable to fly and could hardly stagger. But my man did not catch it. He walked back five miles to tell me that he had seen it. We never saw it again" (117).

As limited as African Americans' acumen for field sports could sometimes be, Rutledge did not doubt their skill in other areas. He described two tenants, Sam and Richard, whom he commissioned to build a cypress canoe. Although "they had never made one before and had never seen one made . . . with an ax and fire and adz they went to work; and by the next afternoon I had as pretty a ducking boat as you ever saw" (120). Yet even Richard, whose craftsmanship Rutledge praised, was soon criticized as incapable in the field. While shooting ducks one day, Rutledge asked Richard, who served as his boatman, to leave the boat and circle around a group of nearby ducks to drive them toward the boat. According to Rutledge, Richard could not handle even such a simple direction. "More than a mile he had gone, swimming nine huge old canals; then he had come in on the ducks from that direction," Rutledge recalled with both frustration and amusement. "On his return he took those nine canals on his stride, and when he reached me, mud and water from heel to head, he was all smiles because I had killed two mallards" (123).

The images of black sportsmen in Rutledge's stories—as instinctual yet unskilled, experienced yet unintelligent, loyal yet incompetent—reflect the common assertion that African Americans remained poor sportsmen because of essential racial characteristics. Yet despite the frequency with which Rutledge used stories of African Americans' sporting inadequacy to entertain his audience, he almost as frequently provided examples of personal experiences with black sportsmen—men like Galboa, Phineas McConnor, and others—who had "an instinct about problems of this kind that a white man rarely has" and were thus some of the finest hunters and fishermen in the Lowcountry.[101]

Whites' accounts, then, oscillated between presenting African Americans as inept, bumbling sportsmen and as savvy, veteran masters of hunting and fishing. Some even combined the two. A *Forest and Stream* contributor, commenting on the myth that African Americans lacked the skill to shoot birds on the wing, described "three negroes in the country . . . who regularly shoot quail on the wing," and he recalled meeting them in the field and hearing of their prowess. Yet the white contributor found a way to devalue blacks' sporting skill and exalt his own. One day in the field, an African-American sportsman who claimed mastery of shooting birds on the wing led him to a gang of partridges, where he claimed he once bagged twenty-three with twenty-five shots. "Doubting his ability to repeat the performance, I offered to lend him my gun, as I should be delighted to see the best record wiped out with my Harrington & Richardson." The black sportsman, however, despite his claims, was too inexperienced with and intimidated by such a modern firearm to attempt a repeat performance. "He declined on the ground that he didn't understand 'dem new fangled guns widout no hammers,'" the white man noted with satisfaction, happy to have salvaged some personal pride out of the situation.[102] African Americans may, regrettably, have become competent sportsmen, but only under limited circumstances. They may have some skill that might impinge on white huntsmen's privileges, but in method, technological advancement, and sheer courage they remained inherently inferior to their white counterparts.

Hunting and fishing by African Americans posed a dilemma for white sportsmen. If whites acknowledged the damage done by black sportsmen, they risked calling attention to lost racial control and narrowing the distance between themselves and their supposed sporting inferiors. If, preferring to uphold whites' supposed mastery of the Southern sporting field, they held to the notion that African Americans could not be effective sportsmen, they risked downplaying the wildlife depletion and delaying its remedy—the restriction of blacks' customary rights. In the end, they chose a middle approach that explained both African-American sportsmen's regrettable effectiveness and their predictable shortcomings as symptomatic of racial inferiority.

Whether whites characterized African Americans as poor sportsmen, bound by their race to "black game" and improper sporting behavior, or as skilled sportsmen, bound by their race to abuse those privileges and slaughter indiscriminately, inferiority was ultimately the central message of criticisms of African Americans' hunting and fishing in the fifty years after the Civil War. Both in sporting narratives, in which African Americans typically appeared in subordinate, usually unintelligent, and often comical roles, and in sporting periodicals, where white writers vented their most bitter complaints, white sportsmen carefully crafted a multi-pronged message about blacks' sporting habits. African Americans could not be reliable trustees of the South's rich and increasingly valuable natural environment. The major ill of the region, an increasingly recalcitrant and devolving black population, could be seen and understood in microcosm in the sporting field. In other words, writers portrayed the problems that African Americans caused for sportsmen as indicative of the problems they created for the South as a whole. Even if whites could not agree on the specific nature of African Americans' hunting and fishing, they could agree on that larger problem. They also agreed that Southern field sports would be improved immeasurably if blacks' hunting and fishing could be diminished or eliminated altogether.

With these ideas firmly embedded, it took only a small intuitive leap for Southern sportsmen to advocate restricting African Americans' hunting and fishing rights. Indeed, those who called for local and state conservation measures between the 1880s, when these measures began in earnest, and the 1920s, when such protection became a permanent part of lawmakers' agenda, often used alleged abuses by African Americans as one of their prime justifications. African Americans played a critical role in the lives of white, Southern sportsmen, not only helping them establish their own identities but also providing an archetype of bad sporting behavior. That archetype would allow white sportsmen, landowners, and lawmakers to use the "race question" to sidestep objections to fish and game legislation and establish a comprehensive system of wildlife protection in many Southern states—which by the second decade of the twentieth century would regulate not only the region's hunting and fishing but also African-American independence.

CHAPTER 3

"The Art of Serving Is with Them Innate"

African Americans and the Work of Southern Hunting and Fishing

The assistance of a negro is as necessary to the full enjoyment of a coon hunt as cranberry sauce is to the completion of a turkey dinner.

—*North Carolina sportsman*, Recreation, *1901*

White sportsmen had long criticized African Americans' sporting practices as a threat to wildlife and as flouting the codes and methods guiding "proper" sporting behavior. They believed such conduct symptomatic of general black inferiority, testimony that former slaves ravished the Southern wilderness, and further proof that freedom threatened Southern prosperity. Yet, despite the venom with which sportsmen decried blacks' hunting and fishing practices, they did not wish African Americans to be completely banished from the Southern sporting field.

Thus white sportsmen maintained that people of color could and indeed must have a permanent place in hunting and fishing in the South. When carried out independently by former slaves, hunting and fishing revealed all the limitations of liberation, but, when performed for and with their white betters, they represented the subordination that confirmed whites' sporting and social superiority. As independent sportsmen, African Americans threatened Southern wildlife and whites' sporting privilege; as dedicated servants, they became valuable sources of necessary labor and vibrant symbols of white mastery that helped elite white sportsmen reconnect with the idealized racial hierarchy of the antebellum South. African-American labor thus became an indispensable physical and symbolic component of "proper" Southern sport. Put simply, black service became, in the eyes of many whites, a welcome antidote to black liberation.

In 1895, Chicago sportsman Emerson Hough contributed a series of articles to *Forest and Stream* that described his recent trip through Mississippi and strongly encouraged Northerners to head south for their field sports. Hough had several reasons for such enthusiasm. The South had richer resources in fish and game, and provided a friendlier welcome to sportsmen, than any other region. Hunting and fishing had yet to be commercialized in the South to the same extent as elsewhere, and thus provided a field for gentleman, not hunters for market. Finally, and for Hough perhaps most importantly, Southern field sports demonstrated the proper ordering of the races. When Hough experienced firsthand the role of African Americans in hunting and fishing in Mississippi, he liked what he saw. "The negro makes a large factor in the field sports of the South. In the North we do our own camp work, team driving, etc., to a large extent, and when you speak of this to a Southern sportsman it always causes surprise." Southern sporting arrangements differed significantly. "The Southern idea of comfort in camp means a large tent, abundant camp furniture and two or three servants to do the work—an idea which certainly grows upon one, and which one is not disposed to call a bad one after he has gained acquaintance with it." For Hough, the North simply did not compare with the South in the area of available and agreeable sporting labor. Northerners typically performed their own sporting labor in the field. "In the South you simply hail the first negro, and the negro doesn't ask any questions, and doesn't say anything about pay. A good deal of the time he doesn't get any pay, but he has put in the time just the same, and feels as happy."[1]

For the thousands of Northern sportsmen who hunted and fished in the Southern United States in the late nineteenth and early twentieth centuries, African Americans' central but inherently subordinate position provided a reason for heading south and a model of race relations for the rest of the nation. "If I could have one of the most sincere wishes of my heart gratified," Hough wrote, "I would export about four thirds [*sic*] of all the Chicago city Negroes, and I wouldn't send them to Liberia either."[2]

African Americans, then, played a vital role in the sport of white Southerners and visiting tourists who hunted and fished across the South in the decades after the Civil War, making Dixie one of the leading sporting destinations in the United States. Since the early days of slavery, African-American labor had been a central part of white Southerners' sporting ideal. Antebellum elites felt more like masters when they had African-American subordinates on hand to sharpen the distinction between owner and property. After Emancipation, subordination of blacks became even more important to white Southerners.

Wherever elite sportsmen led, African-American laborers followed. Before Emancipation, slaves provided skilled and menial labor as huntsmen and fishermen, packed supplies and equipment, worked as guides, tracked, located, and drove quarry, and performed many other tasks in the sporting field. Just as importantly, they provided key symbols of white-over-black domination. In a system disrupted by war and Reconstruction, elite whites both symbolically resurrected and concretely reinforced their hold on African Americans through the hierarchical relationships of hunting and fishing. Myths of the Old South, which flourished into the twentieth century, enabled whites to celebrate hunting and fishing as important institutions that helped them preserve and relive that lost golden age. The racial subordination created and reinforced in the field provided a remedy for the social, economic, and labor problems posed by independent African Americans' exploitation of Southern fish and game. Reasserting the antebellum sporting ideal—subordinate black labor directed by wealthy white Southerners—provided a strategy for reclaiming lost control. With slavery destroyed and Southern social relations restructured, sportsmen needed black labor more than ever. Having black subordinates in the field returned whites to a mythical era of aristocratic sport and racial control and projected to the world, including Northerners such as Emerson Hough, a solution for the South's "Negro problem."

Thus the presence of black labor remained central to white Southerners' quest to recapture the past and frame the future, and also became part of the experiences of the sporting tourists who flocked to the South after the Civil War. To these visitors, a Southern sojourn created an Old South that provided both enjoyable sport and an authentically Southern experience. Whether wealthy visitors whose sporting vision required fine attire and aristocratic field ethics, or middle-class hunters and fishermen whose primary concerns were steady supplies of fish and game, sporting tourists expected African-American subordinate companions to make their fleeting experience of the now-mythic Old South more realistic.

White narrators described the role of former slaves in Southern sport with a nostalgic longing that, in part, accounts for the thematic symmetry between antebellum and post-Emancipation accounts of African Americans' hunting and fishing. As Nicholas Proctor points out, "white hunters often conceived of the hunt as a portal into an immutable (if substantially fictional) South."[3] Yet accounts of black labor in white sportsmen's hunting and fishing reflected more than an affinity for past achievements in racial domination. Such descriptions also focused on the present by responding to a changing Southern social structure in which whites had lost permanent, legal control of the black populace and faced a serious threat to the labor supply essential to the South's economy. Images of slaves in antebellum accounts of hunting and fishing had a substantial impact on the tenor of post-Emancipation narratives, but one must be careful not to label those later narratives as merely backward looking. While harking back to a lost golden age, the visions of black inferiority and incompetence constructed in hunting and fishing narratives, as in Hough's endorsement of the servitude he found in Mississippi sport, were also responding to contemporary threats to white supremacy. Postwar sporting narratives simultaneously presented a longing for the past, a lamentation for the present, and perhaps a hopeful corrective vision for the future.

If it is incorrect to label such sportsmen's accounts as exclusively backward looking, it is equally problematic to interpret them as reflecting only notions of white supremacy. There is more to be gained from studying accounts of African Americans' labor on whites' hunting and fishing excursions than simply how such accounts solidified and refined images of racial control. A close examination shows that black huntsmen, fishermen, and laborers drew substantial benefits from their involvement in whites' sport. Most obviously, they found a source of steady employment and an avenue of economic improvement that only grew as the South became an increasingly popular sporting destination. Ironically, whites' use of hunting and fishing to confirm racial subordination, which made black labor a permanent part of Southern hunting and fishing, created opportunities for some former slaves, particularly those who were highly skilled in the ways of fish and game and lived in the popular resort areas of the South. For while the stereotypes of racial domination perpetuated by whites in their narratives of Southern hunting and fishing reified racial distinction, they also made the presence of rural blacks an indispensable part of the Southern sporting experience.

African Americans achieved substantial material and financial gains from their work. Aside from wages, black laborers often took home a portion of the day's catch, which supplied meat for personal and family subsistence. Their work often allowed them to earn supplies and equipment, including ammunition, tackle, even old firearms, as payment or gratuity, which provided opportunities to improve their own hunting and fishing. While such financial and material gain neither erased the images of inferiority proffered in white sporting accounts nor changed the inherently unequal power relationships, it is clear that laboring for whites did not benefit whites alone. Some African Americans found a niche for themselves in the new sporting system.

In fact, a close examination of the sporting interactions between whites and blacks uncovers rare accounts in which black sportsmen-laborers did not become the victims of white exploitation and stories in which interactions between blacks and whites did not reinforce images of racial subordination. Some accounts provide glimpses into moments when African-American laborers could turn the tables on their white employers by challenging both the litany of racial stereotypes and the supposed white mastery that demanded their presence in the field. Indeed, the reason whites needed such laborers—for their skill and experience in the sporting field—became an avenue through which African Americans could use hunting and fishing to demonstrate their own expertise, poke fun at their employers, and seize a level of authority they normally could not possess. Just as laboring for white sportsmen gave blacks important economic benefits and greater access to Southern fields, forests, and streams, it sometimes provided opportunities to counterbalance the images of dominance and subordination that Southern elites sought to perpetuate.

AFRICAN AMERICANS' SPORTING LABOR

Although the presence of blacks in white Southerners' field sports remained a constant, the tasks they performed depended on a variety of factors. Different kinds of excursions required different types of laborers. The fox hunts enjoyed by wealthy Southerners in some regions, as well as other excursions designed to mirror aristocratic English sporting traditions (in which full field regalia and large numbers of attendants played symbolically necessary roles), usually employed the largest numbers of black laborers. Such excursions were rare, however. It is easy to exaggerate the number of large plantations with hundreds of slaves in the antebellum South, and the degree to which Southern hunting mirrored the ideal of the English country gentry. Indeed, regal hunts, such as that attended by Edward J. Thomas, a planter of Savannah, Georgia, while vacationing at a relative's plantation in South Carolina, were uncommon for all but the wealthiest sportsmen. "About two o'clock—it was in December—all hands would prepare for a fox hunt," Thomas recalled, "horns blowing the signal would be heard from the stable yards . . . saddle-horses, held by negro chaps in gay caps, would be waiting on the lawn, but not long waiting, for we would all soon be in the saddle and cantering to the forests." Such scenes counted among Thomas's most cherished experiences. "I never had anything to suit my taste as did these fox chases," he declared.[4]

Such extravagant hunts, while rare, demonstrate how the projection of aristocratic ideals remained an important function of elite field sports. The clarion call of horns, the use of expensive livery, and other displays of pageantry proved that planter-sportsmen such as Thomas's South Carolina kinsman Colonel Julius Huguenin, master of the hunt described above, had the necessary refinement to follow the sporting codes perfected by the English country gentlemen they sought to emulate. The sheer size of such excursions, with their well-trained hounds and the finest horses, proved that planter-sportsmen also had the financial clout to provide the most lavish sporting experience.[5] And finally, the presence of the "negro chaps in gay caps," central to Southern aristocratic sport, not only provided labor but symbolically reinforced whites' mastery over the African-American population.

The use of freedmen in these excursions testifies to the aristocratic values at the heart of elite Southern field sports. Consider the language employed by One of the Scribes, as an 1872 contributor to *American Sportsman* called himself, when he described time in camp on a Virginia hunt. The party spent much time "lying like kings upon our royal couch of ceder [*sic*] down, listening to the gossip of the huntsmen and the comicalities of the colored peasantry"; having black labor on hand made the party feel "like kings."[6] The descriptions of Southern hunting and fishing used by native and visiting sportsmen to create this fantasy of aristocratic mastery show the degree to which the appeal of the sporting experience depended on subordinated African Americans. Northerner Edward King embraced this fantasy while touring near Mobile, Alabama. Overcome by the scenes he encountered, he wrote that "the long avenue seemed all my own; I could almost fancy that the coast was mine; the islands and the light-houses were mine, and that the two negro hunters, loitering by with guns on their shoulders, were my game-keepers, come to attend me to the chase."[7] Elite sportsmen coveted such mastery, whether over the natural environment or over African Americans, which they symbolically, and sometimes materially, constructed and reconstructed in the sporting field.[8]

Although the quest for aristocracy would remain an important part of the Southern sporting field, most sportsmen lacked the financial wherewithal to provide such pageantry. Large-scale hunts—such as an 1867 deer hunt on St. Helena Island, South Carolina, described by David Franklin Thorpe, in which "we had nineteen white men, about a dozen negroes and eight hounds, six of them being young dogs"[9]—remained rare. Most Southerners, even elites, hunted and fished on a smaller scale, and therefore most African-American sporting laborers toiled on more ordinary outings. Yet even on such smaller excursions, black laborers maintained their symbolic importance. Occasional larger hunting or fishing trips that carried a greater symbolic or recreational function required more black labor. Most Southern sportsmen who frequently employed former slaves hired but one or two, with more laborers added depending on the wealth of the white sportsmen, the number of people taking to the field, the length of the outing, and the type of game sought. A two-week trip, for example, required more gear and equipment and more portage by laborers than a simple two- or three-day expedition. Hunting or fishing trips in coastal, swampy, or other wetland regions, for which both boats and knowledge of landmarks and waterways were at a premium, demanded more skilled laborers, guides, and boatmen. Large-game hunting, for such quarry as deer, bear, or catamount (mountain lion), required more drivers and shooters and typically called for more laborers than did expeditions for small game such as squirrels or opossums. Yet no matter the size of the excursion, African-American labor remained a necessity, both for the work and for the symbolic ideal of blacks' subordination.

When whites took to the sporting field, they invariably sought out labor suited to that important dual function. The recruitment of labor often went hand in hand with other motivations for entering the sporting field, which involved more than just hunting or fishing. Some sportsmen, particularly visitors from other, more populated and urbanized regions, saw in the Southern sporting field a chance to venture into a wilder, less-developed part of the country that re-created a by-gone America and required a shorter (and safer) trip than the Western frontier. J. B. Burnham, for example, saw a chance to escape crowded Northern cities and modern cultures. "To one whose nerves have been worn to the quick by the ceaseless hurry of city life the easy going ways of the South are balm and healing," he declared. Leaving the North, where he was "condemned to hustle and elbow and push lest he get eternally left," the Northern visitor might envy the South for its "pleasing disregard of Father Time, whom he has been accustomed to respect and worship as coequal with the almighty Dollar."[10] The South, for many sportsmen, held the possibility of escaping modern life. Chester L. Fidlar, when describing a hunt with black guides Ace of Spades, Cass, and Bill, and their dogs, asked: "What was there about following those dogs that was so fascinating? I tried to solve the feeling, and I believe it was because it was primitive . . . We enjoy stepping down from the pinnacle of our civilization, and reverting for a time to the ways of our progenitors."[11] This desire to seek untamed frontiers, to return to a less civilized era without truly abandoning the luxuries and refinements of modern America, seemed to have a more than tangential connection to the South's racial history.

Statements that paired the South's sporting benefits with its race relations appear frequently in nineteenth-century sporting literature. Such discussions specifically included African Americans—or, at least, idyllic memories of African Americans as slaves—as important parts of such experiences. For Southerners, this connection evoked memories of a time (at best exaggerated, at worst fictional) when the world was properly ordered. Wirt Howe, who advertised his shooting grounds near Columbus, Mississippi, in *Outing* magazine, assured potential investors that "the large plantations of the cotton belt, which present the same appearance that they did in ante-bellum days and which are operated upon methods that have been in use for many years, are, from an agricultural point of view, unlike anything existing elsewhere in this country." Moreover, he pointed out, each plantation had its own set of "'quarters,' parallel rows of log cabins where live the negro hands and their families, very much as they did in the days of slavery."[12] Thus visitors could rest assured that their surroundings, physically and racially, mirrored the antebellum ideal that lured them south.

Sportsman "P" clearly revealed this longing for the stereotypical trappings of the Old South. "Of all the sports of the field or forest, mountain or plain, wooded hillside or swampy jungles," he wrote, "none affords such real, genuine, jolly, rollicking fun as the old fashioned possum hunt, which is a peculiarly Southern institution, and can be seen in perfection only on the old plantation and among the darkies." The opossum hunt "is eagerly entered into by all classes, from the learned judge to the irrepressible small boy and the happy-go-lucky cornfield negro." Perhaps lamenting the passage of another "purely Southern institution," P saw in the old-style opossum hunt a glimpse of a broadly appealing past that "always brings sweet memories to the country-raised southerner, and are not appreciated by others." Those desperate to recapture old times must head south with all speed and, most importantly, must remember a critical ingredient of the old-time hunt. "Such an one would be repaid for a journey to the favored land for that special purpose, though tyros should by all means get some Uncle Sam, who is to be found on every plantation, to act as master of the hunt."[13]

Charles Henry Smith, writing under the pen name Bill Arp, painted a typically rosy, paternalistic picture of slavery, presenting hunting expeditions with slaves as an aspect of antebellum life that he missed most.[14] Noting with sadness that "the good old plantation times are gone," Smith recalled days when masters cared for their slaves and slaves reciprocated with loyalty, "times when these old family servants felt an affectionate abiding interest in the family." "We frolicked with their children, and all played together by day and hunted together at night, and it beat the Arabian Nights to go to the old darkey's cabin of a winter night and hear him tell of ghosts and witches." Smith later commented on the recollections of his friend Dr. Curry, who also used the hunt to represent the lost social relations of slavery. "How feelingly he records his companionship with the family negroes," Smith recalled. Hunting excursions comprised some of Dr. Curry's favorite memories. "Oh, the tender and teary recollections of 'possum hunts and coon hunts and rabbit hunts and corn shuckings," Smith concluded, "and eating watermelons in the cotton patch and sometimes finding them while pulling fodder in the hot and sultry cornfield!"[15] For those like Smith and Curry whose sporting memories figured prominently in their reconstruction of a Southern golden age, hunting and fishing provided a window into an ideal past, with whites the kindly masters and people of color the loyal slaves.

Ultimately, white Southern sportsmen's attachment to the antebellum ideal reflected both a longing for a return to a largely mythical age of racial domination and a deep-seated dissatisfaction with the post-Emancipation social order. By constantly returning to hierarchical social relations created and reflected by hunting and fishing, relations they associated with antebellum life, white Southerners critiqued a version of the new Southern society—particularly its race relations—with which they were increasingly dissatisfied. As Jacob F. Rivers III noted in his literary analysis of nineteenth- and twentieth-century Southern sporting narratives, the keepers of Southern hunting and fishing traditions found that "the principles underlying the aristocratic code of Southern sportsmanship provided an excellent cultural framework within which to think about and to articulate the negative changes they saw in their respective societies."[16] Several components linked African-American subordinates to whites' hunting and fishing in the post-Emancipation South. White Southerners' fond recollections of hunting or fishing with slave companions, sporting tourists' idyllic visions of a romantic, aristocratic Old South, and, not least, sportsmen's need for steady labor—all led thousands of sportsmen who traversed the South to rely on the labor of African Americans. For many, such an excursion simply could not be truly "Southern" without it.

Descriptions of African-American laborers permeate narratives of Southern hunting and fishing, from setting off on excursions through scenes of sociable camp life at their conclusion. At all times when in the field, whites kept black subordinates with them to do their work, make them feel more like the aristocratic sportsmen of old, and reinforce feelings of racial mastery. C. Wayne Cunningham, in a 1900 letter to *Outing,* wrote that the arrival of a white sporting party created an exciting social spectacle for African Americans on the Georgia coastal islands, especially for those who labored for white sportsmen. When the party arrived at the wharf, a black deer-driver would blow his bugle to "let the colored people on the island know we were coming, and to be on hand at the wharf." On landing, the party was "greeted by several of the island negroes" and their hunting hounds. Cunningham recalled that "no welcome could have been finer to a crowd like ours than seeing those hounds and hearing their familiar voices." Of the crowd of local blacks that met the party, two stood out for Cunningham: "old Dick Shed, the stalwart, beaming-faced negro, who is kindness personified" and "Daddy Bob, the short and dumpy, whose 'whiskey-cough' is well known to all those who have ever hunted on St. Catharine's Island."[17] Such scenes demonstrate both the possibility of employment for black Southerners and whites' seeing such heraldry as a mark of their superior status and an integral part of the Southern sporting experience.

White sportsmen cultivated the notion that their black laborers experienced as much excitement over the prospect of sporting service as did whites over having black workers at their disposal. As sportsman "C" recalled about his dealings with a gentleman from Maryland named Watkins, "The negroes that country round looked on him as a kind of oracle, and when Massa Watkins arrived every darkey's face beamed with pleasure; and when a coon hunt was proposed the entire darkey community went mad with joy." On these excursions, C continued, Watkins usually took along with him "a small army of darkies, each one of them armed with an axe, or a half-starved, ragged cur," to do the bulk of the work for him.[18] An unnamed *Outing* contributor, recalling a similar enthusiasm for black labor in the furtherance of white sport, wrote of his "loyal henchman, 'Ole Brack Pete,'" and noted that each year, as fishing season approached, Pete would sing excitedly of the upcoming chance to serve:

> She's a long time a-comin',
> She's almost heah—
> She's dun bin erlong time on de way;
> Russle wid dem gum boots,
> Hump y'usef chile—
> Marse Ned's gwine fishing'—rite erway.

"I am no singer . . . but I think I understand the feeling that drives that ebony rascal to caterwauling and bellowing when trout time's a-coming," this contributor noted, explaining his loyal employee's excitement over "Marse Ned's" annual resumption of fishing. "It is the same spirit of restlessness, warmed to life by the first mild breezes, which sets me to rummaging and to fussing with flies and feathers, and to overhauling a certain old tackle-box as it has been overhauled these many years."[19] For laborers such as Ole Brack Pete, enthusiasm for service, optimistically presented as the pinnacle of black social ambition, came from a love of field sports and of laboring for whites.

Once sportsmen departed for the field, they relied on African Americans for all sorts of necessary tasks, including transportation, particularly for visitors who might not know the lay of the land. "To enjoy good fishing at Beaufort the first thing you need is a good boatman," a South Carolinian wrote, under the name Cosmopolitan, in July 1874. "Happily they abound, and Alfred or Henry Boyd, Stephen Turner or Caesar Davis will serve you well for a moderate compensation, procure stout lines and strong hooks, such as are used by the local fishermen."[20] Describing an excursion near Lake Ellis, North Carolina, "J.E.W." recalled that, through the railroad's station agent, his party secured the services of "'Sparks' a genuine North Carolina *collard stuffer*" who, "together with his cart and critter, form the transportation of ourselves and our traps."[21] Northerner Horatio Bigelow recalled that when he and a companion hunted at John's Island, South Carolina, they employed African-American guides. "Bill had Uncle Joe, a coal black negro with a white wooly beard, to shove him around through the marsh, while I drew two small nigs, each with a shoving pole, who managed to keep our clumsy old bateau moving."[22]

Sometimes, acquiring a skilled guide made the difference between success in the field and going home empty-handed. Sportsman Edward A. Robinson of Baltimore, Maryland, recalled a trip through Georgia during which "we stopped at several places as we went along to try the fishing, but did not have much success." Finally, Robinson and his friends "made arrangements with a coal black fellow named Lewis to drive us across the island to a celebrated fishing place called Bluff Creek Hammock."[23] On a duck hunt on the Savannah River, an *Outing* contributor writing under the name Dick Swiveller, unfamiliar with the scores of inlets and marshes that dot coastal Georgia, likewise relied on skilled black guides and pilots. "The bateau was commanded by Niger Joe, a prince of camp cooks, while Aleck, his black friend, guided the shooting craft skillfully down the current, past the bending willows under which the wild fowl are found and flushed at the approach of the boat."[24] Particularly in lowland and coastal regions of the rural South, where slaves had long been employed as huntsmen, fishermen, and boatmen, African-American laborers remained readily available and, more importantly, knew local fields, forests, and waterways better than most. They thus provided the best and most sought-after transportation.

Having reached their destination, sportsmen depended on experienced black hunters and fishermen to locate the quarry and take them to it. As they well knew, this often provided the best chance for a successful expedition. Fishing for tarpon in an unspecified part of the region, Fred J. Wells needed an experienced guide to locate and land the notoriously difficult fish. He chose Louis Collins, "one of the best guides in the South" who had "lived on the banks of the Fish River all his life, and is thoroughly acquainted with the habits and peculiarities of the different species of fish."[25] R. S. Pollard noted that he and his companions also relied on an African-American guide to locate their prey for a Virginia raccoon hunt. "The snow was at least 12 or 15 in. deep, which indicated at once that we were to have a glorious time," he began. Because their host's "old darky Coleman . . . had been reconnoitering the whole time of the day before to find out where the best hunting grounds were, and had just returned, informing us that 'I neber see so many coon tracks before in all my born days,' we knew that our most ardent hopes were about to be realized."[26] If white sportsmen wanted the best chance at catching their prey, they knew they should turn to the area's most experienced black huntsmen and fishermen.

Indeed, sportsmen often found African Americans' knowledge of a region's fish and game to be extensive. Naturalist Bradford Torrey, who toured the South in 1898, wrote with surprise of the knowledge demonstrated by an African-American guide hired in South Carolina. "I quizzed him about birds. Yes, he had noticed them; he had been hunting a great deal."[27] White visitors relied heavily on laborers' experiential knowledge, not only for conveyance but also for information and guidance. On the deer hunt on the Georgia coast described above, C. Wayne Cunningham noted that the guides determined the route he and his companions would take. After finishing their breakfast, the party waited while their three guides, Charles Grant, Dick Shed, and Daddy Bob, "fell to a discussion as to what drive we should first take. First, all three disagreed; then, after much expounding on Charles' part and assenting on Dick's, it was determined that we should take one of the drives near the house to start with."[28] White sportsmen, particularly if not native Southerners, quickly learned what many Southerners had known since slavery: African Americans knew not only where to find fish and game but also the best ways to get them.

An unnamed contributor to *Forest and Stream* in 1885 described this connection between black knowledge and white sport. "While out one day with a friend we were joined by a strapping young fellow who volunteered to take us to every 'gang of pattidges' on the plantation. He informed us that he and another negro had only a short while before bagged twenty-three quail out of twenty five shots."[29] The message to white readers was clear: black Southerners could both find game and, to the distress of some white sportsmen, kill it with efficiency. Harry Worcester Smith, in *A Sporting Family of the Old South*, recalled occasional visits to a friend's plantation for hunting and fishing trips. His friend often consulted "his overseer and factotum, old Black Sam" for advice on sporting matters. "On the farm and in matters pertaining thereto, Sam was the Chief's [Smith's friend's] alter ego and he was universally admitted to be a first-rate judge and manager of farm stock generally," Smith wrote, "but far above this the old darky prided himself on his knowledge of and skill in hunting raccoons, and other nocturnal 'varmints.'"[30]

Not all white sportsmen would admit to relying on black subordinates to find fish and game, but none hesitated to use them for the variety of tasks required once the prey was located. Black labor in those situations became an absolute necessity for many outsiders. F. A. Olds noted in 1900 that "the prerequisites for a hunt are a negro, an elderly one preferred, a couple of dogs, kept up during the day so as to be 'sharp' for the hunt, a light, an ax, and a sack," making clear his dictum that African Americans were one of the starting points for a Southern excursion.[31] "The assistance of a negro is as necessary to the full enjoyment of a coon hunt as cranberry sauce is to the completion of a turkey dinner," a Charlotte, North Carolina, sportsman wrote in 1901. "When starting out to spend a night with the coons, we always took with us 2 or 3 darkeys, 2 sharp axes, and 2 large corn sacks." As an example he described a Virginia raccoon hunt. "One day, about the first of the coon season, Arch [the contributor's friend and hunting companion] sent over a darkey to ask if I would go hunting that night. I sent back word that I would, and would take Ned, Jake, and Dick, my father's 3 hired men, to cut down trees and carry the game."[32]

Frank A. Heywood also wrote of the need for black subordinates. Describing small-game hunting in the Dismal Swamp of Virginia and North Carolina, he noted that "for coon and possum hunting, provide yourself with plenty of 'niggers' and coon dogs, and start into the swamp immediately after dark." For Heywood, hiring black laborers to perform the heavy tasks was indeed necessary, but perhaps in some ways secondary to the spectacle of watching such laborers in action. "It will not be long before the dogs will have treed a coon. Then comes the fun," Heywood noted of watching his hired hands carry out their appointed task. "Muscular negroes attack the tree with sharp steel or mount into its branches. Torches of lightwood blare brightly. The hunters gather about. The tree falls or the coon is shaken from the branches. In either case there is a conglomerate mass of negro, dog and coon." Heywood's description reveals his obvious enthusiasm for such contests. "Thump! The dog has him; and a tussle occurs, but the dog wins. Thump again! A negro has smitten a brother in his anxiety to strike the coon. Yah!

A negro has caught a possum, and inserting the beasts' tail in the clevis of a hickory stick, starts for home, the envy of his sable companions."[33] In these hunts, black labor also served a key psychological function. These scenes—"the height of fun," according to Heywood—that depicted African Americans as simultaneously lacking in grace and civility but still under the control of white sportsmen formed one of the most common tropes of dominance in whites' accounts of Southern field sports.

Black laborers also cared for and managed the dogs, mainstays of hunting sports, on whites' expeditions. Hunting dogs were one of the most effective means for locating a variety of small game, such as fox, rabbit, and squirrel, and even for driving large game such as deer. Calling to mind both European aristocracy and the antebellum planter elite, possession of a well-bred, finely trained pack of hounds symbolized sporting refinement.[34] For Southerners, this function also found expression in the ubiquitous presence of the slave dog-handler, who appeared frequently in antebellum sporting narratives. After Emancipation, the loyal former slave who controlled the pack remained a staple of both Southern sport and sporting literature; with slavery gone, it was a particularly valuable icon for Southern elites who seemed to admire these dog-handlers as much for their symbolic value as their practical benefit.

Andrews Wilkinson, while hunting in lower Louisiana, took to the field in a multiracial party that included a former slave dog-handler, and later recalled this individual in regal tone and with more than a hint of longing for the "old days." Wilkinson's party consisted of seven persons, including "three creoles from neighboring white plantations" and Jean Baptiste, "our colored 'master of the hounds.'" Jean Baptiste was born on a local sugar plantation, where he had served as huntsman, and "during his involuntary bondage he had endured no heavier tasks than were allotted to a hound master, gamekeeper, and venison provider of the old regime." The high status accorded Jean Baptiste did not disappear with the end of slavery, nor did his function as a symbol of aristocracy and racial control. Representative of a continuity in race relations before and after Emancipation, re-created in the Southern sporting field, Jean Baptiste proved that freedom did not "ruin" all African Americans. "Though grizzled with advancing age and by thirty years of freedom, and blackened and warped by the winds and suns of half a hundred hunting seasons," Wilkinson noted, "he still remained the guardian, trainer, and master of our general neighborhood pack of deerhounds."[35]

It was also common, particularly with the end of slavery, for white sportsmen to hire African-American dog-keepers who used their own animals for hunts. F. A. Olds, on a hunt on the Cape Fear River in North Carolina, employed Amos, "a faithful darky, to whom a hunt on Bald Head is a never-failing delight." Amos provided trained hounds for the hunt, in this case "a sort of spaniel named 'Jumbo' and a non-descript cur named 'Pete,'" and managed them in the field. While Amos did not know Pete's exact breed, he did not doubt his effectiveness. When Olds asked about Pete's lineage, "Jes one o' dem standard cur dogs, de most reliablest dog a nigger kin have," Amos responded. "His faith in Pete was justified by results," Olds concluded.[36] While hunting in Maryland, H. M. Howard hired two black dog-keepers, the first a "wiry little, old negro, with ill-fitting and discolored clothes, and run down boots" named Uncle Ned, and the second, "another negro, a strapping young fellow," named Lincoln. They brought along "three dogs of doubtful ancestry, popularly termed coon dogs," called Dash, Spark, and Dandy.[37] The skill of laborers such as Jean Baptiste, Amos, Uncle Ned, and Lincoln, who since the early days of slavery had been among the most skilled hound masters in the South, played a critical role in the success of whites' field sports and in maintaining the illusion of a racial aristocracy that seemed threatened in the decades following Emancipation.

As indicated by an account from an unnamed Tennessee sportsman, describing an opossum shooting party he organized for his sister and a friend who was visiting from Boston, black laborers were often responsible for the success of an excursion—and not just while in the field. Leaving with a large party of perhaps twenty young men and women, in addition to the writer's mother and another married woman who went along as chaperones, the party soon met "the negro I had hired, and his pack of dogs." On the hunt, the dogs located their quarry. They treed an opossum, which was shaken out by one of the laborers and fell to the ground dead. By the end of the evening the party had caught four more. "When we started homeward all agreed we had never had a better time," the narrator recalled. Some of the party members later expressed surprise that a fall from a tree could so easily kill an opossum. What they did not know was that the narrator had again relied on his African-American laborer. "They do not know that when I hired the negro I saw 4 'possums in his cabin and bought them; instructing him to send a small boy ahead of our party to plant dead 'possums in trees at ½ hour intervals."[38] Because it would not do to allow guests to go home empty-handed, the laborer not only had worked on the hunt but, more importantly, had kept his white employer from losing face.

There seemed to be no limit to the tasks black laborers would perform on these hunting expeditions. While at their father's Myrtle Grove plantation south of New Orleans, Andrews and H. W. Wilkinson employed "Tom Howard, our reliable colored cook and camp servitor, and old Jean, the ante-bellum plantation deer-hunter, [who] loaded up our cat-rigged hunting-boat with a big tarpaulin tent, camp-beds, provisions for a week's cruise, and a good supply of hunting and fishing accoutrements."[39] When S. Phelps sought good sport near Pine Bluff, North Carolina, he did so "with a prominent State officer"—whom he met through the recommendation of an officer of the Seaboard Air Line Railway, one of the leading promoters of hunting and fishing in North Carolina—with "his keen scented pointer in front and a well scented darkey behind."[40] C. W. Boyd and a companion set out for a winter shoot in South Carolina, "determined to go in style." One of their first tasks was to find a black laborer to serve their camp. After being "overwhelmed with applications," they settled on Barney, "a genuine Southern negro, with thick lips, broad, good-humored face, and somewhat of a character in his way," who met their needs perfectly. Barney proved a valuable asset. "Not an event of importance took place in local sporting circles of which Barney did not know, and of which he was not magna pars, as Virgil puts it," Boyd noted. "Add to this that he was a first-rate cook, and in social intercourse constantly inclined to risibility, with a never-failing flow of conversation, and no one, I think, can disapprove of our choice."[41] It was important for Boyd and his friend to employ an experienced sportsmen, but they specifically sought one with a particular personality type—a "genuine Southern negro," of "good-humored face," who "in social intercourse constantly inclined to risibility"—that fit their preconceived idea of a properly subordinate African-American companion.

Black laborers' role did not end with the set camp, baying hounds, or captured fish or game. African Americans carried the products of these excursions from the field, cleaned and refitted equipment and supplies, even provided entertainment for sportsmen on the return to camp. White sportsmen, particularly those with aristocratic pretensions, would not perform these jobs themselves and believed them to be ideal work for black subordinates. R. S. Pollard, for example, relied on his guide to find a laborer to carry home their game. "It was now impossible for us to carry all our game," Pollard remembered. "We were getting more or less tired from our tramp, so we sent Coleman over to a neighboring colored man's home to ask him if he would not take our game home for us. Coleman soon returned with this man, and after telling him he could take one of the coons for his trouble, we were off again."[42] When a sportsman writing as Mortimer returned with his companion from an excursion near Virginia's York River, they were met by "several of the darkies, who took our traps in charge, and we started for the house."[43]

Even the social life that awaited sportsmen at their destination sometimes included African Americans. Whether in the stereotypical Southern sporting camp of which nineteenth-century sportsmen often wrote or, for well-heeled sportsmen, in the more upscale sporting lodge or resort, black subordinate companions remained visible. One unnamed sportsman, describing an 1875 trip to South Carolina, noted that the presence of former slaves, as well as their activities and behavior while in camp, helped white sportsmen judge the caliber of camp life. Commenting on the social distance between blacks and whites, as well as their respective foods, this contributor again demonstrates the multivaried importance of African-American subordinates. "The negroes were grouped around their own fire at a respectable distance eating their store of provisions contained in one iron kettle, consisting of hominy with the addition of a few birds. We, of the white, or 'plain' skins, as our dusky friends are pleased to call us, made an ample meal of a more luxurious character, and chatted merrily till late hours."[44] Such accounts again suggest that white sportsmen used the presence of African Americans as much to cultivate their own identity as for labor.

The entertainment provided between excursions, which sometimes included black performers, also reveals a close relationship between the presence of African Americans and whites' notions of a complete sporting experience. The program to open the 1889 season at the North Carolina Health and Sporting Resort in Avoca, for example, was made more authentic by the presence of a black chorus. As reported in the Chowan County *Edenton Fishermen & Farmer*, the program consisted of a prayer, a welcome address, a formal speech by an R. B. Creecy, "then an old plantation and fishing beach song by a choir of colored singers then dinner."[45] Such sporting entertainment could even attract a following across the Atlantic. When renowned Massachusetts-born sportsman Harry Worcester Smith, founder of the Master of Foxhounds Association of America and famous for his Southern hunts, took a hunting holiday in Ireland in 1912, he took along his favorite servants, including Norman Brooks, Dolph Wheeler, Sam Webster, Wiley Thrash, and Joe Thomas. These servants reportedly charmed guests at a Christmas gathering at Middleton Park. Smith had arranged numerous American delicacies, including confectionery from New York, ham from Virginia, deerfoot sausages from Massachusetts, and grapefruit from Florida. But nothing proved as big a hit as Smith's servants. The guests "were loud in their praises of the viands and the efforts of my colored cook; and between the courses, Wheeler, my trainer, charmed them with his beautiful double-note whistle, and time and time again the colored quartette would sing and all hands join in the chorus. Finally, after coffee, the table was moved and the rugs withdrawn, and such step dancing as only a Southern darkie can give was shown to those assembled."[46]

Whether at a resort or in camp, on a bateau or in the field, steering or shooting, trapping or carrying home trophies of the day's endeavors, African Americans never strayed far from the thousands of white sportsmen who traversed the South in the decades after the Civil War. These subordinate companions performed the countless, often menial and thankless functions that enabled Southern hunting and fishing (at least as recognized by white sportsmen) in the first place. They also carried out the other crucial function of being black. Sportsmen who hunted and fished in the Southern states demanded the presence of African Americans to make the South seem more like "the South" as they wished to remember or experience it, to help transform white sportsmen into country gentlemen of former days, and to reaffirm, even celebrate, the racial hierarchy that had been muddled by Emancipation. Indeed, African Americans provided their employers not just with luxury and labor, but with an inexorable link to their cherished identities as sportsmen, Southerners, and whites.

THE BENEFITS OF SPORTING LABOR

African Americans found themselves essential to the Southern sporting ideal, because of whites' willingness to profit from blacks' hunting and fishing talents and their desire to use the presence of people of color to validate white identity, but such exploitation was not completely one-sided. Black sporting laborers gained benefits from their centrality to Southern field sports, sometimes substantial benefits, and not just financial or material. Wages, the most common benefit, gave sporting laborers a chance to earn cash income in a money-scarce economy. Particularly in the most popular sporting states of the South, including the Carolinas and Georgia, Florida, Louisiana, Alabama, and Mississippi, sporting labor gave African Americans the opportunity to secure a ready supply of hard money.

Given the geographic and demographic diversity of the South, and that African Americans worked for whites all across the region, it is difficult to determine whether there were standard wage levels for sporting labor. Any standard must have been local and narrators rarely mentioned specific payment to laborers, which complicates any estimation of typical compensation. Cosmopolitan asserted in 1874 that a black laborer "will serve you well and faithfully for a moderate compensation,"[47] a sentiment typical of white sportsmen, who rarely discussed specific terms of employment. B. H. Wilkins, in his memoir "War Boy," noted that "poor folks used to make a few dollars poling the sportsmen around," but provided no detail.[48] J.E.W., by contrast, who hunted near Lake Ellis, North Carolina, offered one of the few examples of specificity. "The best of our guides can be hired for one dollar per day and rations, and almost every man in the country owns one or more hounds."[49]

Evidence indicates that many black sporting laborers sold their services on their own terms, informally, and often not for cash. The jobs provided not only wages but opportunities to earn a share of the fish or game caught or to exchange skill for sporting gear and equipment. The informal economy of the sporting field enabled black laborers, the vast majority of whom did not exclusively hunt or fish for a living, to secure the best deal they could at a given time and use the products of their work, earned in cash or kind, to supplement their normal income. It is impossible to determine with certainty how often whites paid African Americans in cash and how often they paid them in animals, skins, or other goods or services, but narrative evidence indicates that noncash rewards were commonplace.

As described above, Pollard, while hunting raccoon in Virginia with his guide Coleman, solicited a local African American to carry his party's game home "after telling him he could take one of the coons for his trouble."[50] A former slave named John accompanied George Clark Rankin on his nighttime raccoon hunts. John kept the raccoons for his own use because, like many other whites, Rankin perceived raccoons—although great sport to hunt—as food fit only for African Americans. After returning from the field, "a few nights later John would have a coon supper. But right there I drew the line," Rankin wrote. "No coon for me."[51] For his service to Andrews Wilkinson on an expedition near New Orleans, Old Jean, who served as a slave huntsman before Emancipation, received a share of the meat. According to Wilkinson, this was ideal because "we had all the snipe and duck shooting that we wanted, while 'Malviny and the chilluns' [ostensibly Jean's family] were provided with enough smoked coon-meat and pickled *poules d'eau* [small game bird of the rail family] to last them for the remainder of winter."[52]

On Fred Mather's specimen-collecting expedition near Catahoula Lake, Louisiana, with laborer and guide Sam, in addition to paying unspecified wages Mather included several other incentives. To keep Sam happy, he allowed him to sell a portion of the fish and game caught, "as a perquisite, a tip or reward."[53] A single catfish that Sam had landed, which Mather allowed him to sell, brought the laborer "$2.50, about 4 cents per pound," not an insignificant amount of money in 1898.[54] Mather also used new equipment as incentive for Sam. While they were searching for a turtle specimen, Sam noticed Mather's fine set of hooks and lines and remarked, "Golly, I'd like to get some o' dem hooks fo' big catfish, dey's de bes' I ever see." Mather promised Sam that he could indeed earn those same hooks. "Sam, if you can put me where I can get an alligator snapper of 60 lbs. or more, you shall have all these hooks and lines."[55]

Aside from the financial and material windfalls, sporting labor also created rare opportunities for blacks to display skills in the sporting field that many employers believed to be a prerogative of whiteness. Hunting and fishing sometimes gave African Americans a showcase for their mastery over the natural environment and its products, a mastery that whites wished to deny them. At times they could exploit their key role in Southern field sports to challenge whites' authority by embarrassing their employers or engaging in interpersonal behavior with white companions that would be unheard of outside the sporting field. Sporting laborers had a certain amount of social leeway not enjoyed by most other black Southerners, particularly as Reconstruction turned to Redemption and, eventually, segregation. Put simply, because African Americans were indispensable to "proper" Southern hunting and fishing, they could push at the limits of "proper" behavior for people of color.

Whites' accounts of taking to the field with black companions provide occasional glimpses of times when African Americans could display their skills in front of, and sometimes at the expense of, their white employers. Cunningham, for example, on his deer hunt in coastal Georgia, recalled that one of his laborers loudly proclaimed confidence in his own talent by blowing a bugle on arriving at their destination. As noted earlier, the bugle call was used to alert the island's black population to be ready for an approaching white sporting party, but according to Cunningham, "the bugler claimed that the reason he blows his bugle is not so much to warn the colored people of our approach, as the deer. Drawing himself up in a proud manner he would say, 'Boss, when I blow dis horn I can hear dem deer say, "Dere come Chas. Grant."'"[56] Such bravado by a black subordinate in the presence of whites was typically impermissible, but in the context of field sports, within the safety provided by their essential service, African Americans could trumpet, or bugle, their own skill.

This relative safety is shown in an account of a 1902 Pinehurst, North Carolina, hunt written by an unnamed white sportsman who hunted with "Tom, my colored guide." While stalking a bevy of quail, they scared some birds into the air. Both men fired, but with very different results. The employer missed, but "a half a second later Tom's gun scored a kill." Soon after, another group of birds took flight, with the same results. "Try as I might I couldn't pick a bird and at last, I blazed at the bunch," the white sportsman recalled. "Tom's gun had cracked with mine and two birds fell. He had waited until they were in line and killed both!"

Tom's shooting superiority was not lost on his employer. Yet, perhaps not wanting to endanger future employment and most likely well acquainted with the dangers of stepping "out of place" in 1902 North Carolina, Tom downplayed his superior shooting. He even attempted to give his employer credit for one of the kills. "'Berry good shot, sah!' he remarked, indicating that one of the birds was mine, and I was too chagrined to contradict him," the sportsman noted.

The white sportsman had clearly been outdone, a point that neither he nor his guide cared to dwell on. "I knew he had 'wiped my eye' once and killed two birds with his second barrel," the employer admitted, "but I kept quiet and guiltily took the bird and tucked it away in my coat, when the old dog brought it to me." Tom's importance to the hunt allowed him to use his skill to the utmost, in the process proving himself the better marksman and upsetting the notion of African Americans' inherent inferiority as shooters and sportsmen. Notice, however, that Tom minimized his challenge to white racial assumptions and any violation of the codes of behavior in relation to whites by not calling attention to his superior skills. Indeed, that ability probably allowed him to annoy his employer with his magnanimous demeanor. The narrator recalled Tom's discretion on their journey home. "As we rode I held an interesting colloquy with myself, and Tom very kindly confined his remarks to his horse and the dogs."[57]

Providing for the reputation of a sporting employer in this fashion was another requirement of African-American sporting subordinates. Suzanne C. Linder, in her *Historical Atlas of the Plantations of the ACE* [Ashepoo, Combahee, Edisto] *River Basin—1860*, described the sporting histories of several South Carolina plantations (Lavington, Bugbee, The Oaks, Drainfield, Fee Farm, and Godfrey) and recounted the services of "local African Americans [who] served as paddler and guides." One in particular, named Bristow, possessed this quality of prudence regarding his employers. Bristow "was especially valuable because it was said he could paddle with one hand and shoot with the other. Given enough compensation, he could also be discreet about just who did the shooting."[58] As such discretion indicates, black sporting laborers were well aware that their employment often depended on more than skill; it also suggests that they stood in a unique position in which they might benefit from such circumspection.

African Americans' ubiquity in Southern hunting and fishing sometimes allowed them to turn the tables on white sportsmen, with their centrality to "proper" Southern sport offering a measure of protection in the process. Examples of this are rare in sporting narratives—as one can imagine, white narrators were eager to present themselves and their fellows in a good light—but they do exist. An anonymous cartoon in the August 1903 *Recreation*, for example, demonstrates how black subordinates might position themselves to counter an employer's interests. Entitled "How Old Sport Stopped the Game Hog's Little Game," the cartoon depicts the return from the field of the stereotypical white "game hog"—the wealthy sportsman who cared little for the careful management of wildlife and slaughtered more than he should. Accompanying him is Old Sport, a black laborer. In the first panel, Old Sport struggles under the burden of so many animals. Faced with legal limits on how much game he can kill and transport, the Game Hog devises a clever scheme to evade eager game wardens; in the second panel, he is stowing his trophies in his luggage. Old Sport watches the subterfuge with a subtle smile, and finds a way to repay the Game Hog for making him bear such a burden. In the final panel, the Game Hog is smugly awaiting his train, seemingly unaware of the game warden searching his luggage.[59] I do not suggest that black laborers turned in employers who violated bag limits; in fact, I have not found an example of this. But this cartoon does show that sporting laborers, because of their near centrality to whites' field sports and their close proximity to whites while in the field, were very familiar with employers' sporting habits, would know if any laws were violated, and might be able to use such knowledge to their advantage.

William Allen Bruce provides a more concrete example of a laborer stepping "out of place." In his account of a fox hunt in Charlotte County, Virginia ("no where else on earth does fox hunting yield so much pleasure as here, sir!"), a black sporting companion seized the opportunity to prove his skill and knowledge at the expense of his white employers. A particularly sly fox had kept Bruce and his companions at bay for months. Eventually, Bruce organized a large party to dispatch the fox once and for all. Again the fox eluded the hounds and disappeared, a scene that repeated many times. Finally, Bruce called on the opinion of Old Moses, "the 'darkey' hand," who "fairly swelled with pride at being able to enlighten so many white folks on such an important topic." Moses gleefully pointed out a nest in the middle of a hollow scrub oak stump and, "after enjoying the expression of astonishment on our faces," explained how the fox had hidden from the party each and every time.

Moses' proud exhibition of knowledge allowed the party to quickly catch the fox and allowed Moses to display his prowess in that one form of hunting most closely associated with Virginia's aristocracy—a fact that, according to Bruce, Moses let no one forget. "Mose had the pelt to make him a pair of 'glubs' [gloves]," Bruce noted, "and he never tires of telling how this sly old fox was caught."[60] Protected by the real and symbolic value of his labor, Moses earned not only gloves but also a chance to display talents that proved a source of pride long afterward. Such occurrences often annoyed or embarrassed white narrators, but since laborers such as Old Moses resided in an inherently subordinate capacity, these incidents could perhaps be dismissed as aberrations that neither challenged assumptions about blacks' sporting skill nor posed any real threat to the racial hierarchy.

Indeed, one must be careful not to overstate any leveling effect provided by the importance of African-American sporting labor. Though they remained critical to white sportsmen, black subordinates stayed precisely that—subordinate. Ultimately, no matter how skilled the laborer and no matter how much whites claimed to value certain loyal and dear servants, African Americans' key role in Southern field sports could only push so far at the boundaries of the social hierarchy. The ever-growing racial divide limited that ability in the post-Emancipation South. If certain black laborers found opportunities to temporarily "turn the world upside down," those instances remained exceptional. African Americans who relied on hunting and fishing for employment performed difficult and often dangerous work for the benefit of white sportsmen who valued their subordinates only as far as whites' conceptions of proper and enjoyable sport were served.

Consider the story of South Carolina sporting laborer Isaac Polite, who took to the field for the St. Helena Island Rifle and Sporting Club in 1867. Polite set out with a large party that included "nineteen gentlemen consisting of members of the Club both active and honorary, and a number of invited guests from the Navy, from Hilton Head, and from Beaufort." It was a genteel affair and, according to David Franklin Thorpe, the club's recording secretary, everyone had a good time. "The generous good cheer of the tables was discussed with zest, and the songs, the speeches, and exhibitions of heroic valor in the field were heartily enjoyed."[61] An accident involving Polite, which Thorpe described in a letter to an acquaintance, was the only mark on the whole affair. A member of the party, Mr. William H. Alden, not wanting to clean his gun for fear of dirtying his hands, asked Polite to clean it for him. When Polite reached for the gun, it discharged into his left arm, an accident requiring "amputation saving the wrist joint and thumb." Alden gave the laborer fifty dollars, "and a sum was made up at once of one hundred and thirty dolls [sic], but that money can't replace a hand."[62] Thorpe also recounted the incident in the St. Helena Club ledger, asserting that it was "the single untoward incident" of the trip and that "through the generosity of the club, [Polite's] misfortune was mitigated by the prompt contribution of the sum of one-hundred and thirty one dollars, which *was placed in the hands of his employer* for the benefit of his family." In addition to the money given to Polite's employer, "a meeting of the

Club convened at the camp voted a further donation be made at the next meeting."[63] Their concern apparently had limits, however. At the club's next meeting, on February 14, they made no effort to vote additional funds for Isaac Polite, who, ostensibly, would no longer be able to secure part of his living through sporting labor.

SPORTING LABOR AND WHITE AUTHORITY

Despite the benefits to African-American sporting laborers—their chance to earn money, fish, or game, an opportunity to display their skills and experience, and the rare instance in which they could utilize the importance of their labor to poke fun at or embarrass white employers—white sportsmen employed black laborers to serve their own needs and most likely did not particularly care whether their subordinates benefited. Black sporting laborers faced unavoidable limits on how much they could benefit from their work. Such labor served, first, the needs of white employers, as plainly demonstrated by the tragic story of Isaac Polite.

Whites used narratives of sporting excursions involving African Americans to proffer certain images of people of color, to both the sporting and the general reading public, that helped create and reify notions of black inferiority and white supremacy. Just as antebellum narrators of Southern field sports used descriptions of slaves and masters hunting and fishing together to create the archetype of the docile, blissfully ignorant slave, so post-Emancipation sporting narrators, writing in a transitional period of Southern race relations spanning the insecurity of Reconstruction and the racial domination of Jim Crow, used the presence of former slaves to create portraits of black (and, by reflection, white) character that lionized white control over the sporting field and African Americans. In the accounts in sporting periodicals and newspapers, and in sportsmen's published recollections, writers constructed images of black Southerners that meshed with existing stereotypes and helped solidify emerging stereotypes of African Americans as unintelligent, uncivilized, incompetent brutes.

These narratives of Southern hunting and fishing, into the early twentieth century, served a variety of interrelated functions in their construction of particular images of African Americans. They re-created in the sporting field, through images of black loyalty, subservience, and docility, the racial hierarchy swept away by Emancipation. They provided humorous or degrading scenes involving black sporting companions that satisfied white readers' stereotypical associations. They contrasted whites' skill in the field with black subordinates' incompetence and poor behavior, to solidify their own sense of mastery over hunting and fishing. Finally, they depicted African Americans as inferior sportsmen who lacked the skill, intelligence, and moderation in the field required for furthering efforts to conserve the South's fish and game. Put simply, white authors crafted stories of the biracial sporting field to reinforce whites' social and cultural authority, and for that reason such stories abound in narratives of Southern hunting and fishing.

The "Old-Time Negro" became a common device to display white authority. This invention of disgruntled Southerners in the decades after Emancipation revealed a longing for the days of slavery. Such descriptions contrasted elderly former slaves who remained loyal and true to their former masters with the younger generation of African Americans not born into slavery and not as dependent on or deferential to whites. The antebellum archetype of the faithful black sporting companion appears in the story "Moses, the Tale of a Dog," by Francis J. Hagan, published in *Outing* in September 1898. "The Colonel" is on a sporting trip with two servants, one a former slave named Uncle Ephe, the other a young black employee named John White, who has brought along one of his young hunting dogs. The Colonel comments on the dog's obvious good breeding. "[The puppy] looks to me stouter than the sire, and, I dare say, has speed," he says. Forgetting his place, White, "carried away by this need of praise for his idol from such an imminent [*sic*] source," speaks up. "Yes, sah, he pintedly [*sic*] is fast—scuse me, Kunnel, scuse me, sah." White speaks before realizing it is not his business to offer his opinion on such matters. He is "confounded by his own temerity, bowing and scraping, with his hat off." Loyal Uncle Ephe, who knows the propriety of such occasions, admonishes the youngster for his infraction. "'Laws-a-me,' said Uncle Ephe, sotto voce, enviously, 'what's this new generation o' niggers a-comin' to, a-takin' de words out o' their master's mouths?'" [64] For white readers, particularly Southerners, Uncle Ephe would have been a welcome character who provided reassurance that the racial deference of the "Old South" remained alive and well in the sporting field.

Such stories of black loyalty to white superiors were common in accounts of Southern hunting and fishing. For some sportsmen, broadcasting African-American laborers' deference to whites became a worthy endeavor. An unnamed sportsman, describing an 1875 trip to coastal South Carolina, noted that he employed former slaves because the "study of character afforded by the negroes, decidedly the most primitive in manners and speech of the Southern blacks, is extremely interesting." He then recalled the role of African Americans in his hunting party. After the pre-trip meal, "a little darkey popped his head in at the door" to inform them it was time to ready their traps and equipment and prepare to depart from headquarters—"an old Southern mansion with broad piazzas, large high studded rooms, and chimneys built out-side, formerly occupied by the plantation overseer, an important personage in those times." The narrator described the captain of the company's laborers, "a negro by the name of Sergeant Parker." Parker was a kind and skilled hand, but more importantly, "understood his place thoroughly." Whites had their minds set on tractable, dependable black labor and made it a necessary part of their sport. "What servants these colored men are," the sportsman concluded. "The art of serving is with them innate."[65]

White commentators presented the sporting field as a place where racial subordination remained intact, where white sportsmen must and did dominate. African Americans neither controlled the sporting field nor had authority in relation to whites. When the races met in the field, which they often did, whites were in charge and African Americans deferential. Consider the account of "A Quail Hunt in North Carolina" by a contributor writing as H.W.K., during which his party met a group of black huntsmen. "Two of them had guns, the others were apparently unarmed, and they had a half a dozen dogs of as many breeds and colors. Evidently they were rabbit hunters. A North Carolina negro is a born rabbit hunter. A dozen or more of them will get together with possibly two or three guns among them and a horde of dogs of all kinds. Then they will have a rabbit hunt." Apparently the sight of the huntsmen inspired the band of whites to temporarily suspend their search for quail and try for a rabbit. Standing on a railroad embankment, a few of the white huntsmen spied a rabbit and opened fire. They missed their mark, which the black huntsmen, gathered nearby, enjoyed very much. "Of course they were highly delighted, and their remarks were anything but complimentary to our skill; but we didn't say a word—at least not aloud." Then the group of African Americans fired. Apparently believing one of their party made the kill, "a shout of joy went up as one of the rabbit hunter's dogs trotted in with the dead rabbit in his mouth." Their glee soon abated as the whites, either believing they had shot the rabbit or simply sure the animal belonged to them by right, demanded the catch. According to H.W.K., the African Americans offered no debate or resistance. "Upon our claiming the game it was handed over, and the gift of a ten-cent piece sent off the colored contingent with many grins of delight."[66] Properly deferential, the black huntsmen did not question the white men's right to the rabbit, thereby affirming the racial hierarchy of the field. The whites responded by offering a gift of money to show their largesse.

Comic relief provided another obvious function of the frequent inclusion of African Americans in white descriptions of Southern hunting and fishing. Nineteenth-century sporting narratives, designed to sell books, newspapers, and magazines, often contained humorous and farcical occurrences from the field that focused on people of color. These descriptions of Southern excursions appeared just as American racism reached an all-time high. White authors often poked fun at African Americans. Such humor portrayed subordinate companions as unintelligent, unrestrained, and uncivilized in order to contrast stereotypical black character with the intelligence and self-control of white sportsmen.[67] In an account of a Charlotte County, Virginia, raccoon hunt, for example, an anonymous writer portrayed his three African-American companions, Ned, Jake, and Dick, as stereotypically overemotional and unable to restrain their excitable natures. When they reached the field and their hounds began to bay, the excessive exuberance of the three men made it difficult for the white sportsman to clearly assess the situation. "The Negroes could no longer contain themselves and began to yell," he noted.[68] This juxtaposition of white and black sporting behavior is typical of nineteenth-century narratives. The white hunter is in complete control of his emotions while his black companions are not, a contrast that lays bare one of the stereotypes with which white sportsmen maintained the racial divide and labeled African Americans as inferior sportsmen.

To entertain his readers, *Outing* contributor John Mortimer Murphy relied on the popular notions that African Americans had a mortal fear of wild animals and were ignorant of the ways of the natural environment, both staples of nineteenth-century racial stereotypes and sporting narrative humor. Describing shooting in Florida, Murphy commented on African Americans' alleged fear of alligators, noting that "if there is anything [of] which they have a wholesome fear it is an alligator . . . Bayonets have no terrors compared with the jaws of these . . . creatures." Murphy explained that he once asked a guide why he was so afraid of alligators. The guide replied: "'kase in old times, 'bout de flood time, 'gatahs used to live on collude people, and dat made 'em so bad they was kicked out o' d' Ark by Noah or his mudder. Now I don't want 'em to get any blacker by eatin' me; not if I kin help it.'"[69] Here Murphy uses African Americans' supposed dread of alligators, as well as a ludicrous explanation of the alligator's history, to entertain readers probably well versed in assumptions of black intellectual inferiority. The account would also further demonstrate to a white audience that African Americans had an inherent fear and misunderstanding of the natural world and its creatures that both contrasted with whites' keen knowledge and further proved African Americans to be incompetent sportsmen.

Sometimes the "humor" of such narratives came less from poking fun at blacks' character than from placing them in physical danger. Such accounts often had a cruel edge that reveals much about the nature of the Southern racial hierarchy and the racism of the American sporting public. In *Glories of the Carolina Coast,*

James Henry Rice Jr., one-time secretary of the South Carolina Audubon Society who would later become a leading proponent of using the "Negro question" to convince Southerners to accept wildlife restrictions, fondly recalled a contest between an African-American laborer and a tenacious raccoon on St. Helena Island. "One of the most laughable sights I ever witnessed was a fight between a negro man and a 'tiger' raccoon. The negro had cut down a big tupelo in which the raccoon was hiding. I had promised him a dollar for the job." When the laborer went into the tree after the raccoon, a fierce wrestling match ensued. "Such spitting, growling and cursing mixed together I never heard before or since," Rice recalled. "The raccoon was biting off pieces of skin and the negro trying to tear him loose. It was worth a dollar of anybody's money."[70] Rice delighted in watching a subordinate risk his personal safety for his employer's benefit. The enjoyment of that "laughable sight" seemed to come from his subordinate's struggle and from the fact that Rice could cause such mayhem simply by offering a dollar. Such stories, in which African Americans were placed in dangerous, humiliating, and, for some readers, "humorous" situations, became common in sporting narratives and helped sportsmen clarify who was in control of hunting and fishing in Dixie.

"Will Scribbler" wrote of another incident, to amuse the reading public, that also had a decidedly dark edge that would most likely have been understood and appreciated by a Southern audience. His account of a hunt on an unspecified plantation, like so many other sporting accounts, may have been highly fictionalized or told as much to "entertain" or "instruct" as to recount a real incident. Scribbler described a party of white huntsmen who came across a black sportsman in the field. The "native" was hunting with an old musket and a frail hound and volunteered to lead the men to a covey of quail if they repaid him with a few loads of shot. The men agreed and set off with their new companion. The circuitous route led them through a nearly impassable wall of briers and brush that yielded but one rabbit and a single bird. Angry with the "native" for producing poor results, the sportsmen became infuriated when he made another offer: "Hi, gemmen, I tecks yer whar dar's er nudder gang ef gim'e sum mo' loads!" By way of response, the white sportsmen chose to repay the guide for his temerity. "In answer we presented arms as if to deliver the desired ammunition at easy gunshot, but our tormentor tumbling heels over head into a convenient briar patch in a frantic effort to dodge behind a mammoth oak." After the terrified guide embarrassed himself, "we concluded that sufficient retribution had found him out and so left him wondering what effect our nitro powder, wadded with paper, would produce when fired from that rusty musket."[71]

In this incident, the guide failed in his duty to provide Scribbler and his com-

An 1879 Currier & Ives lithograph by Thomas Worth demonstrates the familiar combination of images of African Americans' role in hunting and suppositions of black inferiority. In this case, the accidental peppering of the black subordinate companion provides the scene's supposed humor. (Courtesy of the Library of Congress)

panions with a sufficient quantity of game. For that, the whites made their "tormentor" pay a price by making him fear for his life. Certainly the author intended the story to be humorous, but there are other, embedded messages that would not have been lost on white sportsmen. Incompetent subordinates deserved what they got if their presumptuous claims of knowledge or authority proved detrimental to their betters. African Americans, such as the "native" in this story with his shoddy weaponry and inability to deliver on his promise, could not be taken seriously as skilled sportsmen. Unlike the laborers described earlier, lauded because they made good on the terms of their employment and because their status as trusted servants meant that whites viewed them as extensions of their own skill, a poor sportsman who operated away from whites' oversight and then failed to deliver on his word should be treated with nothing but contempt.

Indeed, even the entertainment drawn from cultivating mastery over African Americans in the field could barely qualify as sporting, at least as presented by some white commentators. When an otherwise refined, white sportsman took to the field with black companions, some asserted, this required stepping down from a higher level of civilization and temporarily embracing a less evolved form of sport. Edward W. Sandys described such excursions with something of a nostalgic longing, even as he made it clear that these endeavors were not true sport as he understood the term. When asked if he was familiar with raccoon hunts, he recalled that "before I ever attained the dignity of a full-fledged sportsman, while yet the complete outfit of cords and canvas, high-priced breech-loaders and well-broken dogs, was a fascinating dream of the future, I knew the coon." Sandys knew that raccoon hunts were not proper for a true sportsman, but admitted that he still secretly engaged in them from time to time. "And, let me confess it," he continued, "long after I down my quail and break my own dogs, I have sneaked away of an August night to join a crowd of 'brack niggers' for a good old-fashioned coon hunt." Notice again the dual message. African Americans cannot be true sportsmen because they do not hunt properly, yet it is perfectly acceptable for whites to join in such occasions because they provide both a temporary escape from the trappings of civilization and a valuable study of black character. "Ah, those old nights!" Sandys concluded. "What jollifications, what carousals of boisterous, harmless savagery were they!"[72]

African-American labor had long been a critical component of antebellum sportsmen's notions of proper sport. For white Southerners of the late nineteenth and early twentieth centuries, the presence of loyal, dedicated black attendants reinforced their sense of mastery over the natural world and dominion over people of color. With slavery gone, the dual function of blacks' sporting labor became even more important. As they recovered from the war and Reconstruction, as they struggled with black independence, as they grew increasingly frustrated with African Americans' slaughter of fish and game, white sportsmen looked to the traditionally hierarchical race relations of Southern hunting and fishing to help resurrect the control and subservience that characterized the slave system and to recapture the mythologized interactions between white superiors and black subordinates that anchored their rosy remembrances of antebellum life.

African-American labor played a central role in the South's emergence as a sporting destination. Sporting tourists saw in Southern locales not only rich supplies of fish and game but also a place where the pressures of Northern industrial life might be set aside, where life remained simpler and more natural, and where society existed as they imagined it had before the Civil War. These romantic longings, applied to the South, meant enjoying pristine natural areas unspoiled by overpopulation and modern development, a physical backdrop that included living reminders of the antebellum South, and, perhaps most importantly, the employment of skilled and loyal African Americans who simultaneously performed necessary labor and placed a capstone on white visitors' reconstruction of a mythologized Old South. This vision connected proper sporting behavior, gentility, intelligence, self-control, and skill to racial domination.

Careful reading of Southern sportsmen's accounts reveals the sporting field as an important site of whites' efforts to construct and reaffirm stereotypes that both harked back to slavery and provided concrete examples of white supremacy in the contemporary United States. Significantly, this process occurred at a time when the race issue exploded onto the national scene and Southerners struggled with what the press often termed the "Negro problem." For their part, African-American subordinate companions found working for whites a valuable source of money, equipment, and fish and game that would normally not be available to them. Beyond these advantages, which should not be understated, taking to the field with white sportsmen sometimes served a less material, though no less important, function. The centrality of black labor to the real and symbolic operation of Southern hunting and fishing sometimes created rare moments when sporting laborers used their skill and experience to counter an employer's vision of social and sporting mastery. But ultimately, for African Americans in the rural South, being a necessary component of Southern hunting and fishing proved a double-edged sword. It provided opportunities for material and psychological benefit, but also gave white sportsmen an arena from which to celebrate white supremacy, invalidate black sporting practices, and cultivate stereotypes of black character that persisted even longer than Jim Crow.

CHAPTER 4

"With the Due Subordination of Master and Servant Preserved"

Race and Sporting Tourism in the Post-Emancipation South

A great country is the South! I love every yard of it; its straggly roads, with pigs, pickaninnies and game cocks always in sight; its pine shake shacks, with mammy in the door, pipe in mouth and mongrel puppy barking at you from the porch . . . Some day I may settle there; or perhaps my youngest son, whose bent is decidedly agricultural, may buy him a plantation there in preference to bucking the game in our cold, hard North.

—*Northern sportsman Warren H. Miller*, Field and Stream, *1918*

By 1902, Theodore Roosevelt was America's best-known sportsman. Cofounder of the world-famous Boone and Crockett Club and a key figure in the rise of the conservation movement, Roosevelt had hunted all over the world. Yet despite his many conquests as big-game hunter, he had yet to land one of the United States' most famous trophies: the Southern black bear. A living symbol of sporting privilege, Roosevelt had long wanted to kill a black bear in the manner practiced by antebellum elites. "I was especially anxious to kill a bear in these canebrakes after the fashion of the old Southern planters, who for a century past have followed the bear with horse and hound and horn in Louisiana, Mississippi, and Arkansas," Roosevelt noted in *Scribner's Magazine* in 1908.[1] With this long-held ambition, and a standing invitation from Mississippi Governor Andrew H. Longino to hunt in the Magnolia State, Roosevelt at last decided to head south. Preparations took months, given the need for secrecy and security, but finally, in November 1902, the president set out by train for the famous hunting grounds of the Yazoo Delta.

The hunt took place largely on plantation lands in Sharkey County, Mississippi, and featured a "who's who" of Northern and Southern sporting elites. The hunting party included Stuyvesant Fish, president of the Illinois Central Railroad, who organized the hunt for President Roosevelt; John M. Parker, later governor of Louisiana, who used his considerable Mississippi sporting connections to arrange the location of the hunt; John McIlhenny, Tabasco Sauce heir and former "Rough Rider"; planter Huger Foote, grandfather of Civil War historian Shelby Foote; and planter and attorney LeRoy Percy, who later served as U.S. senator from Mississippi (1911–1913). These political and financial leaders, all avid sportsmen, eagerly joined Roosevelt's expedition, both for political reasons and to enjoy the famed spectacle of an authentic, old-style, Southern bear hunt.

Parker and his associates did everything to make the hunt a success. They scouted the best hunting grounds, chose the best laborers to accompany the president's entourage, and, perhaps most importantly, contracted with Major George M. Helm, who would lead the hunt, to find the best sportsman in the region to guide the party. Helm chose renowned Mississippi huntsman Holt Collier, a fifty-six-year-old former slave who would become one of the most famous sportsmen in Southern—indeed, American—history.[2] The choice of an African American to lead a party of such important personages may have seemed remarkable to those unfamiliar with Southern hunting and fishing. But to those who understood what sportsmen of the late nineteenth and early twentieth centuries required for a truly "Southern" sporting experience, it came as no surprise.

African-American sporting labor and an "authentic" Southern hunting and fishing experience were in some ways synonymous for many native and visiting sportsmen in the post-Emancipation South. Aside from remaining the preferred source of labor, African Americans, as ideal servants, played a vital role in the growth and popularity of Southern sporting tourism, most notably in the elite sporting clubs and plantations of coastal and Lowcountry regions of the Deep South. These are the regions where African Americans, because of their numbers and the areas' natural bounty, had plied their sporting skills for themselves and their white employers for generations. Wealthy Northerners and local speculators who saw the economic potential of sporting tourism eagerly bought up affordable undeveloped and unused land to attract visitors who wished to indulge in Southern field sports. Between the mid-1880s and the 1920s, largely in the coastal parts of the Carolinas and Georgia, northwestern Florida, southwest Louisiana, south-central Alabama, and the Mississippi Delta, speculators purchased hundreds of plantations and vast tracts of unused or abandoned lands and converted them into sporting retreats where visitors could relive the natural and social worlds of a re-created "Dixieland." Here, sportsmen could experience the stereotypical trappings that made the mythologized plantation South attractive to Northern tourists—Southern hospitality, largely undeveloped natural surroundings, stately plantation houses, and sporting excursions "after the fashion of the old Southern planters." Planters were much admired by sportsmen such as Theodore Roosevelt (his mother, Mittie, was raised in Roswell, Georgia) for both their gentility and their sporting acumen.

Essential for re-creating the social and cultural world of the antebellum South, these hunting and fishing venues required black laborers. From the 1870s, when the movement to establish such tourist retreats began, African Americans provided the best and most readily available sporting labor and, in the process, satisfied visitors' expectations of the Southern experience. In North Carolina, black laborers worked at such places as the Pinehurst Resort, once a renowned sporting and health resort (and now famous as a Professional Golfers' Association tour stop). In South Carolina, black labor dominated in places such as Beaufort's Chelsea Plantation Club, managed by John Edwin Fripp, and the coastal Broadwater Club, which owned the celebrated Hogs Island preserve, reportedly Grover Cleveland's favorite retreat. In Georgia, African Americans added "authenticity" to whites' sport in places such as Brunswick's Jekyll Island Club, once directed by New York's Judge Henry E. Howland and among the most exclusive sporting clubs in the world, and stately Cumberland Island, most famous as the site of Dungeness, the getaway of Lucy Carnegie (sister-in-law of Andrew) of Pittsburgh.[3] At these and other resurrections of the Old South, African Americans worked as scouts, drivers, watchmen, guides, and general laborers. They provided employers with experienced and skilled workers who fulfilled visitors' expectations of a re-created era of racial subordination, which proved a strong lure for tourists seeking to escape from the confines of an increasingly industrialized and urbanized world to a close approximation of the romantic, antebellum South.

Robert Q. Mallard, a planter of Liberty County, Georgia, made the connection between hunting and fishing and the preference for African-American labor even more obvious.[4] Fondly recalling his involvement in his slaves' expeditions "churning" for fish and alligator hunting,[5] Mallard pined for those halcyon days but more particularly lamented the loss of what those black-white interactions meant to Southern society. "It is easy to see how such a life, in which black and white, *with the due subordination of master and servant preserved*, shared the same sports, contributed to the familiar and affectionate relations which so notoriously from childhood bound master and servant together."[6] Such recollections often contained fond memories of masters and slaves interacting while hunting and fishing. Perhaps because, as in Mallard's view, the domination and subordination in these sports mirrored the ideal of the slave regime better than any other antebellum cultural institution, hunting and fishing figure prominently in whites' recollections.

The growing number of visitors who sought this idealized Southern past made tourism an increasingly important part of the Southern economy. As the presence of loyal black attendants became more closely associated with such a re-creation, many African Americans carved out an important and long-lasting economic niche by meeting those expectations.[7] In fact, the association between Southern sporting tourism and African Americans eventually became so indelible that black laborers became a sporting necessity. In the minds of many white sporting enthusiasts, a Southern hunting or fishing excursion was not complete without the presence of blacks. Thus *subordinate* African Americans used hunting and fishing employment to their own benefit at precisely the time when increasing dissatisfaction with blacks' customary rights was leading sportsmen, landlords, and legislators to work to restrict *independent* African Americans' access to Southern fish and game.

The necessity of having skilled African Americans on hand, for practical and symbolic reasons, made conditions right for former slave Holt Collier to lead the hunting party of a U.S. president.[8] A sporting legend while alive, Collier has again become something of a celebrity more than seventy years after his death, at the age of ninety. His exploits are the subject of two recent novels written for children, published in 1991 and 1993, and a scholarly biography published in 2002.[9] In addition, because of Collier's renown as a guide, a historical marker was placed at the site of his hunt with President Roosevelt and, in March 2004, an environmental education and resource management center at the Yazoo National Wildlife Refuge was dedicated as the Holt Collier Wildlife Interpretation and Education Center.[10] As a guide and bear hunter, Collier had few equals. According to his testimony to the Works Progress Administration, and a recent biography, Collier averaged about 125 bears per season. His account book listed, incredibly, more than 2,100 bears killed through 1890.[11] Few Southern sportsmen were unfamiliar with Collier and his sporting prowess. For decades he reigned as the surest shot, keenest tracker, ablest guide, and most famous huntsman of the Mississippi-Yazoo Delta. His reputation led to demands for his services for wealthy landowners, politicians, and sporting tourists from around the country.

The 1902 Roosevelt hunt, along with an October 1907 hunt with President Roosevelt in the northern Louisiana canebrakes,[12] brought Holt Collier national attention and secured his almost mythical place among American sportsmen. Yet despite these achievements and many others in Collier's amazing life, his wide renown remains a bit of a mystery. That an African American in the turn-of-the-century rural South could find such valuable means of support is unusual, considering the limited economic and social opportunities then open to African Americans. That a former slave could become so trusted as guide and huntsman that he would one day hunt with the president of the United States (who reportedly called Collier the best guide and hunter he had ever seen) is remarkable, given the strictures of Jim Crow. And that this African American would become so revered that he would one day be the subject of children's novels and historical markers and have parts of a national wildlife refuge dedicated in his honor seems nothing short of astonishing. Taken together, the events of Collier's life must represent more than just a story of how one man employed incredible sporting skill to create opportunities typically denied to people of color in the decades after Emancipation.

Holt Collier's life tells more than a story of his sporting excellence, and white contemporaries revered him for more than his abilities in the field. Collier's ninety years involved unending labor in the service of whites. Before becoming a legendary sportsman, Collier had been a loyal slave. His fidelity led him to go off to war as personal attendant to his master, Colonel Howell Hinds.[13] Collier became a recognized African-American Confederate combat veteran, fighting as a scout and ranger with the Ninth Texas Cavalry, for which the Sons of Confederate Veterans honored him with a gravestone dedication in 2004.[14] Thus, before becoming a faithful huntsman entrusted with the safety of a U.S. president, Collier was long a devoted slave and servant. He proved his loyalty to the Hinds family by shooting a train conductor who had pulled a knife on his former master.[15] And, if rumor can be believed, he perhaps killed a Freedman's Bureau officer, Captain James King; after beating the aging Colonel Hinds during a business dispute, King was found shot to death in a canebrake in December 1866.[16] Holt Collier, while a remarkable sportsman, always remained a loyal servant.

Collier's current fame may rest on his sporting legacy, but white contemporaries revered him just as much for his fidelity to whites during an age when slavery had ended, control over freed people remained uncertain, and whites were fighting back with a system of segregation to limit black freedoms. During that period, whites remained endlessly uneasy about their status as unquestioned masters of the Southern social structure, and, as scholars have shown, they looked wistfully to the antebellum South as a time when they were truly masters and people of color knew their place. The presence of loyal former slaves such as Collier helped resurrect Southern elites' lost sense of control and allowed them, symbolically and concretely, to reconstruct the lost hierarchy and aristocracy of the antebellum period. Whites built their mythical reconstruction in the sporting field. Sportsmen such as Collier, then, while respected and admired for their sporting prowess, won more renown for their service. Collier's life intersected with stereotypes of African Americans created in myths of the Old South and cultivated at precisely the time that he achieved regional and then national fame. These myths portrayed slaves as loyal, well cared for, and, indeed, happier than freedmen. Collier's life of service, in and outside the sporting field, confirmed the myth and provided a living, breathing example of the ideal, dedicated former slave.

The presence of black sporting subordinates in the postwar South proved a key feature of the region's hunting and fishing for visiting sportsmen. Southern sportsmen and visitors felt more like aristocrats of old when accompanied by African-American attendants. They felt more like antebellum planters with former slaves on hand. Tourists could feel they lived a uniquely Southern experience when hunting or fishing with a black laborer, guide, huntsman, or fisherman. Slavery had passed away, but visitors could recapture the mythological, highly romanticized relationship between benevolent, honorable masters and loyal, contented slaves. By re-creating a key symbol of the antebellum elite in the post-Emancipation sporting field, sportsmen insisted that the racial subordination of the Old South had not died. To put it another way, African Americans remained absolutely necessary for recapturing the version of antebellum social relationships that Southern elites wished to relive and visitors wished to consume.

SOUTHERN SPORTING TOURISM

Some chroniclers of Southern hunting and fishing have argued that the biracial sporting field foreshadowed social integration and was a harbinger of racial equality. Referring to a Southern hunting scene described by planter William Elliott in his famous *Carolina Sports by Land and Water*, literary scholar Jacob F. Rivers III wrote: "There are no lines of caste or class in this scene, no judges or doctors; no neophytes or veterans; no blacks or whites; no masters or slaves. Instead, through their total involvement in the magic of the chase, the men have transcended their societal positions and temporarily exchanged them for their primordial identity as predator."[17] Thus for true lovers of the chase, seeking to escape the drudgery of daily existence in a rapidly changing world, field sports might offer an opportunity to immerse themselves in nature, escape the Southern social structure, and exist only as part of the fraternity of sportsmen. The long-time editor of *American Literature*, Clarence Gohdes, argued that because African Americans figured prominently in whites' hunting excursions, these events became a force for breaking down racial barriers. "Long before the advent of [boxer] Jack Johnson and [baseball player] Willie Mays, hunting was a factor which promoted integration."[18]

Such statements about the leveling power of Southern hunting and fishing do not withstand close scrutiny. The biracial sporting field did not produce racial equality. African Americans had a permanent role in Southern hunting and fishing, but only because of their subordination to whites while in the field. Scholars who see social equality in the sporting field overlook the reasons that elite white sportsmen took to the field in the first place. Sportsmen sought not to erase social differences, but to idealize and more clearly define them. They intended to become members not of a larger, interracial fraternity but of a smaller, more exclusive white one.[19] In the South, where the presence of African Americans had helped draw such lines for more than two centuries, native and visiting sportsmen found it even easier to immerse themselves in such distinctions.

As many scholars of hunting and fishing have noted, white sportsmen had long used these activities to demonstrate their innate class, national, and racial superiority. Hunting and its attendant methods and codes of behavior separated elite white American sportsmen from Native Americans, immigrants, and poorer Americans, whose hunting they despised. For sportsmen such as Theodore Roosevelt, according to historian Daniel Justin Herman, "hunting became more than the mystical source of American manliness; hunting became the mystical source of American national and racial identity."[20] In the South, field sports served a similar goal of allowing the elite to flaunt its domination over the whole of Southern society, particularly African Americans. But unlike elite hunters of the West or the Adirondacks, who used the sporting ethos to disestablish competing traditions of Native Americans, poor whites, or the foreign-born, Southerners did not use sport solely to distance themselves from African Americans; they used black subordinates within the sport to solidify whites' position as masters of Southern society. For Western big-game hunters, their identity as manly defenders of American democracy required rejecting Native Americans' hunting and fishing and completely discrediting their skill and experience.[21] But for elite Southern sportsmen, many of whom were planters and former slaveholders, mastery required the presence of black subordinates and cultivation of the idea that former slaves remained both the best and most natural sporting laborers.

The rise of sporting tourism, predicated on blacks' service and subordination, reached its peak at the time when African Americans' place in the Southern social and political structure reached its nadir. It encapsulated late nineteenth- and early-twentieth-century racism. The inescapable connections between prevailing myths about the antebellum South, the rise of a nostalgia-oriented tourism industry, and whites' ideas of race and racial hierarchy were manifested in the region's hunting and fishing. To understand these connections, one must first have a better understanding of the great changes, both physical and symbolic, that took place in Southern field sports in the period. These changes made the South, particularly its romanticized antebellum version, an important destination for American tourists and sportsmen. The presence of African Americans played a vital role. For potential visitors and investors, black subordination added to the myth's "authenticity." Discussions of the region's hierarchical race relations often appeared alongside descriptions of its natural and sporting advantages.

The North Carolina State Board of Agriculture's guidebook *North Carolina and Its Resources*, published in 1896, emphasized the fine hunting and fishing in the Old North State. Like many other Southern states that used fish and game to lure visitors, North Carolina had worked to make tourism, especially sporting and resort tourism, a centerpiece of its recovery from the physical and economic dislocation marking the final decades of the century. By the 1890s, North Carolina could be counted among the nation's leading vacation getaways. The Board of Agriculture lauded the state's virtues as a pleasure-seeker's paradise worthy of visitation and investment. Yet the attractions thus broadcast, as in other guides published across the South in that period, did not end with natural beauty, mild climate, luxury hotels, and plentiful fish and game. As such literature often makes clear, North Carolina also offered the advantage of the proper ordering of the races. "The people are sociable and hospitable, and the colored people as civil as those whom they like to imitate," the Board of Agriculture noted. Laying bare the common assertion that the South's racial situation played just as important a role as its other attractions, the guide declared North Carolina a white man's country with a properly controlled black population. "No part of the South offers greater attractions to the investor and the seeker for health or pleasure, or is more interesting to the student than this." And aside from its many natural, economic advantages, North Carolina "also has the purest strain of Anglo-Saxon blood in the country, and with the possible exception of Kent and Devon the purest in the world."[22] As such appeals for Northern visitors made clear, the region had important vacation advantages that became linked to equally important racial advantages.

Of the thousands of visitors to the South in the half-century after Emancipation, the two most important groups were Northern investors, who capitalized on the region's depressed economy, low labor costs, and abandoned or undeveloped lands, and an ever-growing number of tourists, who, as investors quickly learned, came for the South's unique combination of natural bounty and real and mythologized history. Indeed, that combination became a godsend to those who wished to focus part of the region's economy on leisure and tourism. After decades of waiting in vain for real economic recovery and growth, Southerners realized that such a transformation could offer, in the words of historian Edward Ayers, "a way for places that had languished for years with unpromising agriculture finally to come into their own."[23] For the *Baltimore Journal of Commerce*, "the capitalist seeking profitable employment for his money finds in the South a rapidly developing country, where the growth is absolutely solid and permanent, and where money is in demand, yielding large profits, whether invested in banking, in manufactures, in railroad building, or in real estate."[24] With Southern landlords increasingly frustrated over the inefficiency of the tenant system and the general problem of labor control, many Southerners pinned their hopes on outside investors.[25]

The decline of rice-growing in the Georgia and South Carolina Lowcountry perhaps best illustrates the process whereby owners turned agricultural land to other uses. After the war, the economy of the Lowcountry, once home to the wealthiest Southern planters, fell into ruin. The migration of black labor, the widespread adoption of small farming by former slaves, a lack of operating capital caused by the war, growing international competition, and, in the 1890s, severe damage caused by intense storms—all marked the end of commercial rice cultivation in South Carolina.[26] By the turn of the century, according to J. William Harris, coastal plantation lands "were receding into the wilderness from which they had been created."[27] When the rice lands declined, the area decayed into poverty. As landowners worked to solve their postwar difficulties, many sought alternatives to large-scale tenant labor and searched for ways to exploit the huge amounts of available land and large supply of fish and game that remained their best assets. Lowcountry elites and other landowners across the South increasingly realized that financial advancement, even survival, required finding wealthy investors. "Lord, please send us a rich Yankee," South Carolina planter Sam Stoney Jr. declared in 1920, echoing a half-century of hopes and frustrations of area landlords.[28] They found such investors in the many Northerners seeking vacation destinations to combat their unease with urban life. Hunting and fishing, which by the last third of the nineteenth century were perhaps the most popular outdoor amusements for the middle and upper classes, became a key attraction.[29]

The South entered a golden age of elite hunting and fishing. At no other time did field sports enjoy such a combination of middle- and upper-class involvement and national acceptance as in the Gilded Age.[30] Because so many from the upper and middle classes became devotees of the sporting field, hunting and fishing became lucrative endeavors for sporting goods manufacturers, fish and game dealers, sporting laborers, and resort owners, prompting an increasing number of landowners and speculators to turn land to sporting uses.[31] Moreover, because that popularity put great pressure on national fish and game supplies, sporting enthusiasts searched for new regions to exploit, which became more difficult as the century drew to a close. By that time, the South ranked among the richest wildlife regions in the United States. Speculators realized that many fish and game regions, such as New York's Adirondack Mountains, faced both depletion of wildlife and overcrowding, and Southern lands that produced a fortune in lumbering and mineral rights might also create fortunes in sporting tourism. "Dakota is shot out. Wisconsin is fished out. The Adirondacks were tramped out long ago. The tide of sporting travel is settling back on itself," conservationist Emerson Hough declared in 1895. "There will be plenty of it turn and go in the South. The longer the South has attractions, the longer it will go."[32]

The Southern states did indeed face wildlife depletion, but the region's natural richness, a relative lag in wildlife slaughter compared with other regions of the country, and the rise of protected club lands purchased by sportsmen and speculators made the South an attractive sporting destination. Agricultural uncertainty after the war proved another reason for the abundance of fish and game in some parts of the South. Volatile cotton prices in the black belt, combined with labor instability, declining crop yields, soil exhaustion and erosion, and boll weevil infestations, led many landlords to abandon significant acreage of cotton land. As a result, according to Mississippi planter Wirt Howe, "these plantations are natural shooting grounds. Covering, as they do, an immense acreage, they present almost every variety of cover, affording not only the best of breeding grounds for the quail, but admirable protection from their enemies and the mild attacks of a climate that is rarely severe."[33] In other words, as agriculture declined and more lands lay fallow, the abundance of certain species of wildlife increased. "An Old Sportsman," lamenting how "the old haunts of the North have become drained," suggested in *Field and Stream* that "of late years it has become a known fact that the only ready good shooting to be had is in the South."[34] Sportsman William Bruce Leffingwell put the matter plainly: "a hunt in this beautiful country will prove a revelation to the Northern sportsman."[35]

Hoping to reach as many potential investors as possible, many Southern landowners advertised their lands in national sporting periodicals. A 1902 *Field and*

Stream article advertised the $20,000 Hutchinson Island Preserve along the Carolina coast, "embracing 12,000 to 15,000 acres of land" and "eligibly situated." "It is ideal as a stock range or game preserve, and is large enough to combine both. It was a famous ante-bellum Sea Island cotton plantation."[36] Some landowners did not sell their lands outright but, wanting to profit from the explosion in hunting and fishing, sold or leased the right to hunt or fish on their holdings. An Elkton, Maryland, sportsman noted that, on the Eastern Shore, "many a farmer, who cares nothing about the pleasure of guns and dog, would be glad to sell the exclusive privilege of gunning on his land for a small sum, to an association, and the price could be graduated to the amount of game on his place, which would be a strong inducement for him to feed and protect the game."[37] As frustrated landowners saw their chance to blunt the effects of agricultural and labor inefficiency, an increasing number turned to selling or leasing land or use rights to the throng of sportsmen and speculators who looked to the South with increasing interest.

The Southern sporting elite eagerly broadcast the region's advantages to Northern investors. Like many others who saw in the region's hunting and fishing a chance to lure outside capital that might revitalize the economy and return the South to its former economic preeminence, elite sportsmen, many from the former planter class, embraced the "second Yankee invasion." As a *Forest and Stream* contributor asserted in 1880, "Here, at the South, the sporting class is, as a general rule, found among the refined and cultivated gentlemen, who were formerly the large slaveholders, and who controlled the sentiment and politics of the South." However, "since the fortune of war has gone against them, they have buried the hatchet, and will be found ever ready to smoke the pipe of peace with their Northern brethren and will go as far as any man toward maintaining the honor and glory of America."[38]

Railroads, including the Richmond and Danville Railroad, the Seaboard Air Line Railway, the Atlantic & North Carolina Railroad, and the Southern Railway, helped Southern landowners and sportsmen advertise available hunting and fishing lands.[39] The Southern Railway, based in Washington, DC, described itself in 1898 as "the Samaritan of the South" because of its role in advertising resort and sporting lands to the Northern public. "No section of the country is comparable to the South to-day in the great variety of game, . . . and visiting sportsmen are always welcome."[40] Even as late as 1927, the Charleston & Western Carolina Railway published descriptions of South Carolina sporting lands, confirming that such lands were the playgrounds of wealthy visitors, not of the average, resident sportsman. "Some of the Beaufortland game preserves are not only spectacular in their acreage, but they are exceedingly costly affairs," the guidebook asserted. "More and more every winter Beaufort is filling up, and many of them are millionaires, with men who spend the season here and who fill up much of their time in hunting, fishing and boating."[41]

Avid hunter Grover Cleveland, who visited Georgetown, South Carolina, in 1894, was drawn south by reports of good sport. When he was hunting near South Island, a stiff wind threw him from his skiff, forcing his host and an African-American guide to rescue him. According to historian George C. Rogers Jr., "This gale proved to be no ill wind for Georgetown, for it also carried news of the President's rescue. The nation thereby became informed of the fine duck shooting available in Georgetown waters. The rich Yankees began to fall in love with the ready-made plantations, all with historic pasts and with the appropriate settings for their gentlemanly sports."[42] Newspaper editor William Page McCarty, who in 1897 tried to sell some hunting land below Virginia Beach, noted that such lands attracted "the class of Northern millionaires who affect the sporting fad like our late 'fat friend' [Grover Cleveland] of the White House and think that to shoot ducks is a certificate of aristocracy that can lift a soap factor or hog packer out of the native patch of mushrooms."[43]

As McCarty suggested, more than just the lure of a presidential retreat or available land teeming with wildlife attracted Northerners. They were also on a quest for what McCarty called "a certificate of aristocracy." Potential visitors fantasized not only about sport but also about an imagined South. As early as the 1870s, Northerners, especially sporting elites, members of the growing middle class, and potential capitalist investors, looked to the South as a place of welcome escape.[44] The appeal of the region thus became a key factor in sectional reunion, making the South, by the late 1880s, a favored middle- and upper-class tourist destination.

Southern locales became increasingly popular with Northern tourists in the late nineteenth century for several reasons. A mild climate, perfect for visitors suffering from maladies including "nervous exhaustion" and various respiratory ailments, provided one major lure.[45] Advertisers and resort managers made the region's healthfulness an important part of marketing strategy, as appeals for visitors made clear.[46] The South, unlike Northern resorts and spa areas such as New York's famous Saratoga Springs, remained unburdened by too many visitors. The region's less well-known and less accessible tourist destinations reputedly offered more spacious and, compared with Northern retreats, more exclusive vacation destinations.[47]

Population growth in Northern urban centers was yet another reason for heading south. Frustrated well-to-do Northerners saw in Southern locales a chance to venture into a wilder, less-developed part of the country and a bygone America. For some visitors, the desire to seek untamed environs, to return to a less hectic era without abandoning modern-day luxuries and refinements, and to experience the legendary trappings of entrenched aristocracy could be achieved only in the South, where time seemed to stand still. An 1881 *Forest and Stream* contributor, celebrating the virtues of the South, urged readers to "leave the false glare and glitter, the hollow show of a city life with a view to some weeks with nature and her charming loveliness, and he may be assured that he will find it, with fair sport added, in North Carolina."[48] This linking of hunting and fishing with a longing for a wilder, more rural, more "primitive" past demonstrates that visitors sought more than just the region's natural advantages.

By reputation, the South seemed friendlier to weary urban dwellers than did other destinations. Such openness to visitors—linked to the mythology of an antebellum planter class of legendary hospitality, which shaped Northern perceptions of the South—became a great inducement for tourists. "I would not change the old conservative ways of the South if I could and hope they never will change," Emerson Hough noted, "and I know all readers of this journal will be glad to rest their future acquaintance with the South upon its unasked and unpurchaseable hospitality."[49] Hinton A. Helper assured visitors to Aiken, South Carolina, of a hospitable local population. "Let him try this experiment of calling at some of the farm houses he may pass, and make any excuse, such as inquiring the way, or offering to purchase a glass of milk, or ask for a glass of water; and . . . he will be surprised to see how ready he will be met and welcomed."[50] Northerners envisioned the South as the model of old-time hospitality; with the economic potential of tourism, Southerners did all they could to confirm that stereotype.

In short, outsiders seemed to admire Southern hunting and fishing as much for its ability to recapture lost aristocracy and gentility as for its sport. As a *Field and Stream* contributor writing as Halcyon Hale noted, "the average American is not insensible to the charm of historic association in his pursuit of sport. He may not deliberately choose his field with a view to its historic surroundings, yet once brought to his attention he is prompt in responding to their sympathetic appeal." No other destination captured the Northern historical imagination as did Dixie. Despite the recent bloodshed, promoters of Southern tourism whitewashed the region's history to the point where its violent past, including the Civil War, became quaint. As Halcyon Hale concluded of hunting and fishing in the Old Dominion, "few places in America offer so rare a combination of good sport and historic interest as the easterly part of Virginia."[51] Even the poverty of some parts of the region might be seen as worthy vestiges of the Old South. "Occasionally for the northern tourist, [vacationing in the South] meant enduring the real experience of drafty old houses and broken-down beds, but it might also mean an up-close encounter with the ruins of an old plantation, a rundown former slave cabin, or an old Confederate soldier," historian Nina Silber writes. "In the tourists' eye these sites were seldom problematic and they were certainly not political; they only heightened the image of Southern distinctiveness which the Northern traveler craved."[52] Publicists cleansed negatives from the region's history; slavery, war, and poverty became monuments that heightened visitors' sense that they were experiencing something uniquely Southern.

NOSTALGIA, RACE, AND SPORTING TOURISM

"Sportsmen, historians, antiquarians and nature lovers will find great delight in visiting Beaufortland," wrote N. L. Willet, Charleston & Western Carolina Railway agent. "This section has a history that is all romantic wonderland . . . It has been a shining mark for wars: Spanish, Revolutionary, Indian and the Civil War with its horrible Reconstruction era. It has been the mother of crops for world use, such as silk, indigo, rice, Sea Island cotton and rock phosphate was mined in large quantities."[53] The war was over and Northerners now craved remnants of the Old South. "There must be amusements, mental and physical, and inducement to out-door life and exercise," F. W. Eldredge declared in a guidebook for Camden, South Carolina, "and certainly nothing more perfect can be wished for in a place of this kind than a quaint, quiet, old village to which nature and history have vouchsafed much that is beautiful and romantic, clinging fondly to its old dwellings, customs, and memories of the past."[54] Sporting tourism relied heavily on such "memories," although it must be noted that the past as tourists wished to see it had little to do with the realities of antebellum or post-Emancipation Southern life. This was especially true for one important part of a fictionalized South —the plantation experience.

The importance of the plantation to stereotypical images of the South cannot be overstated. Southerners had for generations touted the plantation as the seedbed of aristocratic virtue and manly skill, where men learned command of slaves, became intelligent farmers, and engaged in sporting activities that cultivated martial skill. Joseph LeConte, Georgia native and noted scientist who served as chemist for the Confederacy's Nitre and Mining Bureau, credited his plantation upbringing, particularly frequent hunting and fishing excursions, for his mental and physical prowess. "This kind of life is an admirable culture for a boy. It not only contributes to physical health but also to mental health, by continual contact with nature and by cultivation of the powers of observation. In addition, it cultivates in an admirable way quick perception, prompt decision, and persistent energy and patience in pursuit."[55] Many Northerners accepted this romanticized vision. For visiting sportsmen, experiencing the grandeur of plantation life enabled them to enjoy an opulent vacation with a patina of celebrated social hierarchy that they associated with the antebellum plantocracy. The newly arrived elites did not make their fortune in plantations, but they believed such regal estates could best display such wealth. In the words of George C. Rogers Jr., "property in land was no longer the basis for power, but instead property in railroad companies, public utilities, banks, lumber companies, and rice mills. Eventually the holders of new money would wrap themselves in the old plantation myth through marriage alliances, patriotic societies, and an emulation of a style of family living that hearkened back to antebellum times."[56]

Visible continuity between idealized antebellum plantations and the postwar South became an important selling point for land and sporting rights. Buyers wanted reminders of the Old South plantation, complete with stately old buildings, scenic farmland, and African-American dependents. The Southern Railway described lands along South Carolina's Congaree River in just such romantic terms, noting that the river "is a beautiful, navigable stream that winds its way through pine stretches, cotton fields and all manner of plantations. Picturesque is a poor word for its wooded banks, its unexpected turnings, the scenes of cotton and tobacco fields and quaint log cabins galore."[57] According to F. W. Eldredge, these plantations carried on the rich sporting traditions of their antebellum counterparts. "The plantation life was royally hospitable and generous, and as royally reckless and extravagant. A passion for field sports was a part of its very being—an inheritance from the earliest settlers, their ancestors, the English, the Irish and the Scotch." Eldredge declared such traditions alive and well in the New South, noting that "to-day the love of field sports is as keen as ever."[58]

Advertisers stressed that Southern sporting plantation lands both teemed with fish and game and maintained cherished antebellum traditions. Speculators made certain that Southern sportsmen became the logical inheritors of aristocratic sporting traditions in the resurrected Old South. *Outing* contributor Wirt Howe noted that field sports on Columbus, Mississippi, plantation lands had changed very little. There, according to Howe, the cotton-belt plantations "present practically the same appearance that they did in ante-bellum days and . . . are operated upon methods that have been in use for many years," and furthermore are "unlike anything existing elsewhere in this country." A signal feature of this preserved plantation life was the presence of African Americans, as evidenced by "the 'quarters,' parallel rows of log cabins where live the negro hands and their families, very much as they did in the days of slavery."[59] Tourist literature consistently stressed this continuity between the Old South and the New. Those that benefited from the influx of Northern visitors and capital stressed that the basic social structure of the antebellum South, especially whites' domination over a subservient black population, remained intact.

Just as antebellum planters used the presence of African Americans to mark their mastery, so white Southern sportsmen relied on former slaves to assure them of their place in the social order in the post-Emancipation South. For visiting sportsmen seeking to recapture the Old South, African Americans, ideally working for whites just as they had done under slavery, formed an essential part of an authentic reconstruction. In the sporting field, former slaves, such as Holt Collier, played as important a role in re-creating Old South mythology as had skilled slaves for antebellum planters. For Northerners such as sportsman Warren H. Miller, African Americans seemed central to the experience. "A great country is the South!" Miller declared. "I love every yard of it; its straggly roads, with pigs, pickaninnies and game cocks always in sight; its pine shake shacks, with mammy in the door, pipe in mouth and mongrel puppy barking at you from the porch." So attractive was Miller's vision of the South that he believed he might one day leave the North. "Some day I may settle there; or perhaps my youngest son, whose bent is decidedly agricultural, may buy him a plantation there in preference to bucking the game in our cold, hard North."[60] Visiting sportsmen hungry for the Old South expected black servants to be constant parts of the scenery. For how could a reconstruction of Old South aristocracy be complete without those people who made antebellum planters a master class in the first place?

African Americans' importance to reconstructions of the Old South can be seen in the advertising and descriptions of Southern locales in tourist guides, personal accounts, and national sporting periodicals. Soon after the close of the war, for example, David Franklin Thorpe, Sea Island cotton plantation superintendent, wrote to his friend John Mooney that St. Helena would make a fine destination both for its sport and for the presence of African Americans. "You would find a great deal to interest you here in the fields, in the woods, by the shore, and in the water besides what you would find of interest in the character and habits of the negroes lately come out of slavery."[61] Julian Ralph found blacks one of the most crucial parts of his Southern experience, noting that "to me the colored folks form the most interesting spectacle in the South . . . As I think of them, a dozen familiar scenes arise that are commonplace there, yet to a Northerner are most interesting." In his description of fishing along the many canals crossing New Orleans, African Americans completed the scene. "It is delightful to see them. Those open waterways flowing between grassy banks out towards the west end might seem offensive otherwise, but when at every few hundred feet a calm and placid negro man or 'mammy' with a brood of moon-faced pickaninnies sprawling beside her, is seen bent over the edges, pole in hand, the scenery becomes picturesque, and the sewers turn poetical."[62] Such quaint holdovers were essential to re-creating a past, golden age and added to the authenticity of a Southern sojourn. Elite sporting tourists therefore cherished the symbolic importance of African Americans almost as much as, in Old South mythology, benevolent antebellum planters cherished their dutiful slaves.[63]

Yet, although visiting sportsmen needed African Americans to complete their Old South experience, they felt uneasy about them. While advertisers and speculators extolled the presence of "authentic" African Americans living as they had done under slavery, they carefully avoided the impression that the South was anything less than a white man's country. Romantic descriptions of black life went hand in hand with assurances of a clearly drawn racial hierarchy. The message that the South existed first and foremost for white men resonated with many Americans. According to the *Southern Cultivator*, "there is not elsewhere upon the globe as a territory open to the Anglo-Saxon race with such varied and great resources and such propitious and easy conditions of life and labor, so abundantly supplied with rivers, harbors, and with lines of railroad transportation, or so well located to command the commerce of both hemispheres."[64] Fred W. Wolf Jr., of the Jasmine Farms of Green Bay, Virginia, left no doubt about Anglo-Saxon superiority. "'Virginia is heaven,' where the white man is a gentleman—he hunts all day and never works." And African Americans were there to do the dirty work. "The men-folks are off before daylight with their horn, 'hosses' and dog, for deer or fox, while the family's boys do the chores and the plantation work. A colored man servant in Virginia, irrespective of age, is a boy. Imagine an eighty-year-old boy."[65] Sporting tourism relied on African Americans to complete its re-creation of the Old South—provided, of course, that they remained controlled and subordinate.

Advertisers carefully assured potential Southern visitors of both excellent sport and well-behaved African Americans. Sportsman B. W. Mitchell's description of life on North Carolina's Currituck Sound, which noted that African Americans' houses outnumbered those of whites by perhaps four to one, assuaged visitors' fears by highlighting black subservience. "Darkies, darkies everywhere! Of all sizes, shades and conditions; but one and all, old or young, respectful, polite, obsequious; tacitly acknowledging racial inferiority by an extreme deference."[66]

In an undated nineteenth-century stereograph, an African-American boatman attends his white hunting party on an alligator hunt in Enterprise, Florida. The positioning of the laborer, standing at attention, oar at the ready, reinforces the common trope of white-over-black domination that elite white sportsmen worked hard to recreate through biracial hunting and fishing. (Courtesy of Florida Photographic Collection, State Library and Archives of Florida)

H. F. C. Bryant wrote in a similar vein of authentic, old-style fox hunts in Alamance County, North Carolina, and particularly of loyal former-slave laborer Uncle Simon Bolick. According to Bryant, Bolick also longed for the Old South. "The old darkey was in earnest. His memory carried him back and he lived in days gone by. He scoffed at the things of the present." Bryant believed that life had declined precipitously for Uncle Simon since his days of loyal service to Colonel William Bolick. As a slave, Uncle Simon had "hunted and traveled with his old master, who kept fine wines, blooded horses, and fast dogs. Truly, those were glorious days for Simon, and he has never become reconciled to the prosaic life of freedom."[67] Such stories assured Northern audiences that former slaves still served as loyal retainers and that white visitors had nothing to fear from them. The South was not just a sportsman's paradise, it was a white man's paradise.

Even though Southern elites had lost much of their previous authority over African Americans, some mastery could be retained, both literally and figuratively, in the sporting field. No threat to white control would face "those Northerners who spend part of their winters here in hunting and resting" along the Georgia and South Carolina coasts, according to an 1894 *Southern Cultivator* contributor signing himself G.A.G. "The country, although the blackest of black counties, in population, is one of the most orderly in the world," he assured potential sporting visitors. "Crime is almost unknown. This is largely due to the fact that the better class of Negroes, with that characteristic imitativeness of their race, try to copy the manners of their old masters, whom they still look upon as the best of the white race."[68] Real estate agent E. J. C. Wood assured Northern audiences that African Americans near the resorts of Aiken, South Carolina, "are very industrious and saving, and some of them are very lazy and improvident, but all of them are orderly. Indeed, the streets of Aiken are safer than those of New York; and . . . I will add, as safe as any Northern village. Even vicious negroes are not disposed to commit offences against the person."[69] Wood sent a clear message to potential sporting visitors: tractable, well-behaved African Americans could and would perform all necessary labor, and freed people, like slaves before them, knew their place.

New Yorker Henry Wellington Wack, who gained a measure of fame in the early decades of the twentieth century as a landscape artist and illustrator of hunting and fishing scenes, demonstrated both the virulent racism of Southern hunting and fishing and the degree to which Northerners embraced the ideals of domination and subordination proffered by Southern sporting tourism. Wack found black labor to be a key marker of authenticity for his trip to Florida. "To kill tarpon you require first of all an experienced 'nigger.' He is as necessary as bait, from which purpose however, the law exempts him. And I believe Henry Guy Carleton when he says only a 'nigger' will do—no colored person, or darkey or mulatto, but a genuine 'nigger.'" With the peculiar mix of overt racism and respect for African Americans' sporting prowess common among white chroniclers of the Southern sporting field, Wack seemed to draw as much pleasure from the presence of subordinate companions as from the sport itself. He began with advice on how to ensure that one's guide or laborer would be awake for the journey, jokingly suggesting that the employer, to "fix the nigger," should "hang an alarm clock around his neck and arrange with the stable boy to blast a can of giant powder under him at seventeen minutes past three in the morning. Then go to bed with the assurance that you'll have to wake that nigger yourself about five o'clock." Such measures might seem extreme, but were perhaps necessary. "The Florida negro is a specialist on sleep and melons; but properly 'fixed' he is an invaluable aid in your quest for tarpon."[70]

Neither the sportsman's difficulties with the laborer nor his enjoyment of those difficulties ended with such precaution. Warning that, on commencing the day's sport, you would soon "find your nigger fast asleep," Wack proposed a course of action that suggests the degree to which many visitors accepted and desired the racial hierarchy as part of a Southern excursion. "Leave him in peace for the present, but have a club handy, for when the king of game fish starts your line for Jamaica you'll need vigorous inducements to bring that nigger to consciousness. By lambasting his feet you awaken his head; besides, the damage is not so permanent." Once such problems had been dealt with, the sportsman could enjoy the relaxed pleasures of Southern tarpon fishing, pleasures that revealed both an interest in black laborers and a certainty of their overall inferiority. Describing how to pass the time on an excursion, Wack suggested that "some [sportsmen] lounge back in attitudes of the surest comfort and read and smoke; some write, some beguile the wait by discovering that the nigger is an intelligent companion, teeming with ideas about tarpon and local taxes, national politics and peach brandy. I say you may learn all this if your nigger is so obliging as to stay awake."[71]

AFRICAN AMERICANS AND SPORTING RESORTS AND PLANTATIONS

African Americans became so linked with Southern hunting and fishing that the two became almost inseparable. Advertising quail hunting on Shell Road on Alabama's Mobile Bay, Edward Cave assured potential visitors that "one can secure a negro guide there at the rate of one dollar per day."[72] Describing a game preserve on the Virginia and North Carolina border, Herbert K. Job recounted the fine hunting to be had "accompanied by a negro servant on horseback."[73] Robert Pinckney Tucker instructed R. L. Montague, caretaker of a preserve near Marion, South Carolina, that visitors must enjoy the services of "a competent boy employed as waiter during their stay."[74] The public and private hunting and fishing clubs that bought or leased so much of the South's abandoned and fallow plantation and woodland acreage between the 1880s and the 1920s employed large numbers of black sporting laborers.

With the uncertain future of agriculture, dissatisfaction with tenant labor, and a simple desire to make money, landowners across the South sold or leased shooting rights on millions of acres to firms and individuals interested in preserving good sport for themselves and their friends or making money by attracting visitors from across the country. These sportsmen demanded African Americans for both labor and symbolism. Happily, both for white sporting interests and for African Americans seeking employment that would provide at least a temporary alternative to regular agricultural labor, sporting preserves and plantations were typically found in old plantation areas with large black populations. These regions, including the South Carolina and Georgia Lowcountry, the Mississippi and Alabama black belts, and the Mississippi-Yazoo Delta, had no shortage of potential sporting laborers. Indeed, the overall popularity of sporting retreats in these areas perhaps owed as much to the ready supply of African Americans as to the availability of plantation lands. Areas that boasted large black populations could provide cheap sporting labor and more easily fulfill visitors' notions of aristocratic hunting and fishing. Consequently, African Americans in these areas, particularly along the coasts, were better positioned than those in the Southern uplands, the piedmont, and inland cities to take advantage of such employment opportunities.

Portions of the lands purchased as sporting retreats were still cultivated after conversion from strictly agricultural uses, and black tenants or sharecroppers often remained.[75] Permitting African Americans to continue in residence had many benefits. By keeping tenant farms in working order, new owners might make enough money to help finance club operations and reduce the financial pressures on their dues-paying membership. The lands, buildings, and equipment sustaining agricultural operations sometimes became an important part of a purchase. Advertisements for the Altama and Hopeton properties in Glynn County, Georgia, as sportsmen's retreats, for example, emphasized their potential as working plantations.[76] Restoring old plantations to working order provided crops for game, especially quail and other coveted game birds, and made lands more attractive to sportsmen. These sporting retreats, remaining much as they were in the antebellum period, helped craft the "authentic" plantation experience. And the presence of black tenants added to visitors' sense that they had returned to a Southern golden age. Keeping African-American laborers on converted plantation lands also kept a local supply of sporting laborers, often people who had worked on those lands for years.

Extensive, albeit rare, records of sporting plantations that kept careful account of laborers' activities provide glimpses of the valuable employment opportunities available to African Americans and their families. South Carolina's Kinloch Gun Club, located on South Island near Georgetown, left substantial records outlining African Americans' role in Southern sporting tourism. Owned and operated by the DuPont Corporation, headquartered in Wilmington, Delaware, the club was established to provide good Southern sport for DuPont executives and clients and, like many other sporting clubs, was a functioning plantation. Indeed, a majority of the hired hands at Kinloch provided typical plantation labor, and they are listed in surviving payroll records in occupations similar to those on any Southern plantation, including "laborer," "regular hand," "teamster," "gardener," "carpenter," and "plowman." These hired hands were typically listed as less than full-time employees, usually as one-half- or one-quarter-time employees, and they probably served the sporting activities of the plantation as well. In addition to the farming job classifications, many other listings, including "boatman," "watchman,"[77] "marsh hand," "bird-minder,"[78] "driver," and "guide" reflect the club's sporting activities.[79]

Sporting labor, whether in the service of native or visiting sportsmen, rarely provided more than supplementary income, even for laborers at the larger sporting plantations or hunting and fishing clubs. Sporting employees at Kinloch typically worked less than half the month, with some paid daily and others, apparently those who served more regularly, receiving monthly pay. Between early autumn and late winter, when most fish and game were in season and when the majority of Northern sporting tourists were seeking escape from Northern climes, employees worked larger portions of each month. Each job classification received a different pay rate, which the club superintendent recorded in his ledger. Boatmen, apparently the only sporting laborers who frequently worked full time, earned the highest rate of $10.00 for a full month's work. Bennett Wiggins and William Singleton, for example, frequently listed as boatmen in the Kinloch payroll records for 1914 and 1915, earned $5.00 or $10.00 per month, depending, ostensibly, on the number of guests present. Watchmen, who performed the critical task of tracking wildlife and reporting its location, also received good pay at Kinloch. Nelson Anderson, Jim Mitchell, and Toby Vanderhorst earned between $2.50 and $7.50 for their month's work. Peter and Richard Legare served as watchmen for a daily rate. In December 1915, for example, one of the busiest bird-hunting months, the Legares received 50 cents per day and earned a total of $7.50. Other jobs paid considerably less. Bird-minders, including Samuel Glover and Peter Legare (the only employee recorded in the ledger in two separate occupations), received between 25 and 30 cents per day to care for the club's game birds.[80] Although extant Kinloch records only include accounts paid in 1914 and 1915, and changes in individual employees' job status over time cannot be determined, it is reasonable to assume that better-paying positions went to employees who consistently demonstrated the most skill and loyalty.

Kinloch's guides and huntsmen, who were the most visible and, since entrusted with the safety of sporting tourists, probably the most experienced and trustworthy employees, were employed under a different system. Visitors, not the club itself, paid these workers, and each guest kept account with the employee, recording the kind of excursion undertaken and how much time was expended. For a guide and boat for shooting duck and other birds, visitors paid $1.25 per day, or $1.00 without a boat. For a guide for quail, turkey, deer, or other land-game hunting, visitors paid 75 cents per day.[81] Larger parties required more guides and huntsmen. In December 1916, for example, Philadelphia engineer Herbert T. Hartman and two companions spent three days at the club, employing Tommy Anderson, Sampson Edwards, Abram and John Michel, and Bennett Wiggins for a total of $18.75.[82]

African Americans were, unsurprisingly, not the only sporting laborers available to work as guides in Southern fish and game regions. Poorer whites sometimes did so as well. In some sporting areas, particularly where black populations were relatively small, whites had a substantial presence in the sporting labor trade. Many of the sporting laborers along the eastern shore of North Carolina and in popular gunning destinations along the Chesapeake Bay and Currituck Sounds were white. But in black belt regions or areas with a majority black population, the typical sporting guide was African American. The Oakland Club in St. Stephens, Berkeley County, South Carolina, told potential visitors that "colored guides can be obtained at $1.00 per day. White guides are more expensive."[83] This cost difference might indicate two things. First, in an area as predominantly black as Berkeley County, it may have been difficult to find white guides. Second, as the association between African Americans and subordinate sporting labor grew, white laborers might have refused to work for the same wage as their black counterparts, in order to preserve their sense of separation from the black population.

Records indicate that the Kinloch Club primarily relied on African-American guides and laborers. This apparently affected how the club instructed visitors to deal with their contracted sporting labor. The club encouraged guests to settle accounts at the conclusion of their visit and warned them not to offer gratuities. Echoing old assumptions about blacks' laboring and sporting habits, Superintendent R. M. Doar assured visitors that "the guides who received [tips] became utterly and absolutely worthless for a considerable time thereafter, not only causing inconvenience and annoyance to the members and club management, but the tipping was a positive harm to the guides so tipped." Kinloch did find some gifts acceptable, however. "There seems to be no harm in giving the guides cheap cigars and chewing tobacco, of which they are very fond," read the club rules for 1915.[84]

Gifts may or may not have been customary at sporting destinations such as Kinloch, but the records show that some visitors did give presents to their guides. Herbert T. Hartman, for example, sent guide Abraham White "a sweater as a little remembrance," hoping it would "remind him of the sweating he did in pulling that boat through to Duck Creek." DuPont executive R. R. M. Carpenter likewise sent his guide a gift of a sweater, asking Doar to present the sweater to "'Boney,' the guide whom I had when I was at the club, with my compliments."[85] Other sources also provide examples of white sportsmen presenting such gifts. Archibald Rutledge recalled that the most prized possession of his boyhood hunting companion Gabriel Myers was a hunting horn presented to him by John Toland of Philadelphia after Myers helped Toland land a fourteen-point buck on a Lowcountry hunting expedition. "So delighted had Toland been that he had asked his dusky guide what he would like best in all the world" Rutledge recalled, "and Gabe, who had for days been casting languishing glances at the polished horn that hung over the white man's shoulder, had indicated, with the huge shyness of a modest man, that the horn looked to him like a million dollars."[86] After an October 1907 bear hunt in the Louisiana canebrakes, Theodore Roosevelt presented Holt Collier with a Winchester 45-70 model 1886, which became the famous guide's most cherished possession.[87]

Other types of gifts, however, were not permissible—especially liquor. "The House Committee specially urges all members not to give wines or liquors to the guides," Kinloch's Doar cautioned.[88] Worried about the deleterious effects of alcohol, and subscribing to the common stereotype of the drunken, irresponsible African American, clubs wished their employees to avoid the dangers of drink.

Clubs also had other restrictions on their hired workers. They worried that employees would use their extensive knowledge of club lands to destroy area wildlife on independent hunts. For that reason, the Oakland Club of Berkeley County, South Carolina, limited employees' hunting activities as best it could. The club rules for 1908 declared: "No guide or other employee of the Club shall shoot game of any kind on lands owned or controlled by the Club, or on any lands over which Club members may, from time to time, shoot by courtesy, unless so directed to do in writing by a member of the Executive Committee." The rules also forbade "any guide or other employee of the Club" to "shoot game of any kind within five (5) miles of any land owned or controlled by the Club, unless so directed to do in writing by a member of the Executive committee."[89] Such restriction reminds us that, despite their employment of blacks, white sporting interests were still deeply uneasy about African Americans' hunting and fishing and that racial control remained as important as sporting skill as a term of employment. It also illustrates whites' continued resistance to blacks' independent subsistence earned through hunting and fishing.

African Americans worked in many capacities across the richer hunting and fishing regions of the South, leaving an indelible mark on the region's sporting tourism. While serving as overseer for the Chelsea Plantation Club, John Edwin Fripp employed an African-American man named Kit to help him manage club lands and report incursions of poachers and trespassers.[90] In Virginia, Northerner Frank A. Heywood asserted that preserve lands near Virginia Beach proved fruitful provided one had a guide, "an absolute necessity to a stranger." Fortunately for Heywood, guides were plentiful. "Guides can be obtained at all these places, and good horses will be furnished at moderate prices," he recalled. Heywood described one laborer in particular: "Sam Shavender, who appears to have been built after sketches by 'Porte Crayon,' drove me eighty two miles with the rain pouring torrents in eleven hours, changing horses but once. For this service he charged me but $5."[91] In South Carolina, Northern visitors to the Charleston and Georgetown County lands of the Santee Gun Club, founded in 1901 and host to many sporting tourists, enjoyed the option of hiring "the negro Henry Snyder as master of the hunt. His language and grammar are worth the price. He also understands driving."[92]

All across the South, then, white sportsmen called on the services of black subordinates, and such accounts abound. Harry F. Lowe, on a hunt just south of Washington, DC, took to the field with "our negro guide [who] led the way for our party," and greatly enjoyed such "common purpose between black and white kin."[93] When hunting with the Oakland Club's famed African American–trained hounds, Archibald Rutledge witnessed the exploits of renowned "dusky scout" Henry Washington, "a Negro who knows horses, dogs, and deer; who has a voice that carries miles; and who would rather hunt than sleep in the sun—the utmost compliment for any activity that can be paid a negro."[94] A. S. Salley Jr. described white sportsmen's pleasure at being led through the old rice fields of the Santee Country by Isaac, a preacher and sporting laborer "who spends his week days guiding for hunters and his Sundays guiding the spiritual welfare of an ebony-hued congregation of the neighborhood."[95] Nash Buckingham described duck hunting along the Mississippi Sound's Ship Island, especially "with Horace, colored factotum of our Beaver Dam Duck Club," who had charge of white visitors to the island.[96] At these and scores of other hunting and fishing destinations across the South, white sporting tourists eagerly set off with their black subordinate companions. Hunting and fishing activities in post-Emancipation Dixie—integrated, but not bastions of social equality; sources of valuable income for many African Americans, but only because visitors equated black labor with the region's racial legacy—demanded black hunters, fishermen, drivers, and guides who remained loyal, dedicated, skilled, and, above all, subordinated to their white betters.

African Americans' customary attachment to hunting and fishing, and sporting tourists' idealized visions of the South, both of which made black labor indispensable, did not vanish with the turn of the century. The Medway plantation of Berkeley County, South Carolina, perhaps best illustrates the longevity of black sporting labor. Owned before the war by rice planter Peter Gaillard Stoney, Medway was renowned as a hunting plantation. In 1906, Stoney's nephew Samuel Gaillard Stoney converted the property into a well-known tourist retreat. For manpower, he relied on African-American laborers whose families had lived there for generations. Two in particular, a descendant of area slaves named David Gourdine (born at Medway) and Cy Myers, men "whose families have lived and worked at Medway for more than a hundred years," became the plantation's two leading huntsmen and drivers. This multigenerational service did not end there; two of Gourdine's sons, David Jr. and Walter, later worked as laborers, drivers, and huntsmen at Medway.[97] They were followed by David Jr.'s grandson, Sam Washington, who, as late as 1999, still worked at the sporting plantation.[98] Such generational continuity was common. Titus Brown and James Hadley compiled the oral histories of sixteen African-American families that lived and worked on and near Pebble Hill Plantation in Thomasville, Georgia, a popular sporting destination in the first half of the twentieth century. Some Pebble Hill employees worked there for generations, passing on both jobs and important requisite skills from father to son, mother to daughter.[99] Such continuity demonstrates both the degree to which Southern sporting resorts depended on black labor and the desire of some African Americans to preserve long-term employment opportunities.

African Americans drew substantial material, economic, even psychological benefits from sporting labor in the service of whites. But that employment remained sporadic and could never be guaranteed. The steady employment provided by long-term, sometimes multigenerational, service to a sporting club or plantation proved much more valuable, allowing some to use this as a starting point for their family's future economic betterment. Far beyond the first two decades of the twentieth century, which were the true peak of Southern sporting tourism, African Americans continued to play a critical role. Some of the Pebble Hill families, for example, worked at area sporting plantations for more than fifty years. Sam Green, born in 1914, spent thirty-seven years at Pebble Hill (1934–1970), working in the dog kennel and flower garden and driving a hunting wagon. His brother Sidney Green worked there for thirty-six years (1942–1978). Dock Hadley worked at the nearby Fair Oaks plantation for forty-four years (1941–1984), serving as huntsman and working with the plantation's dogs. His long years on a sporting plantation allowed him, on his retirement, to use his savings to buy land, build a house, and live, in his own words, "just like Alice in Wonderland."[100] African Americans such as Hadley remained key sources of sporting labor across the black belt well past World War II.

When W. Ancrum Boykin founded the Boykin Hunting Club near Camden, South Carolina, in 1948, its members relied on black laborers, as Southerners had done for centuries. These employees included Uncle Jimmy Boatwright, who "became a friend of the hunters from across the river"; Little Boy, who was "a welcome addition because he was a good cook and 'help' around the camp"; and three drivers, Spaniard, Rabbit, and Bootie. In describing the work of these valued drivers, Henry D. Boykin II, with a touch of nostalgia, not only called to mind the history of skill that made black labor attractive to white sportsmen, but also showed a clear appreciation for the tradition of service that made African Americans' presence symbolically indispensable. "Listening to the drivers' voices echoing through the swamp, I knew that one day there would be new ways and new drivers, but what makes a driver good?" Boykin wrote. "For me, the talents of Spaniard, Bootie and Rabbit, the fine quality of their voices and the sounds of their horns could never be surpassed. The thrill of many ancient hunters must surge up from the shadows to join the sweet song of those three dark experts. Maybe those good drivers were more of Dad's time than mine. He expected to hunt with the help of his black friends, as he had always done."[101]

Boykin's comment reminds us that, despite the high praise meted out to African-American sporting laborers by white employers, the other side of the dependence on black labor cannot be ignored. While some former slaves, their children, and their children's children carved out lasting advantages by turning hunting and fishing traditions cultivated under bondage into opportunities for regular employment, such opportunities also permitted white Southerners and visiting sportsmen to make the late-nineteenth- and early-twentieth-century sporting field fit their notions of antebellum social and racial relationships. Ultimately, black sporting laborers—such as Archibald Rutledge's companion Gabriel Myers, Kinloch Club's Abraham White and Boney, and Pebble Hill's Sam and Sidney Green—although credited with impressive, sometimes legendary skills, in the end received as much praise for their loyal service to whites. African-American laborers helped Southerners reconstruct the racial hierarchy of the Old South and allowed a variety of sporting and tourism interests to use the long tradition of the biracial sporting field to sell symbolic reconstructions of a vanished plantation South.

Returning now to Holt Collier, the most famous of African-American sportsmen: if African Americans' subordination in the sporting field overshadowed their skill at hunting, fishing, or boating, then we are compelled to ask, again, Is there more to the widespread regard Collier received than just his sporting talents? Did Collier become a legend simply because he killed so many bears? Or was it because he demonstrated, from his days of Confederate service to his hunting trips with Theodore Roosevelt, a ceaseless devotion to white superiors? Did he become such a renowned and respected figure among the white residents of Greenville, Mississippi (and, eventually, the entire region), simply because of his many years of unparalleled sporting excellence? Or was it because during that time he remained, in many ways, a holdover of idealized Old South social relationships that so moved and reassured white observers? Collier never failed to demonstrate the kind of unwavering loyalty that, for white Southerners, characterized the master-slave relationship and, for white visitors to the South, made their sojourn more authentic. He simultaneously showcased what sporting visitors thought idealized African Americans had become and what native Southerners wished they would always be—perfect servants.

In the end we must conclude that while no one can deny Collier's exceptional skill in the field or his remarkable life, the fame he and many other sporting laborers achieved cannot be separated from the fact that white sportsmen valued African-American sporting companions at least as much for what their skilled service symbolized as for that skill itself. While sporting laborers sometimes earned respect and admiration as skilled sportsmen, they also drew praise as loyal servants who exemplified the highest achievements of the Old South. Both native Southerners and sporting tourists frequently lauded and definitely depended on African Americans' skills and experience, but they never saw that role as anything but inherently subordinate. No matter how skilled their laborers, no matter how kindly or admiringly they spoke of them in the field, the hallmarks of these relationships remained service to whites and subordination of African Americans.

CHAPTER 5

"When He Should Be between the Plow Handles"

Sportsmen, Landowners, Legislators, and the Assault on African Americans' Hunting and Fishing

Here we are to-day, going up only because the nigger is
going down, and only by hammering on the subject is it
that we have inspired the legislators with resolution
enough to introduce a bill on the subject.

> —*Member of the Georgia State Agricultural Society,*
> *on the difficulty of enacting laws restricting*
> *African Americans' dog ownership, 1876*

The fight made by the Audubon Society is a fight to save
the birthright of a people, now being wrested from them
by the hireling and the lawless.

> —*James Henry Rice Jr., Secretary,*
> *South Carolina Audubon Society, 1909*

By 1915, after half a century of controversy over African Americans' use—or, as whites saw it, misuse—of Southern wildlife, several key components came into alignment. Landowners, who for decades had broadcast the connection between former slaves' independent subsistence and the problem of labor intractability, eagerly sought to limit blacks' hunting and fishing. Sportsmen, who had long charged people of color with violating elite white sporting codes and contributing to the epidemic of wildlife depletion, joined in the attempt to alert the Southern and national publics to the dangers of unrestricted environmental exploitation by African Americans. Despite these efforts, however, restrictions on hunting and fishing had evolved only slowly, through fits and starts. Then, by the early twentieth century, the pieces finally began falling into place.

With the explosion of sporting tourism in the South, which proved increasingly lucrative for landowners, resorts, and developers, many Southerners began to understand the financial motivation for better protecting fish and game. With the rise of a national conservation movement, which, by the late nineteenth century, penetrated even the recalcitrant South, sportsmen began to accept limits on their own hunting and fishing as perhaps necessary to stop abuses by immoderate, lower-class sportsmen. And with the evolution of Jim Crow segregation, which coincided with a marked increase in racism nationally, Southern and national audiences agreed that blacks' sporting and character flaws were the root cause of Dixie's wildlife woes. The time had finally arrived for a concerted attack on African Americans' right to hunt and fish.

On July 1, 1915, a law requiring state hunting licenses, long sought by sporting enthusiasts, finally went into effect in seventeen of South Carolina's forty-four counties.[1] The new law, known as the Ziegler Bill, required hunters to purchase—at the cost of $1.10 for resident sportsmen and $10.25 for nonresident sportsmen—a state hunting license and a display tag for their guns that identified them as lawful hunters, and to seek written permission from landowners on whose property they hunted or fished. Hunting without a license would earn a fine of $25.00 to $100.00 or, if the offender could not pay, work on the county chain gang—one day for each dollar fined. On August 13, an excited editorial appeared in the coastal *Beaufort Gazette,* heralding the first conviction and sentencing of a local game-law violator: the "incident is one of the most encouraging that have come to the attention of the thousands of people in this region, who want to see game and useful birds saved from extermination." An African-American man, who "has just been given a chain gang sentence because he hunted without the license which the law now requires every hunter to have," became the first target of this new effort to protect fish and game in one of the South's most popular sporting destinations.

That a person of color was one of the first to be sentenced to a chain gang for violating the new licensing law, and that this was reported with such obvious approval, should be no surprise—given the importance of fish and game in blacks' life, their likely inability to afford a license or the subsequent fine, and the frequency with which landowners and sportsmen derided African Americans' ability to hunt and fish. After decades of pointing out the inadequacy of Southern fish and game law and linking blacks' sporting abuses to the problems of wildlife depletion and labor intractability, landowners, sportsmen, and sporting investors could regard the new law with satisfaction. Indeed, the *Beaufort Gazette* left no doubt that the law was specifically intended to combat such problems. "Throughout this region the negro hunter is one of the worst enemies of game and birds. Protective laws mean nothing to him. In season and out of season he goes out with his single-barreled shotgun and kills everything that comes his way." Without comprehensive laws and rigorous enforcement, local law enforcement's ability to deal with such nuisances would be limited. "It is hard to curtail his pernicious activities because if you find him in the woods with his gun in spring or summer time he will tell you that he is just after rabbits and there is no closed season for rabbits," the editorial continued. "As a matter of fact, he is after anything and everything from a redbird to a wild turkey, and the damage that he does by killing game and wild birds during the breeding season is incalculable."[2]

The structure of the Ziegler Bill left little doubt as to its intended target.[3] Of the seventeen South Carolina counties covered by the law, only three had a predominantly white population—Greenville (30.5% black), Lexington (36.3% black), and Oconee (25.1% black)—according to the 1910 census. Thirteen of the seventeen counties had an African-American majority, and in eight (Barnwell, Beaufort, Calhoun, Charleston, Chester, Dorchester, Hampton, and Orangeburg) the black population exceeded 60 percent.[4] Given the frequency of complaints about blacks' sporting abuses and labor intractability, it is difficult to view these population numbers in the counties covered by the law as coincidental.

The long overdue redress in the form of a statewide licensing system, for which a variety of Palmetto State interests had been lobbying for well over a decade, had finally arrived to combat what they considered one of their biggest nuisances. "Now that this law is on the books every one of the thousands of negroes who infest the woods in spring and summer hunting 'rabbits' is liable to arrest unless he can show a hunter's license and unless he has written permission from the owner of the land to hunt upon it," the *Beaufort Gazette* noted. The law finally mitigated "the indiscriminate slaughter practiced by the negroes," and "the Summerville conviction, the first of its kind to be reported, should be regarded as an incident of no small significance."[5] For many white South Carolinians, both the licensing system and its strict enforcement were tremendous victories for the state's beleaguered wildlife. But as my discussions in earlier chapters indicate, neither such laws nor their proponents were concerned exclusively with fish and game.

The early twentieth century witnessed the culmination of elite white Southerners' frustration with blacks' hunting and fishing. The movement to implement fish and game legislation both specifically targeted African Americans and drew on whites' fears of lost racial control to convince lawmakers of the need to act.

Planters and landowners, angry over the possibility of blacks' self-subsistence and resultant ability to avoid agricultural labor; sportsmen, frustrated by perceived abuses of cherished sporting codes; and owners of sporting retreats and plantations, eager to preserve wildlife for tourists—all sought to circumscribe African Americans' hunting and fishing so that they might exercise better control over blacks' subsistence, sport, and labor.

A shared attitude toward black independence became the critical link between these groups of complainants. In the decades after Emancipation, former slaves doggedly protected and openly flaunted their freedom, particularly through hunting and fishing. To the coalition of white interests, African Americans' reliance on wildlife proved doubly vexing. For landlords, it created both labor inefficiency and an irksome reminder of the loss of their slaves. For elite sportsmen, abuse of sporting codes endangered fish and game supplies and former slaves' hunting and fishing infringed on activities ideally reserved for whites. And for purveyors of Southern tourism, who depended on blacks' sporting labor, African Americans' independent pursuit of wildlife jeopardized the real and symbolic reconstruction of the Old South that natives and visitors craved. Threats posed by free blacks had grown more onerous over the decades since Emancipation, as agricultural employers struggled to control labor, as increasing wildlife depletion alarmed sportsmen, and as sporting tourism grew more popular. As a common solution, this conglomeration of interests sought to strengthen fish and game laws and thus circumscribe African Americans' ability to survive independent of whites' control. The future prosperity, wildlife resources, and racial hierarchy of the South had to be defined and dominated by whites alone.

Many white Southerners, however—some of whom were, like blacks, dependent on fish and game for semi-subsistence—were suspicious of hunting and fishing restrictions and had always rejected such legislation. Yet, when couched in appeals to racism and racial control, arguments for wildlife legislation could find a more receptive audience. It is no coincidence, then, that effective and permanent protection of Southern fish and game, seen most notably in the establishment of comprehensive licensing systems and state-level fish and game agencies, took hold at precisely the time when fears about African-American independence were becoming widespread and Jim Crow was laying siege to black Southerners' political rights. Thus the maturation of Southern wildlife conservation became part of the larger goal of "racial conservation." By invoking the need to circumscribe and subvert blacks' subsistence traditions, conservationists helped to implement long-sought, and long-resisted, protective measures. And by directing such measures specifically at African Americans' customary use of the natural environment, they worked toward greater control over African Americans' lives and labors. Ultimately, white Southerners' efforts to restrict blacks' hunting and fishing must be understood both as a faithful reflection of long-standing fears about black independence and as part of the system of segregation created to assuage such fears.

RESISTANCE TO SOUTHERN FISH AND GAME REGULATION

The idea of using fish and game legislation to target African Americans did not begin in the twentieth century. Sportsmen, among the first and loudest to link protecting Southern wildlife with controlling recently freed African Americans, had agitated for protective measures since Emancipation. "For the last ten years I have witnessed the rapid decrease of game with feelings of disgust," asserted a sportsman, under the name Venatoe, in *Forest and Stream* in 1877. "In many places where I used to get good shooting, game is almost annihilated."[6] An anonymous Louisiana sportsman likewise lamented the state of Southern hunting and fishing. "In the ancient antebellum era the hunting grounds of this State were famous throughout the South. All over the State they were preserved and worked in the shooting season, principally by gentlemen sportsmen." But with the end of the war and the sale of surplus firearms, especially to former slaves, "the weapons which had been used in the attempted extirpation of armies were turned to the extermination of our feathered and four-footed game."[7] Since the South presented an ideal sporting location, its wildlife needed a system of laws to protect it.

As another *Forest and Stream* contributor suggested, the need for fish and game protection originated precisely from this point: the region's natural abundance. "There is no other civilized land on all the globe where the supply is so abundant, and the privilege of taking it so free," he began, echoing the common sentiment that the free availability of wildlife was connected to American democracy. The idea that the blessings of American citizenship might require accepting some restriction of this privilege found frequent expression in the pages of sporting periodicals. "The duty imposed on the individual citizen to respect the common interest of all, as embodied in the game and fish statutes," the *Forest and Stream* article continued, "is a duty quite as binding as are other obligations of good citizenship. No one . . . may ignore this principle, set up shooting and fishing license for himself, and yet make claim to good American citizenship."[8]

Eventually, planters and landowners, who were often sportsmen too, and the owners and operators of sporting resorts and preserves joined the cause. But progress did not come easy. Such efforts had for many years been met with, at best, reluctance from a suspicious Southern populace and, at worst, outright hostility from many, rich and poor alike, who viewed wildlife laws as assaults on their liberties. Southern suspicion of hunting and fishing restrictions was tied to elites' position at the top of Dixie's social hierarchy. Poorer Southerners generally took cultural and social cues from the planter class, but they were not willing to do so if that amounted to an outright restriction of their liberties. And they became perhaps even more suspicious of efforts to impose fish and game law because such efforts coincided with serious (and noticeable) wildlife depletion in the region. It seemed to many lower-echelon whites that well-to-do sportsmen were acting not to protect dwindling wildlife for all, but to preserve it exclusively for themselves.

So, despite efforts to reform Southern wildlife protection between the 1870s and the 1890s, criticism from a distrustful public sometimes killed measures before they could reach a vote. Moreover, the ability of counties to opt out of state-approved laws blunted the best efforts by interested parties. By the new century, nearly fifty years of effort to see Southern fish and game protection catch up to that of the rest of the United States, particularly the establishment of statewide fish and game licensing systems, had produced few lasting results.[9] Hunting and fishing clubs and wildlife protection societies spent an increasing amount of time attempting to sway the sporting, landowning, and voting public, but few arguments resonated. The Virginia Fish and Game Protective Association framed the need for legislation in terms of the interrelated economic benefits of maintaining both the region's population and its land values. The association's treasurer, John Ott, assured the public in 1879 that "what is of far greater moment is the keeping of Virginia's own native born sons at home," warning that many Virginians "are attracted to the far off wilds of the West by the great abundance of fish and game reported to exist out there." But the problem did not end with emigration. Ott also asserted that hunting and fishing restrictions would guarantee higher demand for available lands. "If anybody, even in Virginia, has a farm to sell, and there is good fishing and shooting in that locality, he will be sure to advertise that fact, and it will often bring him a purchaser." The Virginia association confidently believed these benefits would create a more positive attitude toward wildlife legislation. "We can personally testify," Ott asserted, " . . . that, in our experience, when the people of Virginia know what is right, they are going to do it."[10] But this justification proved inadequate.

Promoters of tourism, which by the late nineteenth century had become a major source of revenue for Virginia, the Carolinas, Georgia, Florida, Louisiana, Alabama, and other Southern states, made every effort to convince the public of the need for comprehensive protective measures.[11] T. S. Palmer, conservationist, U.S.

Department of Agriculture representative, and one-time secretary of the American Ornithological Union, assured the North Carolina Audubon Society, at Greensboro, in 1904 that "the game is really an undeveloped resource which under favorable conditions can be so managed as to bring in large returns."[12] Sporting tourism could provide fabulous wealth, but only if residents had the will to take the necessary steps. "Anything which tends to increase the number of these visitors must necessarily redound [to] the welfare of the State," Palmer declared, arguing that hunting and fishing could do just that. In 1903, North Carolina issued more nonresident hunting licenses than any other state except Illinois, Wisconsin, and Maine, Palmer noted, and this trend could be further exploited. "Under favorable conditions this travel can be increased very largely, but only by preserving the game which is the chief attraction to this class of visitors — in short by maintaining a comprehensive and well-devised system of game protection."[13]

According to Palmer and his fellow field worker H. W. Olds, "well-devised" game protection provided the key. The South, like the rest of the nation, had done a fair job of enacting fish and game statutes in the late nineteenth century, but general suspicion and local exemptions and amendments weakened them. "In some States certain counties have special statutes or are partially or entirely exempt from the operation of the general game laws," Palmer and Olds wrote. "In . . . Maryland, Virginia, North Carolina, and Tennessee . . . there are probably more game laws for the three hundred or more counties than in all the rest of the United States."[14] Despite their numbers, such scattershot laws could never protect fish and game to proponents' satisfaction. Virginia sportsman and sporting author John Sargent Wise agreed with the assertion that legislation and enforcement were not necessarily the same. "The Southern States still have an abundance of quail, turkeys, ruffed grouse, and in some sections deer; but, so far as legislation goes, they extend very little protection to game and the enforcement of the laws is not seriously attempted."[15]

The North Carolina Audubon Society agreed with Palmer, Olds, and Wise, arguing that, until the early twentieth century, "many magistrates found it difficult to bring themselves to believe that game laws were seriously intended to be enforced, and as a result in a great many cases it was exceedingly difficult to secure convictions for violations of these laws."[16] Not only laws but the will to enforce them, and to fund enforcement, had to be created. As North Carolina naturalist Herbert Hutchinson Brimley put it, "the 'Conservation of Natural Resources' was unknown to us and we blindly went ahead passing additional county game laws at every session of the Legislature. So many people thought—and often still think—that all we have to do to relieve a situation is to Pass a Law."[17] Without both state action and, more importantly, a significant turn in public opinion, supporters feared Southern fish and game would all but disappear.

Finally, by 1910, states that had lagged behind in wildlife legislation, and whose citizenry had resisted bag limits, fixed open and closed seasons, and restrictions on certain hunting methods and weapons, began to catch up. Concerted efforts by state and local governments, local sportsmen's organizations, state and national fish and game protection organizations such as the Audubon Society, and national sporting periodicals such as *Outing, Recreation,* and *Field and Stream* had at last led to limits on access to wildlife. Southern hunting and fishing law had evolved slowly as measures appeared and disappeared with the ebb and flow of public discontent, but between the 1890s and the 1920, some Southerners became more receptive. Laws establishing permanent open and closed seasons appeared on the Southern legislative agenda beginning in the early 1890s. By the turn of the century, statutes requiring written permission from landowners to hunt and fish on their property had become widespread. By the 1910s, some Southern states, including Virginia, the Carolinas, and Alabama, had established permanent state agencies to regulate and oversee wildlife, and some had even enacted the statewide licensing systems long sought by many sporting enthusiasts.

There were several reasons why Southerners finally accepted the need for more permanent, and centralized, restrictions. For one, the pressures of wildlife decline had become obvious to everyone. Like the rest of the country, Southerners begrudgingly accepted the notion that some legal protection would end the slaughter, such as had led to the extinction of the American passenger pigeon in the late nineteenth century. In addition, the profitability of sporting tourism was undeniable. The flow of well-to-do Northerners to Dixie's sporting lands proved a source of income that land and club owners wished to maintain, as demonstrated in their public appeals for legislative action. But the third and central reason—blacks' independence, expressed through their perceived abuses of the right to hunt and fish—has generally been overlooked.

White observers frequently referred to hunting and fishing when complaining about both the paucity of wildlife protection and African-American independence. According to angry Southerners such as Polk Miller of Virginia, the antebellum social order featured "three distinct classes of sportsmen": elite hunters and fishermen, poor whites who hunted and fished for meat, and the "all round sportsman," the slave. Before Emancipation, all kept their appropriate places. But, according to Miller, this social separation had "tumbled down" and the region now was in dire need of effective hunting and fishing legislation, "for there is a certain class of both whites and blacks who never leave their homes to visit a neighbor a mile away without carrying their guns along, and will shoot anything that comes their way in any month of the year."[18]

Indeed, soon after Emancipation, proponents of fish and game laws suggested a connection between wildlife protection and race. Some, like a sportsman of Laurenceville, Virginia, made the connection obliquely. "As yet we have not presumed to indulge in any 'long-range' recreations," he wrote, "for fear his Excellency the President might deem that we are preparing to resist the Civil Rights Bill, and send down little 'Phil' [General Philip Sheridan, one-time head of the military Reconstruction governments of Texas and Louisiana] . . . We have, however, a game association, and our county authorities have taken action to protect our small game from unlawful and unseasonable destruction."[19] Others made the point more directly.

According to Southerner "Cosmopolitan," responding to an editorial by "F.A.B." arguing that legislation was the best way of protecting sportsmen from vagabond "pot hunters," mere laws could not stop such violators, because of the South's experiments with enforced social equality. "The vilest old negro vagabond who takes an old rusty musket which he got for nothing from the United States and goes on a man's land under pretense of shooting, but for the purpose of shooting his fowl or stealing his corn his fruit or his hogs, (as many do in Louisiana)," he wrote, echoing the common assertion that hunting masked blacks' property crimes, "is in the eye of the law just as much a sportsman as anyone else." For Cosmopolitan and many others, the root cause of this predicament lay with Emancipation. "F.A.B. is no doubt well aware of the great struggle going on in this country for years for equal rights and universal suffrage, until one man is just as good as another and better too. How then is the law to make distinctions between sportsmen and vagabonds?" The message was clear. Protective laws had to be strong enough to combat the basic facts of black liberation. "Equality before the law," Cosmopolitan reminded, "don't forget that, F.A.B."[20]

For elite sportsmen and landowners, then, black liberation had to be met with vigorous legal measures to restrict, even deny, blacks' ability to hunt and fish. "The South as a section, is sadly deficient in game laws," a *Forest and Stream* editorial declared in 1874, "which are especially needed at this time, when almost every gunner one meets is an irresponsible negro, delighted with his newly acquired privilege of 'bearing arms,' ignorant of the value and necessity of sumptuary laws, and intent the year round on filling his bag."[21] Such complaints often found their way into the platforms of hunting- and fishing-related organizations. In 1877, "now that the public mind has become quiet, through the restoration of good local government to the several states of the South," a group of sportsmen and landowners created the Virginia Fish and Game Protective Association to coordinate fish and game protection with local and regional groups and to lobby the Commonwealth for legislative action. Among the reasons for founding the association the group included the frightful pace of fish, game, and timberlands destruction, the need to protect wildlife and thus attract immigrants and tourists, and, not least, the need to control the conduct of African Americans. Some thought the problem too complicated to be settled by protective legislation alone. According to sportsman "M," African Americans, ostensibly the prime destroyers of valuable Southern quail, "take entire flocks at a time, and they never set any of the captured birds free for seed . . . Hence they make a regular business of destroying Bob White." To combat that problem, Southern states must combine protective legislation with a campaign "to educate him [the freed man] into the conviction that he is behaving badly, and this, I fear, can never be done as long as Bob White exists."[22]

Such observers had good reason to doubt that legislation would prove a panacea. Despite the frequent linking of African Americans to problems with Southern hunting and fishing, white Southerners' resistance to state and local efforts to limit the free taking of fish and game remained powerful. "The Southern states, as a whole, have been slow in taking a serious and broad-minded view of the problems of game protection and of the conservation of bird-life in general," Herbert Hutchinson Brimley wrote, when describing how the legislative victories of recent years had been long in coming.[23] For decades, each time a politician proposed comprehensive protection, a backlash developed. Fears of class bias and aristocratic privilege, and the trampling of the rights of the middle and lower classes, had been a part of Southern culture for generations and tended to reappear whenever elites challenged free hunting and fishing.

An editorial in *Outing* in 1898 noted that any proposed restrictions would meet heavy opposition "from the men who shoot for the market, and their friends; from the dealers and their friends, and from a certain class of persons who know nothing whatever about game, yet who are always ready to set up a howl against any measure which they fancy tends to give the rich privileges which are denied to the poor." According to the editorial, political pandering created this problem. "'Thou shalt not rob the poor man of his bit of sport' is the burden of their cry, at which the poor man, fancying that something is being done for him, hurrahs most vigorously." Proponents of fish and game law, particularly those eager to restrict former slaves' independence, believed such "clamor for 'equal rights' and kindred nonsense" remained a primary handicap.[24] Poor whites would probably not accept restrictions that smacked of attacks on their own customary rights. Landowning and sporting interests learned the important lesson that they could not limit hunting and fishing in general, and could not crack down on the sporting abuses of all non-elite Southerners, without finding a way to make such restriction more acceptable to the general public.

Starting in the 1870s, dozens of local and regional fish and game associations sprang up across the South to preserve hunting and fishing for elite whites.[25] These included Goslings Hunting Club of Thomasville, Georgia, which became the Oaks Hunting Club in 1876; Currituck Shooting and Fishing Club of Deal's Island, North Carolina, founded in the 1870s; and Otranto Club of Berkeley County, South Carolina, founded in 1872—all dedicating themselves, in the words of the Otranto Club Constitution, "to the increase and protection of game. A game keeper reports poachers and trespassers; and the Club prosecutes them."[26] The Virginia Fish and Game Protective Association, for one, expressed much optimism. "We observe a great deal of interest throughout the State on the subject" of increased protection, it declared in 1877, "and this interest is bound to crystallize into something substantial."[27] Southerners, however, particularly African Americans and poor whites suspicious of fish and game law, proved a difficult challenge.

Even when a law was passed, politicians often would repeal it in response to the cries of enraged voters. For example, a tax enacted by the Virginia General Assembly in 1873 to protect sheep from unrestrained dogs, especially those of freed persons, raised the ire of poor dog-owners by requiring them to pay a fee for each dog owned. This response guaranteed that, according to the *Southern Planter and Farmer*, "when the Legislature came together last winter a howl came up from the vagabond canines and their vagabond masters, demanding a restoration of their ancient rights to despoil, without restraint, the flocks of their neighbors in the counties that had voted the dog tax." Predictably, lawmakers "heard and trembled like the kid at the donkey's bray, in the ancient fable. They took fright and stampeded like whipped spaniels." For the coalition of whites eager for wildlife protection, this was another example of how "the descendants of the proud cavaliers surrendered to a miserable rabble of '*possum hunters*' and '*coon catchers*.'"[28] Such barriers had to be removed before effective fish and game enforcement was possible. As James Henry Rice Jr., secretary of the South Carolina Audubon Society, noted in 1925, "whatever else of blessing may lie in democracy, there can be no denial that natural resources are uniformly destroyed when the people control."[29] Sportsmen and landowners needed a justification that outweighed traditional hostilities. And they found one in fears of black independence. By linking racial control with fish and game laws, white sportsmen and landowners finally found a way to pass protective measures and see them remain in force.

AFRICAN AMERICANS AND THE FISH AND GAME LAWS

The process of developing a comprehensive system of wildlife protection was long, uneven, and directly connected to the region's racial hierarchy. Complaints about the lack of legal protection of wildlife increased immediately following the war, when Southerners first felt the sting of freed people exercising their right to hunt and fish. Not surprisingly, then, many sportsmen looked on the end of Reconstruction as a chance both to establish "home rule" and to begin, in earnest, the work of protecting fish and game from freed people. It is perhaps no coincidence that, as one Louisiana sportsman argued, "it was not until 1877 [the year Reconstruction ended in Louisiana], we believe, that any successful steps were taken to protect our indigenous game from the perpetual warfare of the meat-seeking tyros, who slew the nesting quail and the nursing doe with as much avidity as they slaughtered the gallant five-pronged buck in the 'blue,' or swept away with one shot the autumnal bevies of birds in their 'nooning' retreats."[30] In subsequent decades, complaints connecting African Americans to perceived fish and game abuses appeared regularly, yet the evolution of Southern wildlife protection remained slow.

Not until the second decade of the twentieth century did the combination of agricultural inefficiency, fish and game depletion, the profitability of sporting tourism, and Jim Crow make white Southerners, as a whole, begin to take heed. In agricultural and sporting periodicals, interested parties set out to convince the reading public that blacks' contribution to their common problem had long gone understated. These parties had to persuade audiences that controlling African Americans through hunting and fishing restrictions served larger social interests than just those of sportsmen and wealthy landowners. An unnamed Virginian used a *Southern Planter and Farmer* editorial to link such laws to labor efficiency. Laws requiring a tax on dogs, designed to protect sheep farming by reducing the number of dogs owned by poor whites and, especially, by African Americans, failed because "some of the country people, and especially demagogues seeking office, complain bitterly of the present law, in order to get votes of the grumblers." To overcome these concerns, supporters emphasized the connections between those laws and former slaves. "To every reflecting man these objections are groundless," the Virginian asserted, "in the present demoralization and prostration of our labor system, and in every pursuit, which promises remunerative results for light and easy labor, [such laws] ought to be fostered and encouraged by the state."[31]

The South Carolina Audubon Society used the pages of the *Beaufort Gazette* to remind the public, particularly obstinate landowners, of the connection between blacks' hunting and fishing and property crime. In the push for licensing systems in Texas, Louisiana, and Alabama after Emancipation, the society reminded readers, "conditions in these states were similar to conditions in South Carolina. Negro labor was employed on the farms and in winter, negroes scoured the fields, roaming them at night with fire, often firing timber and thereby destroying both timber and fencing, and sometimes buildings as well. Stock and cattle were also destroyed. But most of all the game and fish were wiped out."[32] Supporters of more vigorous restriction presented their common problem as symptomatic of black liberation. According to sportsman G. G. Ford, the years immediately following Emancipation saw next to no game preservation in the Georgetown, South Carolina, area, "and for several years it was a common thing to ride up on a negro . . . sneaking through the underbrush and trying to walk up on a deer, or we would hear far into the night the yelping of a cur on the trail of some poor deer that had gotten a charge of turkey or squirrel shot." Within a short time, "the entire country was changed, and instead of one of the best hunting grounds for all sorts of game, miles of riding were required to jump a deer or roost a flock of turkeys."[33] Linking African Americans to the South's perceived fish and game shortage in this way became a favored technique of contributors to sporting periodicals.

Throughout the second decade of the twentieth century, a regular column was published in *Field and Stream* called "Unkel David's Letter," in which fictional former slave Unkel David meted out homespun wisdom to white readers. In January 1911, Unkel David editorialized about recent complaints linking immigrants, particularly Italian and Polish laborers, to fish and game depletion. According to Unkel David, if Americans really wanted to get at the heart of the problem, they "shood have said sumthing abowt our cullerd feller voters of the solid South, where the race problem is whitch nigger will beet tothers to the robbin pie." In fact, he asserted, there could really be no comparison between former slaves and European immigrants. "As a gaim killer, I will bak Sambo against a dozen Spagettys & Kazookowskis & keep mi man shet up in the smoak hous haff the time." From there, Unkel David further outlined the problem posed by black independence, framing it primarily as a threat to labor. "The time the nigger is sure deth on game is dooring the cotton seezun, & in that bizzy time a plantashun hand is too valyoobel to be shet up in jail for killing a little wild meet." Yet, despite the value of African Americans' agricultural labor, particularly during the cotton season, the columnist also acknowledged the value of their sporting labor, noting that "a nigger makes a good gide, becos he wunt foarse you to shoote gaim that he has a chance to kill hisself after you go bak hoam." This was a valuable trait, despite black laborers' tendency toward laziness. "Two (2) nigger gides is better than one (1), as you will find when it comes to enny thing like work. If they have a reputashun as hunters you will need twise that menny."[34]

The broader point would have been obvious to American sportsmen. Something had to be done if the South were to be protected from this threat to both labor and tourism. But it would not be easy. Unkel David's column concluded with a word of warning about the difficulty of eliminating African Americans' game abuses: "to choak off a nigger you'd have to kill his dogs, take away his ax & pokkit nife, & then hogtie him with a haff-inch roap." Even using the courts might not prove completely effective. "If you ketch him up in coart, his white boss pays the fine; & if you shet him up in the callyboos, that means a mewl withowt a driver, & a plow standing idul in the furrer." This intersection of landowning, sporting, and tourism interests made the problem a complex one. "Something must be did," Unkel David concluded, "if the Suthern white man hoaps to feed gaim to his projinny, but I can't say off hand what it will be."[35] Fictional former slaves were not alone in looking for solutions.

By the turn of the century, the combination of wildlife depletion, the labor problem, and the profitability of sporting tourism showcasing subordinate African Americans led to concerted efforts to restrict hunting and fishing. Southern fish and game clubs and state and local wildlife protection associations, organizations comprised of frustrated sportsmen, angry landowners, and eager investors, led the crusade. Among these groups, the Audubon Society became the most famous, and perhaps the most active, in the fight for fish and game legislation aimed at African Americans. Initially founded in 1896 in Massachusetts,[36] the society rapidly became one of the most effective organs for permanent fish and game protection in the turn-of-the-century South. The Audubon Society of South Carolina, for example, was organized on January 4, 1900, the first chapter of the society in the Southern states. It worked tirelessly to win over the public, and to carry out the task it dispatched its secretary, James Henry Rice Jr. According to a 1909 society history,[37] "it was urged on all sides that the cause should be carried to the people and taking a cue from this, although the society had spent two years carrying it to the people at its' [sic] own expense, Secretary Rice was sent into the field and kept [there] throughout the year" (3). In 1900 alone, Rice spoke to many groups, including the James Island Agricultural Society, the Christ Church Parish Agricultural Society, the Farmers' Institute at Yorkville, Farmers of Oconee, Farmers at Walhalla, Elenton Farmers' Club, Farmers Union of Newberry County, the farmers of Lee, Clarendon, and Sumter counties at Mayesville, and the farmers of Lexington, Saluda, and Aiken counties at Delmar.

Rice traversed the state, driving home the point to farmers that "the enforcement of game laws requires something more than sentiment; it requires the stern and inflexible determination to make the offender suffer for the offense" (5). And who committed most offenses? He listed the usual suspects, including pot hunters, game hogs, market hunters, and, particularly (and unsurprisingly), African Americans. Rice and the Audubon Society cultivated general acceptance of a licensing measure of $1.00 on each hunter in the state to fund wildlife protection and discourage undesirables, who probably could not afford such a fee. "Is it better," Rice asked, "to permit the vagrant negro and a few exuberant sportsmen in a community to kill all the game and the community get nothing but a vain regret, or make the sportsmen stay within reason and the negro go to work?" (8). Again we see the old message, proffered by landowners for decades, that unrestrained hunting and fishing by African Americans caused "vagrancy in acute form." This threat had to be eliminated, even if "drastic treatment is required to cure it." The state's Audubon Society, and later other local and state fish and game protection associations, argued that African Americans' hunting and fishing challenged future prosperity. "The fight made by the Audubon Society," Rice concluded, "is a fight to save the birthright of a people, now being wrested from them by the hireling and the lawless" (10).

In the case of South Carolina, the phrase "the fight made by the Audubon Society" was literally accurate. Until creation of the office of chief game warden in 1912, the Audubon Society was the state's official enforcement agency in matters relating to wildlife preservation. By 1910, the society had grown weary of this arrangement and had begun to push the state to assume responsibility for passing and enforcing laws and hiring and paying fish and game wardens. According to Audubon Society President B. F. Taylor, "the Society has been very successful in its efforts, and the reason for changing is that we believe it is better for the state to take charge of the enforcement of these laws itself, rather than to commit this work to any society or body of men."[38] That the state was willing to formally assume such responsibilities is a testament to both the effectiveness of lobbying by the Audubon Society and similar groups and the growing public awareness that the interrelated causes of preserving fish and game supplies, maximizing the profitability of Southern sporting tourism, and working to control the black population demanded institutional formalization.

For all of the above reasons, the Audubon Society urged decisive action in locating offenders. "My orders to all wardens are to arrest any men found hunting without a license," Rice wrote in a 1908 *Beaufort Gazette*, "and to bring a case against him for the offense which is a misdemeanor under our laws, punished by fine up to $100 and imprisonment for 30 days for each day's hunting without license."[39] M. G. Vinson, a sportsman of Medoc, North Carolina, argued that a lack of enforcement of existing laws remained the key problem. "We have enough laws for the protection of game," he declared, "but with no one to enforce them they amount to nothing . . . Not a permit has been written; nor has a shot the less been fired. The negro makes war on the squirrel and rabbit, and the white man plays havoc with the quail and turkey."[40] For sportsman "T.H.W." of Kyle, West Virginia, the lack of enforcement played into blacks' tendency toward lawlessness. "Most of the Southern States have excellent laws, made by our fathers, but they are not enforced," he lamented. "The negroes know that it is illegal to trap quails or to dynamite fishes, but they realize the indifference of the authorities and seldom hesitate to break the laws."[41]

For many white observers of blacks' sporting habits, taxes on firearms ownership became a logical partner of the Audubon Society's quest for licensing systems and stricter enforcement of existing statutes. This idea, which had been tried with mixed success across the South since the 1870s, led to hot debates among advocates of wildlife protection. As with many other restrictive measures that met with public disapproval, supporters employed the race issue to make the tax more palatable. They hoped that Southerners, particularly poor rural whites who would probably consider such a measure an attack on their liberty, might begrudgingly consider a tax if born of the need to restrict African Americans' firearm usage. "The negro has a childish love of firearms," attorney Thomas P. Devereux declared in an 1867 letter to the North Carolina State Assembly, "the indulgence of this passion provokes the ill-will of the whites, and to see a negro parading the country with a revolver in his belt has a tendency to produce bloodshed." For Devereux, "the remedy is a heavy tax upon all arms not used in militia drill. Some tribunal might be allowed to license *guns* for the protection of crops from vermin at a reduced taxation; but a revolver, as an article of dress, is more than useless to a negro."[42] Unfortunately for Devereux and others, resistance to such measures remained high throughout the post-Emancipation period, despite supporters continually returning to the "Negro question" to garner support.

By the early twentieth century, proponents had learned to carefully couch such measures, particularly measures that would affect resistant whites, in the language of race. According to K. H. Schuricht of Cobham, Virginia, the *lack* of a tax on guns and dogs put *all* farmers at a disadvantage and led to mischief on the part of the poorest blacks and whites. "As long as every colored and white man is allowed to keep, untaxed, as many curs as he likes to feed upon game . . . and which dogs are compelled by the pangs of hunger to despoil chicken-houses, every farmer must suffer. Is this fair — is this charity, or something worse?"[43] Likewise, the South Carolina Audubon Society reminded voters that the absence of such restriction helped only the very richest and very poorest. "It has been shown time and again that unrestricted hunting and fishing bear with particular hardship on the poor man and the man of average means," the 1915 annual report declared. "The vagrant and the idle rich can spend all their time in woods and fields; the hard working man cannot. He has to trust the State to preserve fish and game, or he will have none."[44] Here the Audubon Society spoke directly to working-class Southerners long suspicious of fish and game law. "The vagrant" meant the independent African American and poor white whose lack of both steady employment and firm guidance from white betters gave them privileged access to fish and game that most whites could not enjoy. Proponents of wildlife law wished to make clear that such measures were not aimed at hard-working whites, but primarily at an increasingly indolent and independent group of people who used hunting and fishing to avoid work. Elite sportsmen, mindful of the perceived sporting excesses of "vagrant" whites and blacks, found in calls for racial control a way to possibly restrict the sport of both groups, while blunting the expected public backlash by claiming to protect working whites. It is likely that proponents relished this opportunity to kill two birds with one stone. They hoped to win support from lower-class whites to simultaneously remove both African Americans and the poorest whites from the Southern sporting field.

Thus advocates of hunting and fishing restriction made clear that farmers and hard-working poor whites had not been targeted, while simultaneously assuaging the fears of sportsmen. Laws requiring written permission from landowners for hunting or fishing on their property, enacted across the South between the 1870s and 1920, seemed to aid both rich and poor landowners. "One of the best game laws which has been passed in our State is the law making it a misdemeanor to hunt on any man's land without his permission," the North Carolina Audubon Society asserted in 1907. "The law was not made with a view of giving trouble to every hunter who goes into the field with a gun, but was made in order that our farmers may have redress under the State game laws when they wish to prevent people from hunting on their lands."[45] Likewise, Polk Miller pledged to sportsmen that "farmers never objected to shooting on their premises by men of respectability, but when these 'game hogs,' as they are called, go prowling about with guns . . . it is but natural that they should ask our legislatures to pass the most stringent laws with regard to trespass."[46] Such statements assured concerned "true" sportsmen that the laws did not threaten them. They targeted false sportsmen, a "worthless class," who, according to Alabama Fish and Game Commissioner John H. Wallace, "would patrol the farmer's lands, and, while ostensibly they were in quest of game, they would knock up the crops, shoot up the cattle, and purloin every species of small stock and poultry that could be easily transported." The regulations did not restrict law-abiding white sportsmen's access to sporting lands, but in fact protected and nourished it.[47]

It is perhaps impossible to know to what degree poor white Southerners found such assurances persuasive. But by about 1905, elite Southern sporting interests could write to national periodicals bragging about the passage of fish and game laws and their use in stopping African Americans' hunting and fishing abuses. Looking back on the actions of his Georgetown, South Carolina, sporting club in the decades since its inception, G. G. Ford noted several accomplishments. "The organization of this club has already put a stop to pot-hunting, and to-day there are more deer in this country than there has been since the close of the war." Yet the club's work could not truly begin until it addressed the African-American question. "A negro is not allowed in the woods with a gun," Ford concluded, "and a negro's dog is not permitted in the woods even if his master carries no gun."[48] By the first decades of the twentieth century, sporting periodicals seemed to have become more critical of African Americans' hunting and fishing than ever before. Northerner T. N. Buckingham's description of a sporting trip to Aberdeen, Virginia, shows how Southern sportsmen continued to unite in support of the notion that blacks' sporting activities had to be restricted. While he was quail hunting with a planter acquaintance named Joe, they encountered a black huntsman stalking prey normally reserved for local whites. Joe explained that, at one time, this situation did not pose a problem, asserting that "we don't mind how many rabbits they kill, but that's just an example of how well the colored brother is learning to shoot when he grabs a chance." Echoing the many complaints that African Americans increasingly went beyond exclusively "black game," Joe noted: "believe me, they never overlook many bets when it comes to killing out a covey [of birds] with one shell." The end result was a cycle of both reckless game slaughter and dangerous behavior on the part of African Americans. "Many a nigger takes a train to town with his battered suit-case full of birds and comes home with one box of shells and the rest in liquor. And that one box will kill many a bird."[49]

Yet, despite the specter of game slaughter, market hunting, killing of "white game," and drunkenness, Buckingham's friend did not turn to legal remedies. Joe had his own solution. When asked if African Americans engaged in similar mischief on his land, he boasted: "my niggers don't shoot our birds unless they take a long chance." He could instill such fear because he learned to "sorter control their dog harvest, not only by a cabin-to-cabin inspection but . . . [through] a terrible hound dog sickness [that] breaks out on my place every fall about open season time."[50] Stories of the growing threat of blacks' independent hunting and proud tales of actions taken to correct it appeared frequently in the sporting periodicals. Many white landowners refused to wait for legislative changes and took immediate extralegal action.

According to some sources, even landowners' common practice of posting their land as off-limits to sportsmen was related to the need for action against blacks' unrestrained hunting and fishing. Writing to inform *Forest and Stream* readers of sporting conditions in the Old North State, Frank A. Heywood asserted that "most lands in North Carolina are posted, but this is chiefly for the purpose of keeping off the negroes, who with a gun in their hands are as dangerous as cans of dynamite. Permission to shoot can be obtained of any owner by any gentleman."[51] Such declarations, with the typical mixture of concern for the sporting privileges of white sportsmen (especially tourists), unease over blacks' sporting practices, and, not the least, fear over blacks' possession of firearms, typified late-nineteenth-century sportsmen's eagerness to broadcast the problem while creating at least a partial solution. Marguerite Tracy, describing restricted lands near Petersburg, Virginia, also indicated that African Americans' excesses drove legal prohibitions. "The laws governing the pursuit of game and protecting the lands from trespass are very rigid as you read them, and penalties for their violation are seemingly severe, but," Tracy pointed out in *Recreation*, "they are necessary, owing to our peculiar population, and are never enforced against gentlemen sportsmen. Personally, I have never had any difficulty in obtaining all the shooting I wanted, either for myself or friends."[52]

The market hunter, who destroyed fish and game for money, remained a common source of complaint for wildlife law advocates. Indeed, hunters who preferred profit to sport had for a long time been targets of gentlemen sportsmen, which accounts for the many state laws enacted to curb market hunting, beginning in the late nineteenth century. Yet white observers often interpreted even these efforts as being partially directed at African Americans. According to an 1897 *Charleston Evening Post* article, a recent law designed to decrease the sale of terrapin at the Charleston markets proved effective mostly because it deterred African Americans. "Perhaps the darkey, who has a wholesome fear of the law, may hesitate about offering the reptile on the home market," the article theorized, "but of one thing we are sure, and that is the people of this section never saw less terrapin offered in this market than there has been in the last year or two."[53]

Supporters of tougher legal restriction tried to reassure an uneasy public, but the slow pace of transforming that ill ease into action remained vexing. Some frustrated sportsmen, landowners, and tourism interests grew tired of waiting and opted for more extreme measures. "W.L.J." of King William County, Virginia, writing of a proposed 1875 tax measure targeting African Americans' dog ownership, asserted that he liked the plan for a heavy tax but had a much cheaper idea than "pleading with our lawmakers" for remedy. According to W.L.J., "every twentieth lock of a fence around my sheep pasture is a negro path" on which "my sheep have been depredated on several times, but fortunately none have been killed." His solution to this problem, like that of Buckingham's planter friend, was more direct. At each gap in a fence, he suggested, "have a small piece of meat, placed with about one grain of strychnia on it in a very secure place, so that nothing will be apt to see it but a dog." With time, this poisoning would deter trespassing. "Any person who has a valuable dog, if he will keep him chained during the day and perfectly fat, will not leave his premises during the night."[54] Since state and county governments remained reluctant to halt marauding by trespassers, more-extreme private action became, for many, a necessity.

Dr. Lavender, speaking before the Georgia State Agricultural Society in 1876, lauded such measures because they seemed the best solution in the absence of real legislation. "I kill every dog that I find prowling on my plantation," he began, "when his master is not with him. I have killed within the last two or three years, about three hundred dogs on my plantation. [Laughter and applause.] They have learned and their owners have learned not to let them come about me." A member of the convention identified as Colonel Howard agreed, noting that private action often forced lawmakers' hands. "Here we are to-day," he asserted, "going up only because the nigger is going down, and only by hammering on the subject is it that we have inspired the legislators with resolution enough to introduce a bill on the subject."[55]

But would the spread of such sentiment—even, as Dr. Lavender and Colonel Howard hoped, among lawmakers—lead to the adoption of effective legislation? Would the widespread antipathy toward African-American independence translate into greater public acceptance of measures Southerners had distrusted for decades? According to many sportsmen, much more was needed to protect Southern fish and game; but popular resistance always tempered such calls to action. "Our game laws are very loosely drawn and are a dead letter upon the Statute

Book," North Carolinian "J.E.W." noted of the situation in the Old North State in 1874, pointing to the general reluctance to accept such laws.[56] Efforts to enact long-overdue protection often failed, even into the early twentieth century. The voting public, legislators, landowners, and even some elite sportsmen were too uneasy over the perceived loss of cherished sporting freedoms and remained, at best, lukewarm. According to Herbert Hutchinson Brimley, each time backers proposed a law, lower-class Southerners asked, "'How are we goin' to git fresh meat in summer if we kaint go out and kill us a deer,' or 'There allus been plenty of chub in the crick and we aim to keep on ketchin' 'em when we damn please.'" Such sentiments, according to Brimley "represent the attitude taken by many of the old-time hunters and fishermen of those days."[57]

Proponents tried numerous means to advertise the positive benefits and benign operations of legal protections. The Virginia Fish and Game Protective Association assured the public in 1878 that "the game laws are founded on the laws of nature, and are not arbitrary in spirit, nor designed to deprive any person of any right that he may possess."[58] A *Forest and Stream* contributor declared that restrictions only hurt those sportsmen "of least advantage to the community," namely, individuals who exploited wildlife for food or profit. "The game supply which makes possible the general indulgence in field sports is of incalculable advantage to individuals and the nation," he concluded, "but a game supply which makes possible the traffic in game as a luxury has no such importance."[59] According to the South Carolina Audubon Society, "it is ridiculous, but true, that the game seasons in South Carolina are practically as long as they were thirty years ago, when game and fish were everywhere abundant and hunters were few."[60] Stacked against age-old hostility to wildlife restrictions, such statements often failed to convince.

Even the idea that laws could control the black population or regulate its sporting abuses sometimes did not resonate. That elites would use the "race card" to convince voters of the need to pass an unpopular measure is not surprising, and legislators and voters knew this time-honored practice well. "Every time a man does some foolish thing politically, he gives as his excuse the fear of the nigger!" declared the South Carolina Lowcountry's *Georgetown Times* in 1905. "It seems to us that certain people will never recover from the fright we all had twenty and thirty years ago. In our opinion, there is no more danger of negro domination in these days than there is of another improbable thing." Frustrated with attempts to sway legislators by cultivating fears of black independence, the editorial reminded readers that "the negro is used to scare everyone into accepting other people's views and opinions as to the expediency of doing this, that and other things they would not think of doing were it not for this bugaboo of nigger." For the editor of the *Times*, such threats had long proved irrational. "We are no longer afraid of the nigger in the woodpile."[61] Yet not all observers shared this view. For many, the need for racial control outweighed the need to preserve the unfettered freedom to hunt and fish at will.

FROM WILDLIFE CONSERVATION TO "RACIAL CONSERVATION"

Advocates of Southern economic and labor reform missed no opportunity to broadcast the dangers of black liberation. "Here are a million negroes who can not claim the roof that shelters them as their own, and yet they are more independent than the richest man in the country," Charles H. Otken declared in his 1894 book *The Ills of the South*, reasserting that African Americans' independence and whites' control of labor were mutually exclusive. "A vast number of them would rather work by the day than by the week, and so on through the other time periods . . . They believe in the blessings of procrastination . . . Do the work as they please, quit when they please, begin when they please—this is the Hamitic idea of labor."[62] To some, this intractability might be traced to the freedom to exploit the natural environment. In 1906, for example, in a *Field and Stream* article entitled "The Fishing of Mr. and Mrs. Bias," sportsman B. W. Mitchell commented on the behavior of "dusky old guide, philosopher and friend of many a camp, Joe Bias," since Emancipation. Although Bias was still an excellent sporting laborer, freedom had made him "a bit more crafty and canny, just a shade more unreliable, and had added vastly to his self-respect—which with him was a mild term of vanity." This change had even made Bias begin to insist on forms of address typically reserved for whites. "The key to old Joe Bias' heart, the best and only way to win to your service all his ancient energies, was never to forget the 'Mr.'" If addressed as "Mr. Bias" the former slave "would willingly perform the most irksome tasks that Joe Bias would have resisted with all the inertia of his race, a well-known form of inertia best spelled l-a-z-i-n-e-s-s."[63]

Whites had for decades used hunting and fishing activities to confirm the most common stereotypes of African Americans. The idea that blacks' sporting practices reflected their idleness illustrated a cherished belief about black life during and after slavery. In the decades following Emancipation, the idea that hunting and fishing guaranteed idleness became a fixture of Southern cultural and sporting mythology. Sporting gospels such as *Forest and Stream* asserted that while true sportsmen ranked among society's best men, those who hunted and fished for survival or profit could be counted among its worst. "The poacher will never work," a contributor declared in 1873, "and is always ready and willing to take his chances in private preserves, to kill game and fish in all seasons. For what benefit? Certainly not for his poor wife and family."[64] For sportsmen, landowners, and, with time, legislators, this unrestrained hunting and fishing posed a common problem. African Americans' ability to make a living for themselves from fish and game challenged the control of labor on which white Southerners depended.

For their part, sportsmen carefully linked concerns about wildlife depletion with concomitant labor issues that spoke to frustrated farmers and landowners. John Ott, treasurer of the Virginia Fish and Game Protective Association, called for vigilance among Virginians and carefully gave a nod to the need for labor, reminding readers that people of the Old Dominion were "addicted to forest and stream and rod and gun and horse and hound *in the intervals of a hard-working life,* and so long as the eye is not dim and the natural force not abated, we shall continue in that practice, and teach our children so."[65] Maryland's *Cecil Whig* also asserted the common interests of sportsmen and agricultural employers, noting that fish and game laws were particularly useful in stopping "the race of Arabs, who lead a vagabond life of hunting and fishing at all seasons and in the most destructive manner," and in curtailing "irresponsible and ignorant parties, who would rather fish and gun than do honest, profitable labor." The article warned that if those who would not perform regular labor were "allowed to work their own pleasure without a wise restraint being placed upon their actions," then "the entire species . . . of wild game and fish will be sacrifice, and none left to propagate."[66] Fortunately for sportsmen and landowners, some proponents of restricting African Americans' hunting and fishing believed they knew precisely what needed to be done.

Even the state Audubon Societies, long-time champions of natural resource conservation in the South, realized the discursive power of laying the region's wildlife woes at the feet of independent African Americans. The South Carolina chapter, for instance, had grown increasingly frustrated with the slow evolution of wildlife protection through the early twentieth century. Its resultant transformation into a standard bearer for confronting the "Negro problem" is a good case study of the way race became a larger part of such organizations' appeals in the early twentieth century.

By 1908, the Palmetto State's chapter of the Audubon Society, commenting on "Existing Conditions" in the Deep South, noted with alarm that "game birds and deer were constantly killed out of season" and "fish were being slaughtered in immense numbers by means of traps and dynamite." Overworked officials, "owing to inadequate pay, lack of State supervision, and for other causes, . . . had been practically inactive, one of them only reporting two convictions for violation of the Game Laws for the year previous." Such a situation raised two issues. First, "the game of the State is being exterminated and that extermination is going on very rapidly." Second, the racial component of wildlife usage, particularly African Americans' use of hunting and fishing to avoid regular agricultural labor, to flout white codes of sportsmanship, and to engage in unregulated market-related activities, had to be fully appreciated and then addressed by both fish and game interests and state legislatures.[67]

"The second fact that impressed me was that negroes and other irresponsible vagrant hunters are responsible in large measure for the disappearance of game," the society's Secretary Rice noted. "A case is known where thousands of ducks have been killed in one day by rice field negroes and these ducks were sold to markets and shipped." Worse than that slaughter, however, the same African Americans "supply town patrons with game in return for ammunition and other supplies furnished. This goes on to an extent that no one would suspect that had not investigated the subject as the Audubon Society has done." The society promoted the dual realization that African Americans' hunting and fishing was a wide-ranging and serious problem and that strong laws must be adopted to directly and specifically target that threat. To protect game from the "great number [of] idle field hands in the fall and winter and their wide dispersion over the State," Rice proposed "the laying of an annual tax of one dollar ($1.00) on every shotgun in the State . . . Such a tax would add a fund to the schools or roads, over and above anything that might be required for enforcing the law, of several thousand dollars in each county."[68] These restrictions would provide revenue for future enforcement, take money away from the detested market hunters, and discourage pot hunting (and, when similar measures were later taken, fishing) by those who could (so it was hoped) neither afford a license nor risk punishments by breaking the law.

From that call in 1908, the Audubon Society stepped up its efforts to implement a licensing system in South Carolina. By the following year, campaigns launched in sporting periodicals and in speaking tours undertaken by Rice and others began to have an impact. In 1909, the society could report that all states except Georgia, Oklahoma, and Nevada required nonresident licenses and that twenty-four states, including "in the South, Alabama, Tennessee and Louisiana," had adopted a licensing measure for all resident sportsmen.[69] Yet South Carolina still lagged behind. To redress this situation, the state society redoubled its efforts to, according to a 1910 report, "keep the question of bird and game protection alive in the press . . . [which] has proved a powerful means of enlisting public sympathy." To do that, the society returned to the common theme of race. An incident in September 1908 underscored the threat from illegal sportsmen. Game warden L. P. Reeves was murdered near Orangeburg by an attacker lying in wait in the woods near the Edisto River, "without excuse, except that Warden Reeves had determined to enforce the law and had thereby incurred the hatred of certain criminals." The society reminded the public that, given such disorder, the failure to act decisively "at the present time, with hunters multiplied by the score, and the negro hunting along with the white hunter, thus bringing another destructive element into play, is so unwise and wasteful that a mere statement ought to be enough to put a stop to it."[70] The report did not claim that African Americans murdered Warden Reeves, but the implication hung in the air. Suggestions of violent outcomes such as this grew stronger, however, as the fight for a state licensing system intensified and the Audubon Society increasingly used race to press its agenda.

In its fifth annual report (1915), the society noted: "Under the lack of system prevailing for fifty years in South Carolina, the laws had the practical effect of putting a premium on vagrancy, for the major benefit of all natural resources was enjoyed by the vagrant alone. The wage-earner and the busy professional man were tied down by the responsibilities, while the vagrant hunted and fished at will." Such appeals resonated with agricultural employers angry over decades of abuses by African Americans who distanced themselves from whites' control through customary activities carried over from slavery. Thus the clarion call to act against such abuses included more than just an appeal to white Southern sporting ethos, conservationist sensibilities, or economic interests; it cried for redeeming and strengthening core social values. "In other words, there will be more liberty, fuller life, for all, and the great principle of American citizenship, 'the greatest good to the greatest number,' will be in operation. This is the only true liberty. The rest is license and lawless living, out of which only the idle and vicious may reap temporary benefits."[71] While the Audubon Society was the loudest voice in decrying "the idle and vicious," it neither did so alone nor only in South Carolina.

By the second decade of the twentieth century, with efforts at implementing state licensing systems developing across the region, proponents celebrated such measures as important not only for the economy, the protection of sportsmen, and the benefit of future generations, but also for protecting white supremacy. In 1912, Virginia conservationists distributed a pamphlet in support of the Moncure and Rutherfoord Bill, which would guarantee the rights of landowners to hunt and fish on their own property, make it more difficult for non-landowners to hunt on another's land, and enact a licensing system requiring all persons to pay a $1.00 county and $3.00 state licensing fee. This bill was "supported by the farmers and sportsmen of the State, the game protective association of Virginia, the Virginia Audubon Society, the National Audubon Society, the American Game Protection and Propagation Association, the United States Department of Agriculture, the Virginia Department of Agriculture, and the Press of Virginia." It had originated in Alabama in 1907 and "in the space of four years, has been copied by twelve States of the Union, Georgia putting it into effect September 1, 1911."[72] Supporters hoped the Alabama law, held up as a model for other states, would spread throughout the South, making clearer the connections between statewide licensing measures and racial control.

The champions of the new law in Virginia and Alabama claimed it would have three distinct results. It would conserve important economic resources. It would bring capital into the state from nonresident sporting tourists. And, most tellingly, it would provide for the "disarmament of a multitude of town and negro loafers, forcing them to legitimate pursuits during the hunting season." The protection of fish and game remained a driving force behind such legislation in the South, but these measures also possessed an inherent racial component. The long-standing connection between African Americans and hunting and fishing—particularly how those activities had, for half a century, helped people of color maximize and (in the eyes of whites) flaunt their freedom—provided an impetus for such legislation that has generally been overlooked.[73]

In an essay appended to the Virginia conservationists' pamphlet, Alabama's Fish and Game Commissioner Wallace wrote that "the farmer . . . has the right to pursue the wild life found on his premises, without license, and, in order for anyone else to hunt, legally, on his lands, a written permission to do so is imperative." Such restriction "keeps out of the fields a class that should not, under any circumstances, have the right to hunt." According to Wallace, African Americans should never have that right. "The sale of single-barrel shot-guns has been cut down at least five hundred per cent, as has the sale of black powder shells, the kind that pot-hunters and negroes used." For Wallace, it did not really matter whether African Americans lost much of their ability to hunt, because, as sportsmen had claimed for decades, they never *truly* hunted in the first place. They merely used customary rights as an excuse to loaf or commit property crimes against whites. Moreover, if such restrictions were passed, rural African Americans would have fewer subsistence options, a condition that employers had sought since the end of slavery.[74] Even if Wallace oversimplified blacks' sporting practices, his zeal in promoting the bill suggests the evolving commitment to using fish and game legislation in the cause of racial control.

Through such state-by-state action, a conglomeration of agricultural and sporting interests gradually embedded in the minds of Southerners a link between fish and game depletion and black independence. The biggest victories, especially the adoption of the Alabama law by other states, came later. In South Carolina, the state government, most notably its game warden, took up the cause. When A. A. Richardson became the first chief game warden in 1913, he found that, although local wardens had been employed in many areas, "in most localities of the State the game laws were looked upon as a joke, and that the wardens had lost interest."[75] To fix this situation, he suggested more money, more wardens, and, most importantly, a resident licensing system. The scheme Richardson endorsed became law on July 1, 1915, and was implemented as described at the beginning of this chapter. He proposed requiring the purchase of either a resident or nonresident fish and game license and a fine of between $25.00 and $100.00, or time on the chain gang, for hunting without a license. To convince doubters, Richardson avoided both vague appeals to Southern values and American democracy and oblique references to the perils of vagrants. Indeed, he went beyond reminding the public of the problems posed by, in the words of the Audubon Society, "hunters multiplied by the score, and the negro hunting along with the white hunter." For the final push to enact a licensing measure, he appealed bluntly and directly to the "Negro problem."

Richardson specifically brought up the central issues of African Americans arming themselves and avoiding regular labor through unrestricted exploitation of the natural environment. He sought a law that would be "constitutional" and would "give every decent citizen of South Carolina the right to hunt and bear arms," but would also "stop the irresponsible drunken Saturday night negro from firing promiscuously up and down the public roads and in front of our homes at all times of the night." Tightly controlled licenses would accomplish both goals. "By refusing to issue a license to such a character he could not lawfully carry a gun," Richardson asserted. By calling for restrictions on hunting and gun ownership, and indeed hinting that state agents should refuse to sell permits to African Americans, Richardson drew on—in fact, counted on—the relationship, in the minds of Southerners, between customary sporting activities, people of color, and ownership of firearms, "which becomes so deadly in the hands of the lawless negro."

Warden Richardson claimed to have personal reasons for being angry over the issue of firearm ownership. In May 1914, three of Richardson's friends were killed in Barnwell County by "the negro outlaw Richard Henry Austin." While reluctant to summarize the incident in his report to the state, Richardson took the opportunity to point out "that had there been a hunter's license, and had each gun been required to be tagged, the chances are that Austin would not have been able to carry a gun in South Carolina, or that the gun would have been taken from him by a game warden before he had committed these terrible crimes." While serving on the posse that chased Austin for twenty-nine days, Richardson was stunned to discover just how many African Americans in the region possessed guns. "I saw negro houses through Hampton and Barnwell counties searched by the posse, and in all these houses were found guns. In some houses only one, in some others two, three, or four, and in some instances as high as six guns, and in nearly all instances they were guns of the latest improved type. In fact, much better guns than those that were carried by the majority of the white men that were on this man-hunt. In this part of the State the negroes are vastly in the majority of the white people. Therefore, you can readily see what I mean when I say that I found conditions that were alarming."

In his report, Richardson summed up these fears by posing a simple question. "I ask you, gentlemen, is there a man in South Carolina who would not be willing to pay one dollar to reduce the number of those guns?" He counted on an affirmative response from a long-suspicious sporting public, a response that would counter traditional objections to such measures. "I wish it understood that I am by no means trying to disarm the negro as a race or in general," Richardson insisted, "but there are certain classes that should be stopped from carrying guns, and as far as I can see the hunter's license is the only constitutional way that you can do it."

Richardson also emphasized other threats posed by African Americans' hunting and fishing, particularly to the South's economic prosperity, as a way of convincing the public of the need for a strict licensing system. The chief game warden reminded his readers that "the greatest destroyer of game out of season, and also of the insectivorous birds, is the negro, who is continually hunting at the very season of the year *when he should be between the plow handles*" (emphasis added). Invoking the decades-long association between hunting and fishing rights and labor evasion, Richardson reminded Southern whites that African Americans "would be abusing a hunter's license if they had one. Therefore, you will further see that the resident hunter's license law will in a great measure improve laboring conditions." Here, proponents of licensing legislation found their most resonant argument. "I feel sure that every farmer in South Carolina will welcome such a law," Richardson declared.

As tenaciously as the Audubon Society had stuck to its essential message since the turn of the century, South Carolina's chief game warden now stuck to his. The following year, Richardson continued to push the need to restrict black liberties as the essential reason for enacting a statewide licensing system. He asserted that three-fourths of South Carolinians favored strong fish and game laws and those supporters "constitute the better element of the people," and that both legislative action and game wardens had their enemies. This was aptly demonstrated by three acts of violence against game wardens in South Carolina in 1914. "A warden in Aiken County was badly beaten whilst making an arrest, another in Dorchester was seriously shot *in a battle with eight negroes*, and the Chief Game Warden was cut and stabbed nearly to death whilst fighting for his life in Barnwell County." Such incidents helped convince a recalcitrant public and an unresponsive legislature to act in the name of wildlife conservation and "racial conservation."[76]

Once state officials such as South Carolina's Richardson and Alabama's Wallace began to lobby for increased funding and legislation, lawmakers began to act. Licensing measures that had previously failed now passed. In South Carolina, the Ziegler Bill (based on the Georgia and Alabama measures), which had failed in the state house by five votes in 1907,[77] finally passed in July 1915. Thus South Carolina joined similar states in enacting statewide systems, such as the Moncure and Rutherfoord Bill passed earlier in Virginia. With establishment of state organizations to protect fish and game and the implementation, in many states, of licensing requirements, proponents of protection laid the foundation for further wildlife regulation and greater restriction of blacks' self-subsistence. "Now that we have an undoubtedly constitutional State-wide Hunter's License Law [the state's] business during the current season is growing by leaps and bound," W. H. Gibbes, then South Carolina's chief game warden, asserted in 1919. Passage of this law presented an opportunity to go farther. "If our game fish are to be saved we must have a State-wide Fishing License Law, and this will double the activities of our Wardens and enable us to pay competent men to specialize in the work."[78] Thanks to the concerted efforts of sporting periodicals, fish and game clubs, semi-official protection associations such as the state Audubon Societies, and, by 1920, the states themselves, sportsmen, landowners, and tourism interests could look at the status of Southern fish and game with growing satisfaction.

Objections to blacks' subsistence and sporting practices, like other criticisms of African Americans' behavior lodged by uneasy whites during Jim Crow, did not end with establishment of state fish and game departments. But such objections seemed to be voiced with a greater hope that they would be answered. N. B. Landy of Lynchburg, Virginia, acknowledged that, while abuses remained a problem, they could be addressed. "Aside from an occasional severe winter," he wrote in

Field and Stream in 1919, "the greatest hindrance to the birds of our State is the immense number of mongrel dogs around every Negro cabin and tenant house, but these we are gradually 'weeding out' by State laws, more efficient game wardens, and county officials."[79] African Americans' sporting, laboring, and subsistence habits had frustrated white Southerners since Emancipation, but by the early decades of the twentieth century there was much for long-complaining whites to celebrate. The struggle for fish and game protection, while unfinished, had produced tangible victories that provided for the future protection of wildlife and the continued restriction of blacks' customary rights.

While African Americans did not, and indeed never would, abandon hunting and fishing, it became harder for them to use such traditions to provide food for themselves and their families, engage in marketing activities of their own design and control, and escape dependency on regular agricultural labor in the service of whites. Through private-property and posting laws, written permission requirements, comprehensive licensing systems, and stricter penalties for fish and game violations, whites made it more difficult for African Americans to draw a considerable portion of their livelihood from practices they had cherished and protected for generations. Indeed, a brief yet telling comment from former Kentucky slave Samuel Sutton to his WPA interviewer illustrates that wildlife reformers had perhaps achieved some of their desired results. When asked whether he and other former slaves still hunted as in the old days, Sutton responded: "No huntin' no mo . . . They aint' wuth the price ob a license no mo."[80] At first glance, such a statement may seem like a simple financial decision to abandon a once widely used means of acquiring food or money. Yet when considered in the larger context of the more than half-century of whites' complaints about African Americans' hunting and fishing, Sutton's decision might be seen as the culmination of a long process that many white Southerners would have viewed with satisfaction. Indeed, it was a state of affairs that many whites had worked for since Emancipation. As Alabama's fish and game commissioner, John H. Wallace, wrote, African Americans "have become, completely disarmed under the game law, and must now pursue the avocation of an honest and industrious life."[81]

The restrictions lauded by Wallace circumscribed African Americans' ability to freely use the South's natural environment. With fines, licensing fees, and jail and labor-gang sentences, and the many other legal and extralegal methods employed to combat unrestricted hunting and fishing by African Americans, the weight of public attention and the legal system was brought to bear on deeply rooted cultural traditions that had served slaves and former slaves for so long. By the time Southern race relations reached their nadir in the 1920s, African Americans' free use of the natural environment, not coincidentally, had also declined. The long assault on blacks' customary hunting and fishing rights, occurring at precisely the time when whites were stripping black Southerners of their civil and political rights, must be seen as part of the broader evolution of efforts at racial control. For just as whites hoped to divide Southern society into white and black, so sportsmen, landowners, and lawmakers hoped to impose a similar division on Southern hunting and fishing. In the end, the long campaign to disrupt blacks' time-honored traditions became part of a larger strategy that included disfranchisement, chain gangs, lynchings, and segregation, all of which were deployed to erode African Americans' control over their lives and labor.

Conclusion

*Contradiction and Continuity in
the Southern Sporting Field*

In October 1911, a group of wealthy Lowcountry denizens gathered in Berkeley County, South Carolina, for a meeting of the St. John's Hunting Club, an organization founded before the Civil War. Since 1900, the organization had ceased to be a functioning hunting club and had become solely a social club for wealthy South Carolinians. But although the club had abandoned hunting as its central activity, it did not completely give up the traditions associated with it. Hunting continued to play an important symbolic role for the club's membership.

Although the club was no longer directly involved in field sports, for its members, its long history of hunting in the Lowcountry was a connection to an immutable past, a time when hunting both reflected and solidified white elites' position at the top of the Southern social structure. And, while clinging to the tradition, if not the act, of hunting, club members preserved the connection between hunting and race relations that elite sportsmen had long cultivated. At the October 1911 meeting, for example, members gathered around to listen to a poem entitled "Opening the Hunt" by M. E. Ravenel. The poem, written in the stereotypical black dialect common to sporting literature of the period, left no doubt that the symbolic place of hunting, as a reflection of elite white status and African-American subordination, remained important to club members:

> Look sharp dere boys, quit your foolin' roun',
> It's time you was ready for true;
> Uncle Quash done loadin' ol' Maussa gun,
> An' de hosses don saddle too.
> An' quick as de brekfas' is done at de house

Ole Maussa gwine blow 'im a blas'.
So he 'spectin' de dribers and dogs waitin' den
To git in de woods bery fas'.

Written from the perspective of a devoted servant named Pompey, the poem confirms both the importance of African Americans' labor to Southern hunting and fishing and the centrality of the ideal of blacks' service to elite white sportsmen. Indeed, the verse seems to celebrate racial subordination as much as the tradition of hunting. Pompey goes on to enthusiastically describe both the degree to which "ol' Maussa" depends on him and his fellows for their service and his own excitement at the opportunity to meet his master's expectations:

For Maussa got cump'hy wid 'im today
Which he anxious to gi' dem some shootin';
He countin' on Pompey to clean up dese woods
An' bring out de game a-skootin'.
An' I says moreober on cashuns like dis,
Do its me dats doin' de praisin',
(What perhaps I isnt ought to) but yet I does say
Dat I gin'rally shows my raisin'.[1]

Nearly half a century after the end of slavery, Ravenel's poem, complete with its loyal black servant eager to impress his employer with his skilled service and the chance to "rally shows my raisin'," reminded St. John's Hunting Club members that while the club's active sporting days had ended, its lofty social position, typified by the historical white-over-black mastery found in the hunting field, lived on. By 1911, Jim Crow was firmly in place and the legislative assault on blacks' customary rights was in full swing in Virginia, Alabama, South Carolina, and elsewhere in the South. But it seemed that, at least at the St. John's Club, preserving and celebrating the racial significance of hunting had perhaps become more important than hunting itself. By the early twentieth century, some Southern elites had abandoned hunting as a pastime, but not as a vibrant symbol of white supremacy.

Yet even if hunting and fishing—or, in the case of Ravenel's poem, the memory of hunting and fishing—are understood to have been an important part of the evolution of the Southern racial divide, such "racial conservation" did not affect all African Americans equally. Indeed, ironically, the process coincided with the booming popularity of Southern sporting tourism that guaranteed African-American hunters and fishermen a permanent, if limited, place at fish and game plantations and sporting resorts. The establishment of private clubs and preserves may have dramatically decreased the amount of land available for the free taking of wildlife, but some African Americans nonetheless carved out a long-term place for themselves in Southern hunting and fishing. Even as the creation of state fish and game departments and the employment of a growing number of game wardens challenged African Americans' ability to hunt and fish freely, native and visiting sportsmen's dependence on black labor—or, again, in the case of the St. John's Club, the memory of such labor—guaranteed that Dixie's sporting field would not be lily white. While whites celebrated the restrictions on African-American independence, their desire to recapture the mythical Old South guaranteed that part of the region's sporting field would remain permanently biracial.

For well over a century, only when the sporting exploits of slaves and freed persons were conducted in proximity to white superiors did they escape criticism. When hunting and fishing were done away from white oversight and exclusively for the betterment of African Americans and their families, and particularly when used, after Emancipation, as powerful symbols and key protectors of black independence—then, whites cried for action. The cultivation of independence was the most important benefit African Americans drew from their long-standing reliance on such customary rights. That independence became the most convincing reason offered by whites in their efforts to make those practices more expensive and more exclusive. The realization that whites had more to protect than fish and game, that hunting and fishing had a strong racial component, and that the Southern conservation movement used racism to garner support is central to any understanding of the fight to protect wildlife.

Thus the story of the place of African Americans in Southern hunting and fishing between 1865 and the 1920s is one of apparent contradictions. The sporting field became, for blacks, a place of economic opportunity where valuable wildlife, marketing opportunities, and steady employment awaited them. For former slave Jake Williams, who relied on hunting with his loyal hound Belle for subsistence after escaping bondage, and later with Belle's offspring to cultivate independence after Emancipation (as recounted in the Introduction), hunting and fishing stood as bellwethers for freedom. Yet they also helped elite whites reconstruct a racial hierarchy swept away by Emancipation. For Southern elites, particularly landowners, the sporting field became both a site where they celebrated continued mastery over people of color by re-creating the old master-servant relationship and an arena in which they expressed their fears about black liberation through their antipathy toward unrestricted customary rights. For sportsmen, in Southern hunting and fishing they celebrated their own traditions and acumen and, at the same time, lamented blacks' apparent rejection of whites' sporting codes, a rejection that both threatened fish and game supplies and challenged whites' sporting dominion. All those, both black and white, who were directly touched by former slaves' long relationship with the pursuit of Southern wildlife knew the story to be a complex and multi-sided one. Hunting and fishing reflected African Americans' ability to use long-cultivated subsistence traditions to better their lives, and whites' willingness to circumscribe that freedom to combat the negative consequences of black independence. Simultaneously providing economic competence and racial subordination, guaranteeing long-term employment and economic exploitation, and foretelling both physical and symbolic liberation and emerging segregation, hunting and fishing encompassed all the racial tensions of the late-nineteenth and early-twentieth-century South and thus defy simple labels.

It is therefore difficult to describe hunting and fishing in the post-Emancipation South as exclusively a source of either black independence or white supremacy—an ambiguity demonstrated by the uncertainty of even contemporary observers. When Archibald Rutledge described a former-slave sportsman as possessed of a "kind of eerie skill instinctive to him and a few others of his race but denied the white man," while also declaring that "if he brings home a rabbit or a squirrel or a 'possum, he will be both lucky and happy," he expressed the inescapable fact, for elite whites, that African Americans' hunting and fishing could be good or bad, effective or immoderate, depending on the observer's point of view.[2] Likewise, when Henry Wellington Wack asserted that black subordinates were "teeming with ideas about tarpon and local taxes, national politics and peach brandy" and thus made valuable companions, he nonetheless warned readers to "have a club handy, for when the king of game fish starts your line for Jamaica you'll need vigorous inducements to bring that nigger to consciousness." Wack thus furthered the notion that while hunting and fishing could reflect African Americans' competence and skill, those traits were invariably bound by the limitations of black character.[3] And when C. W. Boyd described hunting with "a genuine Southern negro" named Barney whose sporting "accomplishments were considerable," and "not an event of importance took place in local sporting circles of which Barney did not know," he was careful to point out that Barney remained a devoted servant who "in social intercourse constantly inclined to risibility." Thus Boyd further demonstrated that whites recognized black sporting skill only if accompanied by tacit acknowledgment of white supremacy.[4] At first glance, then, few observers of African Americans' hunting and fishing failed to at least begin to grasp these contradictions. Yet if one examines such statements closely, the apparent contradictions begin to unravel.

Despite the often-conflicting descriptions of hunting and fishing by people of color, there is an essential component of all these descriptions that makes the story clearer: the attitude of white observers toward black independence. When commentators such as Rutledge, Wack, Boyd, and scores of other whites criticized blacks' hunting and fishing, they were invariably referring to times when people of color hunted and fished on their own and for their own benefit. Away from white oversight, hunting and fishing by African Americans represented a loss of white Southerners' power and reminded them that former slaves now had the freedom to earn a living apart from exclusively white-directed labor, and to express that freedom by trespassing on Southern cultural traditions that ideally should be reserved for whites.

While taking to the field in the service of white elites, African Americans did so as extensions of the sportsmen whom they served. In these instances, blacks' skill ceased to be a threat because, while in the field with their employers, everything African-American subordinates did came under the umbrella of service. In that context, white sportsmen believed, all challenges to assumptions of white supremacy and black inferiority proved fleeting. Even the great skill demonstrated by so many African-American hunters and fishermen, when plied under a rubric of subordination, testified to whites' own position at the top of the racial and sporting hierarchy. As independent sportsmen, African Americans might threaten whites' economic and cultural interests, but as subordinated laborers, they could only serve and reinforce them. The relative levels of freedom expressed through hunting and fishing thus became the axis on which whites' assessments of such activities turned. For elite white observers, struggling to come to grips with the loss of their slaves and eager to maintain control over black labor, independent hunting and fishing expressed the worst consequences of black liberation. Yet at the same time, when black subordinates hunted and fished for and with white superiors, those same activities proved a proscriptive for the many problems posed by that liberation.

The two great transformations in Southern hunting and fishing between the end of the Civil War and the 1920s—the rise of the tourism industry and the rise of the conservation movement—reflect these two distinct sides of African-American liberation. Much of the popularity of Southern sporting tourism may be explained by the lasting appeal of the idealized antebellum master-servant relationship, which both comforted native whites and created for visitors a sense of Southern authenticity. The central role of black labor in maintaining that relationship made hunting and fishing a powerful celebration of whites' sporting and social supremacy and an effective means of exploiting African-American skill and labor for the continued benefit of white elites. Likewise, much of the force behind the drive to enact wildlife protections in this period may also be laid at the doorstep of black liberation. For as much as hunting and fishing by subordinate African Americans helped native and visiting whites resurrect an era of control over people of color, independent hunting and fishing by former slaves, with its specter of self-subsistence, labor intractability, and open challenges to white sporting privilege, reflected the consequences of losing that control. If advertising former slaves' abilities as sporting laborers became an indispensable way for elites to profit from and express their belief in continued racial subordination, then creating a comprehensive legal apparatus to restrict blacks' customary rights became an essential strategy to minimize the freedom African Americans expressed through independent hunting and fishing.

Despite such efforts, however, African Americans would never completely abandon hunting and fishing. As demonstrated by the long relationship between African-American sporting employees and resorts and plantations such as Pebble Hill in Thomasville, Georgia, and the Medway plantation in Berkeley County, South Carolina, the presence of black subordinates remained a crucial part of Southern hunting and fishing for generations. Physically dependent on black labor and, more importantly, tied to the tradition of racial subordination it symbolized, white Southerners refused to give up African-American sporting labor. White Southerners hoping to use the sporting field to recapture the social and racial trappings of the antebellum era, even well into the twentieth century, found the presence of black laborers a continuing comfort. Indeed, as South Carolinian Henry D. Boykin insisted with his romantic description of his father's loyal huntsmen, Spaniard, Rabbit, and Bootie, "the thrill of many ancient hunters must surge up from the shadows to join the sweet song of those three dark experts."[5] For many white sporting enthusiasts, African Americans remained a key part of a particular version of Southern sporting and racial relationships that had to be preserved and celebrated.

White Southerners and visiting sportsmen, however, did not remain the only champions of the biracial Southern sporting field. Despite the decades-long struggle to restrict blacks' customary rights, and despite the imposition of legal measures to circumscribe their access to hunting and fishing, whites failed to eliminate such practices altogether. In time, African Americans emerged as notable advocates of the hunting and fishing tradition. In 1996, the United States Fish and Wildlife Service conducted the *National Survey of Fishing, Hunting and Wildlife-Associated Recreation*, with the aim of gathering information on how and why different population groups spent their time engaged in wildlife-related recreations and to better identify those groups whose participation traditionally lagged. The study found that "hunting and fishing have predominantly been white male activities since at least 1955 when the Fish and Wildlife Service began tracking the demographics of hunters and anglers. Participation rates of females and minorities have consistently been below the national average."[6] Then, in a 2000 addendum, *Participation and Expenditure Patterns of African-American, Hispanic and Women Hunters and Anglers,*[7] it became clear that although African Americans' participation trailed that of white hunters and fishermen by a wide margin (5),[8] hunting by blacks was far more concentrated regionally than hunting by whites. According to the study, 73 percent of all African-American hunters, and 64 percent of all African-American fishermen, lived in the South (8, 16).

Two facts emerge from the 2000 addendum. The first is the noticeably large gap in the prevalence of hunting and fishing by white and black Americans. According to the Fish and Wildlife Service, that gap exists because of "cultural differences" that are "deep-seated enough to transcend the effects of income, education, age and other factors normally assumed to have a large influence on behavior" (16). Yet one must wonder if a more persuasive answer might be found by looking at the historical relationship between African Americans' hunting and fishing and attacks on these activities, beginning in the late nineteenth century. In considering why minorities tend to hunt and fish far less than whites, Fish and Wildlife researchers might wish to consider whether the present-day disparity represents exactly what beleaguered elite white sportsmen fought for over so many decades—a sporting field dominated by whites. They might also consider the possibility that "cultural differences" between white and nonwhite Americans could be a less critical factor in modern-day differences in hunting and fishing than was the creation, in the early twentieth century, of wildlife regulations that privileged men of means and, at least in the South, specifically targeted African Americans.

The other key fact that emerges from the addendum is that African Americans in the Southern states are far more likely than African Americans nationally to hunt or fish. As noted above, in 2000, nearly three-quarters of all African-American hunters and nearly two-thirds of all African-American fishermen lived in the South. These statistics, aside from reflecting the predominantly Northern, urban nature of the country's black population since the Great Migration, perhaps confirm the deep roots of these customary practices for black Southerners and demonstrate that efforts to eliminate blacks' independent hunting and fishing in the early twentieth century proved incomplete. Even if whites' participation in hunting and fishing nationally outstripped blacks' participation by more than three to one, the concentration of blacks' hunting and fishing in the South indicates that the roots of these practices run deep. This was confirmed by another study, undertaken two years after the original U.S. Fish and Wildlife survey.

Given the lag in minorities' participation in hunting and fishing, and the desire to increase participation in order to make outdoor recreation and boating industries more profitable, in 1998 the Sport Fishing and Boating Partnership Council commissioned the report *Women's, Hispanics', and African Americans' Participation in, and Attitudes toward, Boating and Fishing.*[9] This report was drawn from ten focus-group interview sessions with female, Hispanic, and African-American volunteers. The results show that some African-American participants not only were well aware of the long-standing connection between people of color and hunting and fishing traditions, but also worked to cultivate that heritage. According to one African-American woman, "I was a born fisherman . . . I come from a long line of fishermen . . . A lot of African Americans before us didn't have a lot of things to do. It's been passed down through the generations . . . For our ancestors, there was nothing else for them to do" (8).

Other interviewees confirmed this appreciation for the deep, generational roots of African-Americans' use of wildlife. "I've got an uncle who just passed. He could go out and catch fish to fill his table," a black resident of Tampa, Florida, noted. "I just inherited it from him I guess. It's a family thing. At family reunions, we all go fishing" (9). A third participant, clearly aware of the historical connection between hunting and fishing and the African-American community, noted that such tradition influenced his choice to continue hunting and fishing. "When I was little, you fished or hunted because you had to," the subject noted. "I still hunt (and fish) . . . there's not very good hunting in this area, but I still enjoy it. Since my family has been connected to it for over 200 years, I still do it" (9).

African Americans' participation in hunting and fishing activities may be low for the United States as a whole, but the testimonials of these individuals indicate that this rich tradition has not died. Such findings in fact suggest that at least some contemporary African-American hunters and fishermen continue to roam Southern fields, forests, and streams for food or sport, well aware of the historical connection between hunting and fishing, people of color, and the struggle for independence. Despite elite whites' attempts to drive blacks out of the sporting field, the decline of the Southern sporting tourism industry since mid-century, and the life and death of Jim Crow segregation, this rich tradition has endured and continues to influence how African Americans interact with the natural environment, feed themselves, spend their leisure time, and honor long-standing, important traditions that have served them for so long.

Acknowledgments

Research and writing can be a daunting and isolating experience at times and, for that reason, is never a truly individual endeavor. This study could not have been completed without the intellectual, emotional, and moral support of many fine people, and it is a great pleasure to acknowledge my debts. My deepest appreciation and gratitude goes to my family, friends, and colleagues for their help, guidance, and patience through this challenging and sometimes difficult process.

I first developed an intense love for studying the past while a history major at Hiram College, in Ohio. There I had the great fortune to learn from Wilson Hoffman, now Emeritus Professor of History, and Glenn Sharfman, now Vice President and Dean for Academic Affairs at Manchester College. In classes, in their offices, or just talking around the big table in Pendleton House, Wil and Glenn inculcated an appreciation for the twists and turns of history and provided an outstanding model of teaching, advising, and mentoring. My eventual decision to pursue a career in academics was based in part on their example and I would be remiss in not expressing my gratitude to them.

My thanks also go to the members of my dissertation committee at the University of Pittsburgh for their efforts reading, criticizing, and sharpening my work over the years. Without welcome advice and keen insight from Professors Kathleen Blee, Seymour Drescher, and Marcus Rediker this project would not have been possible. My work and my own understanding of history are much stronger for their efforts, and I sincerely thank them for their interest and guidance.

I especially wish to express my deepest appreciation for the unbending support of my valued graduate advisor, Professor Van Beck Hall. Dr. Hall's mentoring over the long years, from our explorations of Southern history in early independent studies (during which I first glimpsed the full scope of his terrifying but inspirational knowledge of the region) to the final stages of writing, showed me what it truly means to be a dedicated scholar, thoughtful educator, and concerned advisor and friend. I intend to follow his fine example as best I can in my own career.

Numerous organizations provided generous financial support for the research and writing of this book. I was fortunate to twice receive the Samuel P. Hays Research Award from the Department of History of the University of Pittsburgh, which greatly aided in locating and, later, completing the necessary research. In between those awards, I received valuable support from the Virginia Historical Society in the form of an Andrew W. Mellon Research Fellowship that funded my work in Richmond. For my work in the Southern Historical and North Carolina Collections at the University of North Carolina, I benefited from the Archie K. Davis Research Fellowship from the North Caroliniana Society. In addition to the above grants and awards, the Lillian B. Lawler Predoctoral Fellowship provided most valuable assistance that enabled me to complete the majority of my research. I sincerely thank each organization and the individuals involved for these much-appreciated awards.

I also wish to acknowledge the librarians and archivists at the sites I visited for my research. Their help and interest in my study made the research process much easier. I especially thank the staff of the Hillman Library at the University of Pittsburgh, particularly the Inter-Library Loan and Microfilm departments, which were a great help for this project. I also thank the staff of the Library of Virginia and Virginia Historical Society in Richmond, the North Carolina State Archives in Raleigh, the South Carolina Historical Society in Charleston, the South Carolina State Archives and the South Caroliniana Library, University of South Carolina, in Columbia, and the Southern Historical and North Carolina Collections at the University of North Carolina at Chapel Hill.

For a junior scholar navigating the world of publishing for the first time, I benefited greatly from working with the fine people at the Johns Hopkins University Press. Robert J. Brugger showed interest in and support for the study before the dissertation draft had even been completed and was extremely helpful in shepherding the manuscript toward completion. He also found an anonymous reader whose comments and criticism proved both encouraging and helpful. In addition, the Press assigned a wonderful copyeditor, Linda Strange, whose careful attention to the book improved it greatly. I thank Bob and the staff of the Press for their efforts.

I wish to make special mention of the many friends and colleagues whose friendship over the years, from my days as a graduate student at the University of Pittsburgh to my time at Culver-Stockton College in Canton, Missouri, has been so important, personally and professionally. Without their interest in my work and their steadfast intellectual and emotional support, this project would not have been started, let alone finished. Whether in seminars, over lunch, on research trips, via telephone and e-mail, or at conferences, that network of friends proved invaluable. I deeply thank Tania Boster, John Donoghue, Mike Ervin, Jeff Forret, Patrick Hotle, Jack Kapluck, Jayme Long, Steve Long, Mike McCoy, Dave Recht, Chad Statler, Vanessa Sterling, and Andy Walsh for their friendship and valuable contributions to my work.

Special thanks go to those friends and colleagues who have read all or parts of the manuscript over the years as it changed from master's proposal to dissertation to book, and generously lent their time and honesty toward pointing out the study's strengths and weaknesses. Andrew Haley, Craig Marin, and Ellie Walsh generously gave their time to this project since the beginning, discussing the research, helping shape the argument, and reading and critiquing chapter drafts. I am forever grateful for their efforts. Their questions, suggestions, and criticisms are an important reason why the work has reached this stage. Any places where the book falls short, of course, reflect my shortcoming and not theirs.

Finally, I wish to acknowledge the love and support from my family that made my studies of history possible in the first place. Without the tireless and unwavering support from my parents, John and Judy Giltner, I could never have reached this point. I thank them for their patience during this long process and for their faith that it would someday reach a conclusion. Ultimately, the existence of this book is much more a testament to their hard work and dedication than to mine.

Notes

Manuscript collections and depositories cited in the notes are identified by the following abbreviations:

DocSouth	Documenting the American South Collection
NCC	North Carolina Collection
NCDAH	North Carolina Division of Archives and History, Raleigh, NC
NCSA	North Carolina State Archives, Raleigh, NC
SCDAH	South Carolina Division of Archives and History, Columbia, SC
SCHS	South Carolina Historical Society, Charleston, SC
SCL	South Caroliniana Library
SHC	Southern Historical Collections
UNCCH	University of North Carolina at Chapel Hill, Chapel Hill, NC
USC	University of South Carolina, Columbia, SC
VHS	Virginia Historical Society, Richmond, VA

INTRODUCTION: HUNTING, FISHING, AND FREEDOM

1. George Rawick, "Alabama Narratives," in *The American Slave: A Composite Autobiography* (Westport, CT: Greenwood Press, 1972), 6(1): 123. Rawick provides scores of Federal Writers' Project interviews with former slaves. The Writers' Project was a program of the Works Progress Administration (WPA).

2. As numerous scholars have demonstrated, such sources as the WPA narratives, while providing invaluable information on slave life, can be highly problematic as primary evidence. Given the problems with subjects' memory and their tendency to exaggerate or distort the truth (for a variety of reasons), scholars must use these narratives with care. For two essays that deal with this problem, see John W. Blassingame, "Using the Testimony of Ex-Slaves: Approaches and Problems," *Journal of Southern History* 41, no. 4 (1975): 473–92, and David Thomas Bailey, "A Divided Prism: Two Sources of Black Testimony on Slavery," *Journal of Southern History* 46, no. 3 (1980): 381–404.

3. Charles Ball, *Slavery in the United States: A Narrative of the Life and Adventures of Charles Ball, a Black Man, Who Lived Forty Years in Maryland, South Carolina and Georgia, as a Slave under Various Masters, and Was One Year in the Navy with Commodore Barney, during the Late War* (New York: John S. Taylor, 1837), 352.

4. Scott E. Giltner, "'Whatever I Could Git': Slave Hunting and Fishing in the Plantation South" (MA thesis, University of Pittsburgh, 1998). The thesis has since been published as "Slave Hunting and Fishing in the Antebellum South," in *"To Love the Wind and the Rain": African Americans and Environmental History*, ed. Dianne Glave and Mark Stoll (Pittsburgh: University of Pittsburgh Press, 2005).

5. J. William Harris, *Deep Souths: Delta, Piedmont, and Sea Island Society in the Age of Segregation* (Baltimore: Johns Hopkins University Press, 2001), 5.

CHAPTER 1: "YOU CAN'T STARVE A NEGRO"

Epigraphs. [Editorial], *Southern Planter and Farmer*, November 1872, 671; George Rawick, "Alabama and Indiana Narratives," in *The American Slave: A Composite Autobiography* (Westport, CT: Greenwood Press, 1972), 6(1): 201–2.

1. Letter to George Washington Trimble, December 29, 1900, Kelly Walker Trimble Papers, 1770–1954, manuscripts, Mss10: no. 120, VHS (emphasis in original).

2. For a discussion of slaves' hunting and fishing—particularly how those activities helped make life under bondage more bearable by providing food, money, and material goods, creating time for family bonding, and even carving out opportunities to resist slavery itself—see Scott Giltner, "Slave Hunting and Fishing in the Antebellum South," in *"To Love the Wind and the Rain": African Americans and Environmental History*, ed. Dianne Glave and Mark Stoll (Pittsburgh: University of Pittsburgh Press, 2005). See also Nicholas W. Proctor, *Bathed in Blood: Hunting and Mastery in the Old South* (Charlottesville: University of Virginia Press, 2002), esp. chap. 7, "Slave Perceptions of the Hunt."

3. "Mutual Confidence and Reciprocal Fidelity Will Secure the Material Prosperity of the White Man and the Negro," *Southern Planter and Farmer*, August 1867, 400 (emphasis in original).

4. "Hints on the Labor Question," *Southern Planter and Farmer*, October 1867, 53 (emphasis in original).

5. Goodwyn Agricultural Club, "Essay on the Subject of Labor," *Southern Planter and Farmer*, March 1871, 135–36.

6. Elizabeth Ware Pearson, ed., *Letters from Port Royal, 1862–1868* (New York: Arno Press, 1969), 221–22.

7. Major-General David Hunter, commander of the Union forces in the South Carolina and Georgia Sea Islands, gained fame for his general order of May 9, 1862, declaring martial law and abolishing slavery in South Carolina, Georgia, and Florida. Issued without approval, the order was rescinded by President Lincoln, who feared the political impact of such action on the border states. James McPherson, *Battle Cry of Freedom: The Civil War Era* (New York: Oxford University Press, 1988), 499.

8. Pearson, *Letters from Port Royal*, 37–38 (emphasis in original).

9. Rawick, "North Carolina Narratives," *American Slave* 14(1): 336.

10. Rawick, "Alabama and Indiana Narratives," *American Slave* 6(2): 93.

11. George Washington Cable, *John March, Southerner* (New York: Charles Scribner's Sons, 1899), 52.

12. Rawick, "Virginia Narratives," *American Slave* 16(5): 14. It did not take planters long to realize that the ability to live off the products of the land slowed the process of returning former slaves to the service of their former masters. According to Steven Hahn, "planters recognized that customary use rights, along with the availability of public domain in some states, jeopardized labor supply and discipline and, by extension, the revitalization of the cotton economy." Hahn, "Hunting, Fishing, and Foraging: Common Rights and Class Relations in the Postbellum South," *Radical History Review* 26 (1982): 36–64.

13. Ethelred Philips to James Philip Jones, September 5, 1866, James Philip Jones Papers, SHC #972, UNCCH.

14. James Philip Jones to Ethelred Philips, December 19, 1866, James Philip Jones Papers, SHC #972, UNCCH.

15. Ruth McEnery Stuart, *In Simpkinsville: Character Tales* (New York: Harper & Brothers, 1897), 13, DocSouth, UNCCH.

16. Archibald Hamilton Rutledge, *Hunter's Choice* (New York: A. S. Barnes and Company, 1946), 21.

17. Edward King, *The Great South: A Record of Journeys in Louisiana, Texas, the Indian Territory, Missouri, Arkansas, Mississippi, Alabama, Georgia, Florida, South Carolina, North Carolina, Kentucky, Tennessee, Virginia, West Virginia, and Maryland* (Hartford, IL: American Publishing Company, 1875), 60, 430, 321, 593, 372.

18. Rawick, "Texas Narratives," *American Slave* 5(3): 240–41.

19. Rawick, "North Carolina Narratives," *American Slave* 14(1): 299–300.

20. Rawick, "Florida Narratives," *American Slave* 17(1): 227.

21. Alan Brown and David Taylor, eds., *Gabr'l Blow Sof': Sumter County, Alabama, Slave Narratives* (Livingston, AL: Livingston University Press, 1997), 69–70.

22. Rawick, "Alabama and Indiana Narratives," *American Slave* 6(1): 201–2.

23. Rawick, "Unwritten History of Slavery: Autobiographical Accounts of Negro Ex-Slaves," *American Slave* 18(1): 95.

24. Milton Meltzer, ed., *In Their Own Words: A History of the American Negro, 1865–1916* (New York: Ty Crowell Co., 1965), 4.

25. James Henry Rice Jr., *Glories of the Carolina Coast* (Columbia, SC: R. L. Bryan Co., 1925), 89, SCHS.

26. Julian Ralph, *Dixie; or Southern Scenes and Sketches* (New York: Harper & Brothers, 1895), 376.

27. H. B. Frissel and Isabel Bevier, *Dietary Studies of Negroes in Eastern Virginia in 1897 and 1898*, U.S. Department of Agriculture, Office of Experiment Stations, Bulletin No. 71 (Washington, DC: Government Printing Office, 1899), 11. That African-American families living along the edges of the Great Dismal Swamp relied heavily on hunting and fishing is no surprise to students of slavery in Virginia and the Carolinas. The Dismal was one of the richest fish and game regions of the South, and due to its renowned impenetrability was a famed destination for runaway slaves. Alexander Hunter noted the Dismal's role in runaway life, asserting in 1895 that "the Great Dismal, in the *ante-bellum* days, was a famous resort for runaway slaves, and once in its

recesses they were never heard of more." Hunter, "The Great Dismal Swamp," *Outing* 27, no. 1 (October 1895): 71 (emphasis in original).

28. Frissel and Bevier, "Dietary Studies of Negroes in Eastern Virginia," 40.

29. J. A. Dickey and E. C. Branson, "How Farm Tenants Live," University of North Carolina Extension Bulletin, 1922, NCC, C378 UJ3, UNCCH. Cooperative Extension Services were an important government institution in the history of modern rural America, and existed primarily as offshoots of early-twentieth-century efforts by the U.S. Department of Agriculture (USDA) to improve agriculture, bring advances in farming techniques and technologies to farmers in isolated rural areas, and generally serve as a liaison between farmers and various branches of state and federal government. Extension services became especially active in the South, where problems of agricultural efficiency and technological backwardness proved particularly detrimental to the region's prosperity. Ultimately they also became one of the few government agencies that worked to help black farmers—in the words of historian Jeannie Whayne, to "make conditions better for blacks in the South while at the same time avoiding the appearance of challenging the racial status quo." Whayne, "'I Have Been through Fire': Black Agricultural Extension Agents and the Politics of Negotiation," in *African American Life in the Rural South, 1900–1950*, ed. R. Douglas Hurt (Columbia: University of Missouri Press, 2003), 156.

30. Dickey and Branson, "How Farm Tenants Live." Unlike the study undertaken by the USDA in Virginia, which focused specifically on African Americans, the North Carolina study documented life for white and black farm tenants. The study revealed an unsurprising similarity between the subsistence patterns of the two groups. Faced with comparable economic challenges, particularly as the South's agricultural economy became increasingly volatile between the 1880s and the 1920s, white and black tenants and sharecroppers relied heavily on hunting, fishing, and foraging to guarantee their subsistence.

31. J. William Harris, *Deep Souths: Delta, Piedmont, and Sea Island Society in the Age of Segregation* (Baltimore: Johns Hopkins University Press, 2001), 51.

32. Despite prohibitions against possessing dangerous weapons, slaves often obtained them in a variety of ways. Former slave Jacob Stroyer suggested some of the ways in which slaves could acquire weapons, all of which distressed slave owners. "My readers ask, how had they obtained arms and what were they, since slaves were not allowed to have deadly weapons? Some had large knives made by their fellow negroes who were blacksmiths, others stole guns from white men, who were accustomed to lay them carelessly around when they were out hunting game. The runaways who stole the guns were kept in powder and shot by some of the other slaves at home, who bought such from poor white men who kept little country stores in the different parts of the South." That slaves would take such risks is testament to the value of these weapons, not only for hunting but also as potential tools of freedom. Stroyer, *My Life in the South* (Salem, MA: Salem Observer Book and Job Print, 1885), 65, DocSouth, UNCCH.

33. Agitation over African Americans' gun ownership rights became inherently connected to intense debate over their hunting rights. After a relative lull in the evo-

lution of Southern hunting and fishing laws, the uncertainty of the immediate post-Emancipation years—when many elite white Southerners called for limits on gun ownership—led many to consider widespread restrictions on the previously near-universal right of all Southerners to hunt and fish. Such restrictions, in the words of a white South Carolinian, would "keep the negroes more confined." Hahn, "Hunting, Fishing, and Foraging," 46.

34. Quoted in "Louisiana Game Interests," *Forest and Stream*, September 16, 1886, 146. *Forest and Stream* was late-nineteenth century America's largest and most influential sporting magazine.

35. Henry Edwards Davis, "'Old Betsy': Stories of Hunting with the Old Percussion Muzzle Loader and Its Successors" (typescript), 21, manuscripts P, SCL, USC. Davis is considered one of the most influential turkey hunters in American history. He wrote the influential *The American Wild Turkey* (Georgetown, SC: Small Arms Technical Publishing Company, 1949), which still stands as the classic treatise on the subject.

36. "Notes on Dogs and Game in Mississippi," *Forest and Stream*, July 2, 1874, 326.

37. Norman R. Yetman, *Voices from Slavery* (New York: Henry Holt and Company, 1970), 315. According to White, one particular occasion when he borrowed a gun from Ed Davis had violent results. In his narrative he recounts how, against his normal habit, he left the gun loaded, which became important later that evening when the Ku Klux Klan paid Davis a visit. "When dey told him to open de door," White recalled, "he heard one of 'em say, 'shoot him time he gets de door open.' 'Well,' he says to 'em, 'Wait till I can light de lamp.' Den he got de gun what I had left loaded, get down on his knees, and stuck it through a log and pull de trigger. He hit Newt Dobbs in de stomach and kilt him" (315).

38. For slaves, opportunities for gun ownership were both rare and valuable. At the risk of oversimplifying, there were essentially three ways slaves could enjoy the use of firearms in their independent hunting. First, the state or county could legally bond a slave to carry a hunting weapon. Second, a master could give a slave permission to hunt with firearms, in the absence of government sanction. Finally, slaves could obtain firearms without permission. For an example of the latter, see the WPA narrative of former North Carolina slave George Rogers, who recalled "borrowing" guns to hunt when his master was away. "We used to kill squirrels, turkeys, an' game wid guns. When Marster went off some o' us boys stole de guns, an' away we went to de woods huntin'. Marster would come back drunk. He would not know, an' he did not care nuther, about we huntin' game." Rawick, "North Carolina Narratives," *American Slave* 15(1): 222.

39. Davis, "'Old Betsy,'" 10.

40. Rawick, "Unwritten History of Slavery," 251.

41. "Coahoma," "The Possum 'Sulls,'" *Forest and Stream*, June 25, 1891, 455.

42. Alexander Hunter, "Sport—Past, Present, and Future, Part I," *Outing* 5, no. 13 (December 1888).

43. Archibald Hamilton Rutledge, *Santee Paradise* (New York: Bobbs-Merrill Company, 1956), 155, 169.

44. Yetman, *Voices from Slavery*, 200.

45. Hunter, "Sport — Past, Present, and Future."

46. "Rabbit Hunting with Uncle Ned," *Forest and Stream*, December 15, 1887, 406.

47. "Will Scribbler," "In November," *Forest and Stream*, December 22, 1894, 334.

48. For a detailed account of the role of dogs in slaves' subsistence, the depth of the attachment between slaves and their dogs, and whites' attempts to limit such ownership, see John Campbell's "'My Constant Companion': Slaves and Their Dogs in the Antebellum South," in *Working Toward Freedom: Slave Society and Domestic Economy in the American South*, ed. Larry E. Hudson Jr. (Rochester, NY: University of Rochester Press, 1994).

49. J. Vance Lewis, *Out of the Ditch: A True Story of an Ex-Slave* (Houston, TX: Rein & Sons Co., 1910), 17, DocSouth, UNCCH.

50. Bill Arp [Charles Henry Smith], *Bill Arp: From the Uncivil War to Date, 1861–1903* (Atlanta, GA: Hudgins Publishing Co., 1903), 48. Under this pen name, Smith was known for writing satirical editorials about political and military matters during the Civil War and was later famous for his letters recounting the simple pleasures of Southern country life.

51. Harry Worcester Smith, *A Sporting Family of the Old South* (Albany, NY: J. B. Lyon Co., 1936), 91, general collection, SK 33.S63, VHS.

52. "Sarah S. Carter Diary, 1866," 3, manuscripts, Mss5:1C2467:1, VHS.

53. Clifton Johnson, *Highways and Byways of the South* (New York: Macmillan, 1904), 336.

54. Charles Hallock, "Wild Cattle Hunting on Green Island," in *Hunting in the Old South: Original Narratives of the Hunters*, ed. Clarence Gohdes (Baton Rouge: Louisiana State University Press, 1967), 67.

55. Rutledge, *Santee Paradise*, 156.

56. For descriptions of such devices, see the narratives of former slave Peggy Grigsby, in Rawick, "South Carolina Narratives," *American Slave* 2(2): 215; and former slave "Aunt" Esther Green, in Rawick, "Alabama and Indiana Narratives," *American Slave* 6(1): 167; and Frederick Law Olmsted's *The Cotton Kingdom: A Traveler's Observations on Cotton and Slavery in the American Slave States: Based upon Three Former Volumes of Journeys and Investigations* (New York: Mason Brothers, 1861), 267.

57. "Any Old Way Will Catch a Coon," *Forest and Stream*, September 17, 1898, 228. Alexander Hunter confirmed the existence and efficacy of such log traps, noting that "the darkeys catch them [raccoons] in a peculiar trap; a great log, some eight feet long, is laid on the ground, and fenced in by shingles or palings being driven down on either side, thus when one of the logs is raised there is apparently a hollow running beneath it. A trigger is set and baited, and the coon has his life crushed out if he meddles with the dead chicken or fish on the end of the blade." Hunter, "Great Dismal Swamp."

58. "Chasseur," "The Nottoway Region," *Forest and Stream*, December 30, 1875, 322.

59. William Elliott frequently criticized fire hunting, noting that "the practice of fire-hunting, forbidden by the laws, is nevertheless but too much pursued in certain

parts of the country. It is the author's aim . . . to expose the dangers to property and to life, attendant on this illicit practice. It is nearer akin to poaching than to legitimate hunting; and he professes no personal acquaintance with it." Elliott, *Carolina Sports by Land and Water: Including Incidents of Devil-Fishing, Wild-Cat, Deer and Bear Hunting, etc.* (New York: Derby and Jackson, 1859), 258.

60. Rawick, "Ohio Narratives," *American Slave* 16(4): 17.

61. John Fox Jr., *Blue-Grass and Rhododendron: Out-Doors in Old Kentucky*, (New York: Charles Scribner's Sons, 1901), 180.

62. Henry William Ravenel, "Recollections of Southern Plantation Life," *Yale Review* (1936): 753–55, SCL, s.c. p917.57 R191r, USC.

63. "James Lee Love Recollections: Volume Three," 90, James Lee Love Collection, folder 67, SHC #4139, UNCCH.

64. Johnson, *Highways and Byways of the South*, 240.

65. Davis, "'Old Betsy,'" 22. This method of camouflaging a boat or shooting skiff was particularly effective for both white and black sportsmen of limited means. According to Davis, "the more expert market hunters, both white and negro, developed the method I have described in another chapter of camouflaging the front of a boat with brush so to make it resemble a floating tree, concealing a gunner in the boat and having a skillful paddler who would propel the boat slowly to a raft of ducks floating on the water. This method got results even with the old muskets" (1).

66. Peter Randolph, *From Slave Cabin to the Pulpit: The Autobiography of Reverend Peter Randolph: The Southern Question Illustrated and Sketches of Slave Life* (Boston: James H. Earle, 1893), 159.

67. Simeon H. Duffer Diary, 1866, manuscripts, Mss5:D8735:1, VHS.

68. "Thomas Henry Carter Account Book, 1859–1888," manuscripts, Mss5:3 C2468:1, VHS.

69. B. F. Fly, "Arkansas Sport," *National Sportsman* (Boston), November 1907, 575.

70. John Edwin Fripp Papers, ser. 1.2, folders 1–7, Account Books, v. 4, SHC #869, UNCCH.

71. Former Arkansas slave Scott Bond, for example, remembered fellow slave Slade, "whose duty it was to hunt all night" for the then frontier plantation. "He could not bring in all the game he killed, hence the hands on our place would divide themselves into squads and take time about hunting with Slade at night until he had a load of coons, and they would then carry them home and go to sleep, leaving Slade to make the rest of the night alone. The meat secured in this way would last several families for some time." Daniel A. Rudd and Theophilus Bond, *From Slavery to Wealth: The Life of Scott Bond; The Rewards of Honesty, Industry, Economy and Perseverance* (Madison, AK: Journal Printing Company, 1917), 34, DocSouth, UNCCH.

72. Ambrose E. Gonzales, *The Captain: Stories of the Black Border* (Columbia, SC: State Company, 1924), 81.

73. Anne Simon Deas, "Recollections of the Ball Family of South Carolina and the Comingtee Plantation" (1909), 171, SCHS.

74. Lewis, *Out of the Ditch*, 10.

75. B. H. Wilkins Memoir, 1856–1876 (typescript), manuscripts, Mss5:1W6544:1, VHS. Many African-American plantation huntsmen described in postwar writings served in that same capacity under slavery. The fact that so many huntsmen remained in service after Emancipation is indicative of the strong attachment many slave owners and their families developed for loyal slaves working as hunting attendants, which so powerfully symbolized white mastery in the antebellum South. Noted African-American author and poet Charles W. Chesnutt, born to free black parents in Fayetteville, North Carolina, in 1858, included a postwar reunion between a former slave huntsman and his former master in his novel *The Colonel's Dream* (New York: Doubleday, 1905). For the fictional old colonel, the sight of his former charge brings back thoughts of a by-gone era. "This meeting touched a tender chord in the colonel's nature, already tuned to sympathy with the dead past of which Peter seemed the only survival . . . Through the golden haze of memory the colonel's happy childhood came back to him with a sudden rush of emotion" (26).

76. B. H. Wilkins Memoir, 1856–1876.

77. Pattie Jane Watkins Scott Diary, 1881–1885, "February 9, 1883," manuscripts, Mss5:1Sco853:1, VHS.

78. For examples of such government-sponsored bounties in the antebellum period, see *Acts of Assembly* for Virginia, 1820, chap. 38; 1821, chap. 43, 1829, chap. 121; 1845, chaps. 141, 142; 1847, chap. 118; 1849, chap. 63 (Richmond: State of Virginia, various years).

79. Of course there were regional variations in which animals had bounties placed on them. The best example is the fox. In many parts of the South the fox was seen merely as an annoyance, a pest to be eliminated. Many states had fox bounties on the books throughout the post-Emancipation period. Yet in regions where fox hunting endured as an aristocratic tradition — most notably in Southside Virginia, the South Carolina Lowcountry, parts of Mississippi and Louisiana, and other small, isolated pockets of "horn and hound" — foxes were coveted and thus protected from depredation. As J. H. Montague Jr. of Richmond, Virginia, noted in an 1899 editorial, "there is no bounty offered for his scalp in this region and any man caught shooting a fox would be severely censured by all true lovers of the sport." Montague, *Recreation* 10, no. 2 (February 1899): 125.

80. Clubs such as the Chelsea Plantation Club depended on men like Fripp. During the sporting season, Fripp had the responsibility of organizing the hunts, arranging guides, and managing equipment; during the off-season, he protected game on club lands from poachers and trespassers. He rode around the plantation each day, keeping track of game animals and investigating any cases of animals found shot. In such a position he had substantial contact with local African-American hunters and fishermen, through paying them bounties or attempting to curtail their hunting and fishing activities.

81. "Daybook of Accounts with Chelsea Club," John Edwin Fripp Papers, ser. 1.2, Account Books, vol. 7, SHC #869, UNCCH.

82. Archibald Hamilton Rutledge, *Days off in Dixie* (London: Leonard Parsons, 1925), 228.

83. Fletcher Coyne, "In the Lowlands of South Carolina," *Frank Leslie's Popular Monthly*, March 1891, 286, SCL, USC.

84. Rudd and Bond, *From Slavery to Wealth*, 34.

85. Rice, *Glories of the Carolina Coast*, 118.

86. Examples of slaves' marketing of the products of hunting and fishing abound. Former North Carolina slave George Rogers recalled how he and others traded fish to the folks in the "big house." "We fished a lot in Briar Creek. We caught a lot o' fish . . . We would trade our fish to missus for molasses to make candy out uv" (Rawick, "North Carolina Narratives," *American Slave* 15[2]: 222). The Reverend Squire Dowd found such arrangements ideal for obtaining currency to purchase extra goods. "We hunted a lot, and the fur of the animals we caught we sold and had the money" (ibid., 14[1]: 267). Sam T. Stewart noted: "We caught birds and game, sent it to town, and sold it for money. We caught birds and partridges in traps. Our master would bring them to town, sell them for us, and give us the money" (ibid., 15[2]: 318–19).

87. Johnson, *Highways and Byways*, 298. Tar burning was a tedious occupation involving melting down pine and other softwood tar to produce coating and sealant for the shipping and construction industries.

88. Yetman, *Voices from Slavery*, 27.

89. Frank Farner, "A Southern Bear Hunt," *Recreation* 16, no. 4 (April 1902): 264.

90. "Lawtonvillian," "Sports in South Carolina," *Rod and Gun and American Sportsman*, October 28, 1876, 50.

91. Frances Butler Leigh, *Ten Years on a Georgia Plantation since the War* (London: Richard Bentley & Son, 1883), 20.

92. King, *Great South*, 593.

93. Rice, *Glories of the Carolina Coast*, 118–19.

94. Patience Pennington [Elizabeth Allston Pringle], *A Woman Rice Planter* (New York, 1914), 139.

95. M. L. Murdock, "Pop Peters' Pups," *Recreation* 10, no. 1 (January 1899): 76.

96. Alexander Hunter, "A Coon Hunt," *Outing* 5, no. 18 (September 1891): 457–61.

97. "Chasseur," "Nottoway Region," 322.

98. Davis, "'Old Betsy,'" 23–24, 1.

99. King, *Great South*, 274.

100. "Delmo," "Terrapins," *Rod and Gun and American Sportsman*, February 20, 1875, 331.

101. Edward A. Robinson, "A Trip to Georgia," *Forest and Stream*, March 18, 1899, 202.

102. By the 1890s, properties such as Pringle's, located in or near resort regions, or stocked with vast quantities of fish or game, or situated in areas blessed with renowned natural beauty, became much sought after. Interested parties from across the nation, particularly wealthy Northern businessmen wishing to pursue hunting or fishing, came South in droves. By the turn of the century, the resort and sporting regions of the South contained scores of such properties held by outside interests. If intruders reduced the available fish or game of a given property, as in the case of Elizabeth Allston Pringle's mountain home, it would not be as attractive to potential buyers.

103. Pennington [Pringle], *Woman Rice Planter*, 51–52, 142–43, 293.

104. Irving E. Lowery, *Life on the Plantation in Ante-Bellum Days, or, A Story Based on Facts* (Columbia, SC: State Company, Printers, 1911), 139.

105. "Alston v. Limehouse Case Records, 1892–1902," Mitchell and Smith Records, 152.04.01, box 12, SCHS.

106. Robert Barnwell Roosevelt, *Florida and the Game Water-Birds of the Atlantic Coast and the Lakes of the United States* (New York: Orange Judd Company, 1884), 51–52, 60, 327.

107. "Memories," Sally Hawthorne Reminiscence, 109, p.c. 743.1, NCDAH.

108. Ibid, 141.

109. *The Land We Love: A Monthly Magazine Devoted to Literature, Military History, and Agriculture* 5, no. 6 (October 1868): 525.

110. R. L. Dabney, "The Negro and the Common School," *Southern Planter and Farmer* 37, no. 4 (April 1876): 256.

111. Leigh, *Ten Years on a Georgia Plantation*, 24.

112. Susan Dabney Smedes, *Memorials of a Southern Planter* (Baltimore: Cushings & Bailey, 1887), 252.

113. W. F. Robert, "Chinese Immigration," *Southern Cultivator*, January 1870, 15 (emphasis in original).

114. "To the People of Virginia," *Southern Planter and Farmer*, July 1877, 474.

115. Thomas Pollard, "Agriculture in the South: Will Farming in the South Pay?" *American Farmer*, December 1, 1883, 333–34.

116. [Editorial], *Southern Planter and Farmer*, November 1872, 671.

117. Andrews Wilkinson, "An Understudy in Black: The Excommunicated Fisherman of Huckleberry Hollow," *Field and Stream*, February 1906, 1035

118. Jas. H. Oliphant, "A Very Important Question—Where Are We Drifting To?" *Southern Planter and Farmer*, November 1875, 635.

119. Leigh, *Ten Years on a Georgia Plantation*, 295.

120. Philip A. Bruce, *The Plantation Negro as a Freeman: Observations on His Character, Condition, and Prospects in Virginia* (New York: G. P. Putnam's Sons, 1889), 220–21.

121. Allen Family Papers, 1850–1910, Diaries, 1858–1895, manuscripts, Mss1A1546c, VHS.

122. Pennington [Pringle], *Woman Rice Planter*, 217, 212, 217, 250.

123. "From North Carolina," *Forest and Stream*, January 27, 1881, 505.

124. "N.A.T.," "The Freedman and the Quail," *Forest and Stream*, March 1, 1883.

CHAPTER 2: "THE POT-HUNTING SON OF HAM"

Epigraph. Doctor Macklin quoted in "A Christmas in 'The Forks,'" *Richmond Whig*, December 25, 1872, James Booth Walters Papers, manuscripts, Mss1W1714a, VHS.

1. "Game Preserving in Louisiana," *Outing* 11, no. 6 (March 1888): 533–35.

2. "Chivalrous Southrons," *Southern Review* 6 (1869).

3. William Temple Hornaday, *Thirty Years' War for Wildlife: Gains and Losses in the Thankless Task* (Stamford, CT: Gillespie Brothers, 1931), 42–44.

4. According to environmental historian Albert E. Cowdrey, Southerners' resistance to restrictions on exploitation of the environment began in the colonial era. "The South tended to exalt, sometimes with a special anarchic heedlessness, the contemporary American standard of exploitation without limit." Cowdrey, *This Land, This South: An Environmental History* (Lexington: University of Kentucky Press, 1996), 83.

5. Hornaday, *Thirty Years' War for Wildlife*, 42.

6. Nicholas W. Proctor, *Bathed in Blood: Hunting and Mastery in the Old South* (Charlottesville: University of Virginia Press, 2002), 23.

7. Daniel Justin Herman, *Hunting and the American Imagination* (Washington, DC: Smithsonian Institution Press, 2002), 145–47. Breech-loading technology was a key development in military and sport shooting, revolutionizing firearms in the United States. Before this advance, most firearms were muzzle-loaded, meaning that the charge was rammed down the barrel of the gun. When the trigger was pulled, a small amount of burning powder was sent into the barrel, igniting the main charge and forcing the bullet out of the gun. Because muzzled-loaded rifles and shotguns required several steps to load, it took a long time (compared with breech loading) between discharges, decreasing the rate of fire. Moreover, because gunpowder created residue that clogged a weapon's barrel and internal mechanisms, the range and accuracy of muzzle-loaded weapons could be limited if they were not properly cleaned. By contrast, breech-loaders use ammunition contained in a single cartridge inserted directly into the end, or breech, of the weapon. Breech-loaded firearms can be reloaded more rapidly than muzzle-loaders; hence a greater volume of fire can be maintained.

8. The Civil War provided a break in the wildlife slaughter that characterized the antebellum period. But the abatement would not last. Alexander Hunter recalled that sportsmen in his native Virginia, "who loved sporting, and had the good luck to return to the homes of their youth with their arms and legs intact, had a rare and royal time among fur and feather, and a moderate shot would return in the evening and show such a bag as the result of the day's sport as would last the family for a week." Hunter, "Sport—Past, Present, and Future, Part II," *Outing* 13, no. 4 (January 1889): 321–27.

9. Hunting without restraint remained a key characteristic of Southerners' hunts before the late nineteenth century, according to historian Ted Ownby. "This widespread demolition of the South's resources seemed selfish, improvident, or unsportsmanlike only to a tiny, if growing number. For most hunters and fishermen, such self-indulgence was the reason for sport." Ownby, *Subduing Satan: Religion, Recreation, and Manhood in the Rural South, 1865–1920* (Chapel Hill: University of North Carolina Press, 1990), 34.

10. Robert Barnwell Roosevelt, *Florida and the Game Water-Birds of the Atlantic Coast and the Lakes of the United States* (New York: Judd Company, 1884), 5

11. Henry B. Ansell, "Tales of Knotts Island," 90, Henry B. Ansell Papers, p.c. 1431.1, NCSA.

12. Ibid.

13. Walters, "Christmas in 'The Forks.'"

14. "Southern Shooting Grounds," *Forest and Stream*, February 26, 1885, 86.

15. Both firearm production and per capita gun ownership rose dramatically in the decades after the Civil War. These concurrent increases, tied to the supply of firearms from factories converted to arms production during the war and the huge increase in the number of men trained to use such weapons, made the ability to own firearms nearly universal. Herman, *Hunting and the American Imagination*, 146.

16. Alexander Hunter, "A Deer Hunt in Old Virginia," *Outing* 17, no. 1 (October 1893): 61.

17. "Report of L. L. Polk, Commissioner of Agriculture, for 1877 and 1878," Legislative Documents, 14–15, NCSA.

18. "Prospectus of the Shocco Game Association" (1894), NCC, Cp971.93s, UNCCH.

19. Robert Pinckney Tucker to B. R. Kittridge, Carmel, NY, August 9, 1904, Robert Pinckney Tucker Papers, SHC #1010, folder #99, UNCCH.

20. "Chasseur," "In the Old Virginia Lowland," *Forest and Stream*, October 19, 1882, 204.

21. "G.T.N.," "Sport in the South," *Rod and Gun and American Sportsman*, September 4, 1875, 339 (emphasis added).

22. J. Turner-Turner, *Three Years Hunting and Trapping in America and the Great Northwest* (London: Maclure & Company, 1888), 12. Note that in the sporting literature "quail" and "partridge" were often used interchangeably, although these are different groups of birds. Both are also sometimes referred to as "Bob White."

23. James Henry Rice Jr., *Glories of the Carolina Coast* (Columbia, SC: R. L. Bryan Co., 1925), 97.

24. Arney R. Childs, ed., *Rice Planter and Sportsman: The Recollections of J. Motte Alston, 1821–1909* (Columbia: University of South Carolina Press, 1999), 77.

25. "B.C.H.," "The Pot-Hunting Son of Ham," *Forest and Stream*, December 29, 1881, 431. The phrase "Pot-Hunting Son of Ham" refers to the biblical "Curse of Ham," a central justifying myth of transatlantic slavery. Noah's son Ham saw his father lying naked in a drunken stupor and invited his brothers, Shem and Japheth, to join him in mocking their father. On learning of his son's disrespectful act, Noah cursed Ham's youngest son, Canaan, and his progeny to be slaves to Ham's older brothers and their descendants. Slavery apologists used this story to explain how and why God ordained bondage for people of African descent. For two detailed analyses, see Benjamin Braude, "The Sons of Noah and the Construction of Ethnic and Geographical Identities in the Medieval and Early Modern Periods," *William and Mary Quarterly*, 3rd ser., 54, no. 1 (January 1997): 103–42; and William McKee Evans, "From the Land of Canaan to the Land of Guinea: The Strange Odyssey of the Sons of Ham," *American Historical Review* 85, no. 1 (February 1980): 15–43.

26. "B.C.H.," "Pot-Hunting Son of Ham."

27. Dr. Macklin, "Christmas in the Forks" (emphasis in original).

28. John Edwin Roller, "Doomed Race," Roller Family Papers, 1837–1917, manuscripts, "Miscellany," "Notes and Essays" folder, Mss1R6498A2, VHS.

29. "Chasseur," "Old Virginia Lowland." At the core of this vision of the antebel-

lum South was the common, yet fundamentally false, notion that the South was dominated by large plantations manned by hundreds of slaves. The Old South, as remembered by elites and sportsmen, reflected a longing for an age of aristocracy that never existed.

30. Ibid.

31. "N.A.T.," "The Negro and the Game," *Forest and Stream*, March 22, 1883, 148.

32. Edward King, *The Great South: A Record of Journeys in Louisiana, Texas, the Indian Territory, Missouri, Arkansas, Mississippi, Alabama, Georgia, Florida, South Carolina, North Carolina, Kentucky, Tennessee, Virginia, West Virginia, and Maryland* (Hartford, IL: American Publishing Company, 1875), 778.

33. "M," "Quail in Virginia," *Forest and Stream*, December 21, 1882, 409.

34. "Letter from N.A.T., Palestine, TX," *Forest and Stream*, March 1, 1883, 87.

35. Hunter, "Sport—Past, Present, and Future, Part II," 322–33.

36. "Letter from N.A.T., Palestine, TX."

37. "Coahoma," "The Possum 'Sulls,'" *Forest and Stream*, June 25, 1891, 455.

38. "H.P.U.," "The Ideal Sportsman," *Forest and Stream*, December 20, 1881.

39. According to historian Nicholas Proctor, elites designed the criterion of the hunting fraternity to separate elite sportsmen from their supposed inferiors. "Hunters desired companions, but fraternities balanced their inclusiveness with exclusivity. By limiting the pool of possible initiates and imposing various social barriers, a hunting fraternity became a bastion of social power." Proctor, *Bathed in Blood*, 30.

40. Ibid., 76–78; Herman, *Hunting and the American Imagination*, 152–56.

41. Eugene P. Odom, ed., "Brief Biographical Sketch of H. H. Brimley," in "H. H. Brimley: North Carolina Naturalist. Selections from His Writings," Herbert Hutchinson Brimley Papers, p.c. 203.1, NCSA.

42. "The Absolute Prohibition of Traffic in Game," *Forest and Stream*, February 10, 1894.

43. A. M. Scudder, "Stop the Sale of Game," *Forest and Stream*, June 2, 1894.

44. "J.D.H.," "Some Georgia Game Hogs," *Recreation* 10, no. 2 (February 1899): 143.

45. "F.P.W.," "The Hog behind the Gun," *Recreation* 10, no. 4 (April 1899).

46. "The Pot Hunter," *Rod and Gun and American Sportsman*, December 11, 1875, 168.

47. A. S. Salley, *The Happy Hunting Ground: Personal Experiences in the Low-Country of South Carolina* (Columbia, SC: State Company, 1916), 15.

48. "Pot-Hunters," *Forest and Stream* 18, no. 2 (April 20, 1882).

49. As Proctor notes, this ideal had strong English roots. "Imported from Great Britain and quickly adapted for American audiences by the sporting press, the concept of sport elevated the act of hunting and the concomitant display of prowess, self-control, and mastery over the simple accumulation of corpses." Proctor, *Bathed in Blood*, 88.

50. Henry Edwards Davis, "'Old Betsy': Stories of Hunting with the Old Percussion Muzzle Loader and Its Successors" (typescript), 1, manuscripts P, SCL, USC.

51. E. Hough, "The Sunny South—Part VI," *Forest and Stream*, March 16, 1895, 206.

52. *Forest and Stream* 14, no. 2 (February 12, 1880): 32.

53. Hunter, "Deer Hunt in Old Virginia."

54. "Coahoma," "The Possum 'Sulls.'"

55. "P.," "The Possum Hunt," *Forest and Stream*, November 21, 1891, 326.

56. John Fox Jr., *Blue-Grass and Rhododendron: Out-Doors in Old Kentucky*, (New York: Charles Scribner's Sons, 1901), 189.

57. In his *Subduing Satan*, Ownby argues that this unrestrained hunting characterized all Southern sportsmen, even elite whites. The emphasis on self-control in the sporting field, Ownby suggests, did not emerge among elite Southerners until a wider campaign against all forms of immoderation by Southern evangelicals, which provided a basis for accepting the conventions of the growing natural conservation movement. By the end of the nineteenth century, then, elite Southern sportsmen complained vociferously about behavior by African-American hunters and fishermen that they themselves had long practiced.

58. The notion that African-American hunters and fishermen did not care for sport does not survive scrutiny. Although the majority who hunted and fished did so for semi-subsistence and were thus less free to emphasize pure sport, narrative sources reveal African Americans' enjoyment of sporting activities. As former-slave narratives make clear, material and recreational benefits were not mutually exclusive. According to Isaam Morgan, although slaves hunted out of necessity, "it is sho' nuf' fun, dough, to go a-railin' th'ough de woods atter a possum or coon." James Mellon, ed., *Bullwhip Days: The Slaves Remember* (New York: Avon Books, 1988), 44.

59. Archibald Hamilton Rutledge, *Those Were the Days* (Richmond, VA: Dietz Press, 1955), 108.

60. "H.P.U.," "More Light on the 'Possum Puzzle," *Forest and Stream*, July 21, 1881.

61. Aspersions against blacks' sporting practices served an interesting dual purpose. They allowed elite sportsmen not only to attack African Americans' subsistence habits but to launch veiled assaults on poor white sportsmen who, like former slaves, typically relied on hunting and fishing for subsistence and market. By invoking blacks' sporting abuses, sportsmen could publicly decry lower-class sporting habits, and even demand legal restriction of the rights to hunt and fish, while not directly assailing poor whites. For elites, criticizing African Americans was both rhetorically more effective and politically more cautious.

62. "Blue Ridge," "The South Carolina Season," *Forest and Stream*, November 21, 1889, 347.

63. F. A. Olds, "A North Carolina 'Possum Hunt," *Outing* 36, no. 1 (April 1900): 33.

64. "Coon," *Outdoor Life: A Magazine of the West* 9, no. 4 (1904).

65. T. S. Palmer, "Some Possibilities for Game Protection in North Carolina" (address to the North Carolina Audubon Society, Greensboro, 1904), NCC Cp799P17s, UNCCH.

66. "Rallywood," "The Negroes and the Birds," *Forest and Stream*, February 1, 1883, 7.

67. "N.A.T.," "The Negro and Game."

68. F. C. Ford to James Henry Rice Jr., November 19, 1909, Conner Family Papers, "Henry W. Conner II Correspondence," 282286, SCHS.

69. In the early twentieth century, before most states had fish and game commissions or game wardens, and before state legislators were willing to commit substantial funds to such endeavors, the task of disseminating and enforcing fish and game laws often devolved to private clubs or protection societies. For a time, in some states, including South Carolina, that power rested with the Audubon Society. This arrangement, while blurring the line between public and private wildlife protection, proved popular with many Southern sportsmen who were convinced that state agencies would never adequately protect fish and game and that the gentlemen sportsmen who comprised the membership of organizations such as the Audubon Society were the most willing and able to carry out the task.

70. Ford to Rice, November 19, 1909.

71. H. P. Wilder, "A Virginia Game Country," *Forest and Stream*, November 10, 1898.

72. "B.C.H.," "Pot-Hunting Son of Ham."

73. "Letter from N.A.T., Palestine, Texas."

74. Fred Mather, "In the Louisiana Lowlands—I," *Forest and Stream*, September 24, 1898, 247–48. The U.S. Commission of Fish and Fisheries, generally called the U.S. Fish Commission, was the nation's first federal conservation agency (founded in 1871). The commission was charged with investigating supplies of food fish along the coasts and in lakes and rivers and with recommending strategies for preserving and protecting them. This early effort gave rise to the U.S. Fish and Wildlife Service.

75. Mather, "Louisiana Lowlands—I."

76. Fred Mather, "In the Louisiana Lowlands—II," *Forest and Stream*, October 1, 1898, 272.

77. Herman, *Hunting and the American Imagination*, 223. The idea that nonwhites inherently lacked sportsmanship illustrated white sportsmen's belief that hunting and fishing encapsulated the hierarchy of races. An 1888 *Forest and Stream* editorial, for example, argued that hunting would play a role in an inevitable war between the races. Asserting that the "Sclav [*sic*] and Tartar and Latin races are not going to bow themselves politely out of the earth to make room for us," the editor reminded readers that population pressures might someday lead to a "universal struggle for existence" between the races of the world. "For these inevitable wars, the hunting field is the best training field. It improves a man's physique, gives him readiness of hand and eye, familiarity with weapons of war, inures him to hardship, and gives him that self-reliance born of assured skill in the handling of his weapon which is so much conducive to victory." Concluding that, since "the United States at any rate is not likely to drop out of the struggle for existence so long as the love of hunting continues to be a leading characteristic," the editor declared such training essential for inculcating the attitudes and skills American men owed to the future. "The Ethics of Hunting," *Forest and Stream*, November 22, 1888, 1.

78. "Letter from N.A.T., Palestine, Texas."

79. In addition to their disapproval of excessive killing of game, elite sportsmen

also detested the practice of pursuing fish and game during the breeding season or, in the case of wildfowl, the migrating season, when wildlife replenished itself and was more vulnerable to capture. Sportsmen credited such practices with much of the wildlife depletion in the late nineteenth and early twentieth centuries. For a discussion of the controversy surrounding spring shooting along the Mississippi flyway, the nation's largest bird migratory route, and the efforts by sportsmen to eliminate such practices, see Karel D. Bicha, "Spring Shooting: An Issue in the Mississippi Flyway, 1887–1913," *Journal of Sport History* 5, no. 2 (1978): 65–74.

80. "Game Preserving in Louisiana," *Outing* 11, no. 6 (March 1888): 533–34.

81. "E. Wanders On," "Letter from Virginia: Charlottesville, December 12, 1872," *American Sportsman*, February 1873, 77.

82. "M," "Wild Turkey Hunting," *Forest and Stream*, October 20, 1881, 229. Notice that M declared turkey trapping fit only for African Americans and poor whites. These groups were sometimes lumped together in complaints about lower-class sporting practices, illustrating that much of the controversy over Southern hunting and fishing depended on class differences. Poor whites, in fact, remained targets of elite ire, but sporting periodicals, particularly Southern contributors, reserved special criticism for African Americans. The unrestrained, unintelligent African-American sportsman became an archetype of poor sportsmanship, even at a national level, suggesting that the conflicts were as much about race as about hunting and fishing.

83. David Brainard Whiting Reminiscences, 49, p.c. 1822.1, NCSA.

84. Turner-Turner, *Three Years Hunting and Trapping*, 3.

85. "J.E.W.," "The Game of North Carolina," *Forest and Stream* 2, no. 3 (February 1874): 36–37. In the late nineteenth century, breech-loaders were relatively new inventions, particularly for a poor gunner like Sparks who was forced to rely on older firearm technology far longer than more affluent sportsmen, such as his white employer.

86. Ibid.

87. William H. Frazer, ed., *The Possumist, and Other Stories* (Charlotte, NC: Murrill Press, 1924). Dialect stories were a popular literary genre of the late nineteenth and early twentieth centuries that relied on tales of supposed humor and homespun wisdom from African Americans, told in stereotypical black dialect. Frazer's collection is an example of literature in the "plantation tradition," which romanticized the antebellum South and portrayed slavery as a benign institution. It was part of a genre that found considerable popularity with white audiences once the mythical Old South took hold in the American imagination in the late nineteenth century. For a well-known example, see Thomas Nelson Page's *In Ole Virginia, or, Marse Chan and Other Stories* (New York: Charles Scriber's Sons, 1887).

88. Frazer, *Possumist*.

89. "L.J.M.," "How 'Ras Fools the Divers," *Forest and Stream*, March 24, 1894, 244.

90. A. J. Lipton, "Jim, I and the Bear," *Recreation* 10, no. 1 (January 1899): 41.

91. Davis, "'Old Betsy,'" 24.

92. Edward King, *The Southern States of North America* (London: Blackie & Son, 1875), 303.

93. "M," "Quail in Virginia," *Forest and Stream*, December 21, 1882, 409.

94. "Rallywood," "The Negroes and the Birds," *Forest and Stream*, February 1, 1883, 7.

95. "M," "The Freedman and the Quail," *Forest and Stream*, March 1, 1883, 87.

96. "Letter from N.A.T., Palestine, Texas."

97. "A.F.R," "Freedmen and Quail," *Forest and Stream*, April 12, 1883, 207–8.

98. Archibald Hamilton Rutledge, *Hunter's Choice* (New York: A. S. Barnes & Company, 1946), 22.

99. Ibid., 21.

100. Archibald Hamilton Rutledge, *Home by the River* (New York: Bobbs-Merrill Company, 1955). Page numbers in the following text refer to this source.

101. Rutledge, *Hunter's Choice*, 74.

102. "Southern Shooting Grounds," *Forest and Stream*, February 26, 1885.

CHAPTER 3: "THE ART OF SERVING IS WITH THEM INNATE"

Epigraph. "Coon Hunting in Virginia," *Recreation* 14, no. 3 (March 1901): 193.

1. Emerson Hough, "The Sunny South—Part VIII," *Forest and Stream*, April 1 1895, 284.

2. Ibid.

3. Nicholas W. Proctor, *Bathed in Blood: Hunting and Mastery in the Old South* (Charlottesville: University of Virginia Press, 2002), 171.

4. Edward J. Thomas, *Memoirs of a Southerner, 1840–1923* (Savannah, GA, 1923), 25, DocSouth, UNCCH.

5. The use of grandiose sporting traditions and methods available only to the very wealthy was one of many Southern sporting legacies that began early in the colonial era, carried over into the antebellum period, and remained vital after Emancipation. Southern elites, whether antebellum slaveholders or postwar sportsmen seeking to recapture lost aristocracy, used the barriers of class and race inherent in such sporting codes for "promoting the idea that while a hunter was a man, a sportsman was a gentleman." Proctor, *Bathed in Blood*, 87–88.

6. "One of the Scribes," "Coon hunting in Virginia," *American Sportsman*, October 1872.

7. Edward King, *The Great South: A Record of Journeys in Louisiana, Texas, the Indian Territory, Missouri, Arkansas, Mississippi, Alabama, Georgia, Florida, South Carolina, North Carolina, Kentucky, Tennessee, Virginia, West Virginia, and Maryland* (Hartford, IL: American Publishing Company, 1875), 321. *Scribner's Monthly* dispatched King because it "desired to present to the public, through the medium of their popular periodical, an account of the material resources, and the present social and political condition, of the people in the Southern States" (i).

8. As Proctor notes, "the feeling of community that [elite field sports] helped create bound white males together. These ties supported abstract notions like white supremacy by providing concrete representations of white power." Proctor, *Bathed in Blood*, 118.

9. David Franklin Thorpe to John Mooney, February 6, 1867, David Franklin Thorpe Papers, SHC #4262, folder 10, January–May 1867, UNCCH.

10. J. B. Burnham, "Notes of a Shooting Trip South," *Forest and Stream*, January 13, 1894, 29.

11. Chester L. Fidlar, "A Possum Hunt," *Forest and Stream* 35, no. 3 (December 1899): 240.

12. Wirt Howe, "With the Quail among the Cotton," *Outing* 33, no. 3 (December 1898): 245.

13. "P," "The Possum Hunt," *Forest and Stream*, November 12, 1891, 326.

14. Bill Arp [Charles Henry Smith], *From the Uncivil War to Date, 1861–1903* (Atlanta, GA: Hudgins Publishing Company, 1903). For forty-two years, Smith wrote his newspaper articles in the guise of simple farmer Bill Arp. Later in life, he compiled these letters in several books, including *Bill Arp's Peace Papers* (1873), *Bill Arp's Scrap Book* (1884), *The Farm and the Fireside* (1891), and *Bill Arp: From the Uncivil War to Date, 1861–1903* (1903).

15. Arp, *From the Uncivil War to Date*, 54, 327.

16. Jacob F. Rivers III, *Cultural Values in the Southern Sporting Narrative* (Columbia: University of South Carolina Press, 2002), x.

17. C. Wayne Cunningham, "A Deer Hunt on the Coast of Georgia," *Outing* 35, no. 4 (January 1900): 370.

18. "C," "A Coon Hunt," *Forest and Stream*, April 21, 1887, 273.

19. "Fishing," *Outing* 32, no. 1 (April 1898): 93.

20. "Cosmopolitan," "A Paradise for Sportsmen," American Sportsman, July 18, 1874, 246.

21. "J.E.W.," "The Game of North Carolina," *Forest and Stream* 2, no. 3 (February 1874): 36–37 (emphasis in original). Railway interests became some of the most common and influential champions of Southern fish and game. Expanding rapidly after the war, railroads sought to bring Northern and Western sportsmen to the South for the purpose of expanding their passenger traffic. For this reason, railroad companies, such as the Southern Railway Company, the Norfolk and Western Railroad, and the Seaboard Air Line, published a large portion of the advertisements and sporting tourism manuals that promoted Southern hunting and fishing. See, for example, Richmond & Danville Railroad, *Summer Resorts and Points of Interests of Virginia and Western North Carolina and North Georgia* (New York: C. G. Crawford, 1884), NCC Cp917.5 R53 s1, UNCCH.

22. Horatio Bigelow, *Flying Feathers: A Yankee's Hunting Experiences in the South* (Richmond, VA: Garrett and Massie, 1937), 22.

23. Edward A. Robinson, "A Trip to Georgia," *Forest and Stream*, March 18, 1899, 202.

24. "Dick Swiveller," "Duck Shooting on the Savannah River," *Outing* 27, no. 6 (March 1896): 419.

25. Fred J. Wells, "An Adventure with a Tarpon," *Outing* 25, no. 5 (February 1895): 389.

26. R. S. Pollard, "A Coon Hunt in the Snow in Old Virginia," *Forest and Stream,* February 15, 1895, 140.

27. Bradford Torrey, *A World of Green Hills: Observations of Nature and Human Nature in the Blue Ridge* (Boston: Houghton, Mifflin and Company, 1898), NCC C917.5 T69w, UNCCH.

28. Cunningham, "Deer Hunt on the Coast of Georgia," 371.

29. "Southern Shooting Grounds," *Forest and Stream,* February 26, 1885, 86.

30. Harry Worcester Smith, *A Sporting Family of the Old South* (Albany, NY: J. B. Lyon Co., 1936), 133, general collection, SK 33.S63, VHS.

31. F. A. Olds, "A North Carolina 'Possum Hunt," *Outing* 36, no. 1 (April 1900): 33.

32. "Coon Hunting in Virginia."

33. Frank A. Heywood, "The Game of the Dismal Swamp," *Forest and Stream,* May 5, 1892.

34. According to Proctor, elite whites' possession of and control over the animals used in hunting, including horses, hounds, and hunting dogs, became another component of slaveholders' sense of mastery of the world around them. Proctor, *Bathed in Blood,* 65–66.

35. Andrews Wilkinson, "Horn and Hound in Grande Cheniere, Louisiana," *Outing* 29, no. 5 (February 1897): 437.

36. F. A. Olds, "A Christmas Morning in Carolina," *Outing* 33, no. 4 (January 1899): 383.

37. H. M. Howard, "Coon-Hunting in Maryland," *Outing* 24, no. 5 (August 1894): 345–46.

38. "A 'Possum Shooting Party," *Recreation* 14, no. 4 (April 1901): 287–88.

39. Andrews Wilkinson, "Christmas Week among the Lagoons of Lower Louisiana," *Outing* 31, no. 3 (December 1897): 211.

40. S. Phelps, "In the Carolina Woods," *Recreation* 15, no. 5 (November 1901): 336.

41. C. W. Boyd, "Winter Shooting in South Carolina," *Outing* 8, no. 5 (February 1889): 401.

42. Pollard, "Coon Hunt in the Snow."

43. "Mortimer," "A Trip to the York River, Virginia," *Rod and Gun and American Sportsman,* January 9, 1875, 243.

44. "Shooting in the South," *Forest and Stream* 5, no. 15 (November 18, 1875): 226.

45. "Avoca; the Health and Sporting Resort — A Big Time Ahead," *Edenton Fishermen & Farmer,* February 1889.

46. Harry Worcester Smith, *A Sporting Tour through Ireland, England, Wales and France in the Years 1912–1913* (Columbia, SC: State Company, 1925), 214.

47. "Cosmopolitan," "Paradise for Sportsmen," 246.

48. B. H. Wilkins, "War Boy," B. H. Wilkins Memoir, 1856–1876, manuscripts, Mss5:1W6544:1, VHS.

49. "J.E.W.," "Game of North Carolina," 37.

50. Pollard, "Coon Hunt in the Snow."

51. George Clark Rankin, *The Story of My Life, Or, More Than a Half Century as*

I Have Lived It and Seen It (Nashville, TN: Smith & Lamar, 1912), 67. Small game such as raccoon and opossum was often not eaten immediately. If the hunter had time to spare, to make the dinner as palatable as possible, he kept the animal alive to fatten it up by feeding it special food such as cornbread and milk. It was also common to hang the carcass for a day or two to remove the animal's strong "gamey" taste.

52. Andrews Wilkinson, "Christmas Week among the Lagoons of Lower Louisiana," *Outing* 29, no. 5 (December 1897): 216.

53. Fred Mather, "In the Louisiana Lowlands—II," *Forest and Stream*, October 1, 1898, 272.

54. Fred Mather, "In the Louisiana Lowlands—I," *Forest and Stream*, September 24, 1898, 247.

55. Ibid., 248.

56. Cunningham, "Deer Hunt on the Coast of Georgia," 370.

57. "With the Quail! A Day Afield at Pinehurst," *Pinehurst Outlook*, November 28, 1902.

58. Suzanne C. Linder, *Historical Atlas of the Plantations of the ACE River Basin—1860* (Columbia: South Carolina Division of Archives and History, 1995), 309.

59. "How Old Sport Stopped the Game Hog's Little Game," *Recreation*, August 1903, xxviii–xxx.

60. William Allen Bruce, "How a Sly Old Fox Was Caught," *Recreation* 5, no. 3 (September 1901): 193.

61. David Franklin Thorpe, Ledger of the St. Helena Rifle and Sporting Club, David Franklin Thorpe Papers, SHC #4262, UNCCH.

62. Thorpe to Mooney, February 6, 1867.

63. Thorpe, Ledger (emphasis added).

64. Francis J. Hagan, "Moses, the Tale of a Dog," *Outing* 32, no. 6 (September 1898): 576.

65. "Shooting in the South," *Forest and Stream* 2, no. 3 (November 1875): 226.

66. "H.W.K.," "A Quail Hunt in North Carolina," *Forest and Stream*, February 27, 1890, 104.

67. As Proctor argues, the gentleman sportsman remained calm, self-assured, and restrained. Antebellum planters had to exude such confident control at all times to maintain the social order of a slave society. The sporting field, because of the increased likelihood of chaos, fear, and emotional outbursts, became an ideal place for elites to display their ability to keep their passions in check (Proctor, *Bathed in Blood*, 63–65). This emphasis on self-control, particularly as a foil to stereotypes of blacks' behavior, remained part of the culture of Southern field sports after Emancipation.

68. "Coon Hunting in Virginia."

69. John Mortimer Murphy, "Alligator Shooting in Florida," *Outing* 15, no. 4 (January 1890): 303.

70. James Henry Rice Jr., *Glories of the Carolina Coast* (Columbia, SC: R. L. Bryan, 1925), 90–91.

71. "Will Scribbler," "In November," *Forest and Stream*, December 22, 1894, 334.

72. Edward W. Sandys, "Paw Ducket's Coon-Hunt," *Outing* 26, no. 6 (September 1895): 434.

CHAPTER 4: "WITH THE DUE SUBORDINATION
OF MASTER AND SERVANT PRESERVED"

Epigraph. Warren H. Miller, "With Tad and Gosh in Cotton Land," *Field and Stream,* February 1918, 847

1. Theodore Roosevelt, "In the Louisiana Canebrakes," *Scribner's Magazine* 43, no. 1 (January 1908): 47.

2. Minor Ferris Buchanan, *Holt Collier: His Life, His Roosevelt Hunts, and the Origin of the Teddy Bear* (Jackson, MS: Centennial Press, 2002), 154–57.

3. J. William Harris provides a detailed discussion of the process whereby lands such as Carnegie's Dungeness became part of a large migration of Northern capital into the Georgia Sea Islands. Harris, *Deep Souths: Delta, Piedmont, and Sea Island Society in the Age of Segregation* (Baltimore: Johns Hopkins University Press, 2001), 144–48.

4. Robert Q. Mallard, *Plantation Life before Emancipation* (Richmond, VA: Whittet and Shepperson, 1892).

5. Mallard referred to his slaves' fishing as "a sport in which I sometimes shared," but the large number of slaves participating, as well as Mallard's direct supervision, suggests this was a commercial endeavor, done for market, fertilizer, or food. According to Mallard, slaves "churned" for fish by wading into a river with empty flour barrels that had both ends knocked out. In unison, slaves brought the barrels to the bottom, trapping fish inside. Once the fish were trapped, the slaves threw them to slave children on the shore, who put them on a string (ibid., 26).

Georgia rice fields required occasional alligator hunts, according to Mallard, because alligators nesting there often fed on "uncured bacon" or "the tail of some thirsty cow." Slave huntsmen waded into the paddy with a large wooden pole with an iron hook attached to one end, felt around to locate an alligator, wrapped the hook around a leg, and dragged the thrashing creature to shore, where its head was lopped off "by a well-aimed blow of the axe" (27).

6. Ibid., 28 (emphasis added).

7. For a discussion of the process whereby tourism, due to declines in some large-scale agriculture that created a vast acreage of superfluous land, became both a critical part of the Southern economy and a key way for Northern capitalists to invest in the region's development, see Harris's outstanding *Deep Souths,* esp. chap. 4, "Capital at Work, Capitalists at Play"; and Nina Silber's *The Romance of Reunion: Northerners and the South, 1865–1900* (Chapel Hill: University of North Carolina Press, 1993), esp. chap. 3, "Sick Yankees in Paradise: Northern Tourism in the Reconstructed South."

8. Holt Collier was not the only African American on the hunt with Theodore Roosevelt. Collier selected guides Frank Dorsey, Calvin Dorsey, Bill Ennolds, and Thomas McDougall to attend the president's party while in the Delta. In addition,

John M. Parker employed African Americans Ben Johnson and Freeman Wallace as guards, charged with maintaining the perimeter of the hunt to keep out reporters who might seek to intrude on the president's outing. According to Buchanan, this outraged both reporters and local whites, who strongly objected to being kept away at gunpoint by African Americans. Buchanan, *Holt Collier*, 158, 162–63.

9. See Jim McCafferty's *Holt and the Teddy Bear* (Gretna, LA: Pelican Publishing, 1991) and *Holt and the Cowboys* (Gretna, LA: Pelican Publishing, 1993); and Buchanan, *Holt Collier*. McCafferty's novels, intended to entertain children with the colorful exploits of this legendary figure, are based on a romanticized version of Collier's life. They are not intended to be factual accounts.

10. The dedication to Collier was part of a 2003 Congressional bill, sponsored by Mississippi Second District Congressman Bennie Thompson, which established a federal wildlife refuge in the part of the Yazoo-Mississippi Delta known as the "Lower Delta." House of Representatives of the United States, H.R. 2894, "Theodore Roosevelt National Wildlife Refuge Act," 108th Congress, 1st Session, July 24, 2003.

11. Buchanan, *Holt Collier*, 138–39.

12. Reportedly, Collier solemnly promised the president he would get a bear on that hunt. Collier stunned and hobbled a black bear, which the party then presented to Roosevelt. According to Collier's account, "I said to him, with my head down, 'Don't shoot him while he's tied,'" referring to the code by which a true, elite big-game hunter would avoid killing helpless quarry (George Rawick, "Mississippi Narratives," in *The American Slave: A Composite Autobiography* [Westport, CT: Greenwood Press, 1972)], suppl. ser. 1, 7[2]: 455). The other hunters called for Roosevelt to shoot the bear, but he refused. Soon after, accounts of the outing, particularly the incident with the bear, began to receive wide circulation in the national press. Numerous cartoonists, most famously Pulitzer Prize–winner Clifford Kennedy Berryman of the *Washington Post*, began to include images of helpless bears, often released by the honorable Roosevelt, in depictions of the president. These bears, which occasionally accompanied Roosevelt in cartoons for years afterward, were soon dubbed "Teddy Bears." Capitalizing on the popularity of the "Teddy Bear" image, toy manufacturers began attaching the name to their new lines of stuffed-animal toys (Buchanan, *Holt Collier*, 171–72, 178–83).

13. According to his WPA interviewer, when Collier asked for permission to accompany Hinds and his son to war, he was refused. Collier was only about fourteen at the time and they deemed him too young to fight. "I begged like a dog, but they stuck to it—'You are too young,'" Collier recalled. He would not be dissuaded. When Howell and Thomas Hinds departed for Memphis by steamboat, the young slave stowed away. Apparently impressed with such persistence, Hinds dropped his objections and Collier spent the war serving his master and fighting at his side (Rawick, "Mississippi Narratives," *American Slave*, suppl. ser. 1, 1[1]: 449–50). Buchanan gives an excellent account of Collier's service in Company I of the Ninth Texas Brigade, providing a detailed look at both the battle-by-battle movements of the company and Collier's contributions at Shiloh, Vicksburg, Corinth, and Holly Springs. See Buchanan, *Holt Col-*

lier, esp. chap. 5, "Ninth Texas Cavalry"; chap. 6, "Boots and Saddles"; chap. 7, "Vicksburg"; and chap. 8, "Delta Rangers."

14. "Confederate Headstone Dedication to Holt Collier, Private; Company I, Ninth Texas Cavalry," Mississippi Division, Sons of Confederate Veterans, July 2004, www.mississippiscv.org/collier.htm.

15. Buchanan, *Holt Collier*, 109–10.

16. Ibid., 110–17.

17. Jacob F. Rivers III, *Cultural Values in the Southern Sporting Narrative* (Columbia: University of South Carolina Press, 2002), 18. Rivers's reference is to William Elliott, *Carolina Sports by Land and Water: Including Incidents of Devil-Fishing, Wild-Cat, Deer and Bear Hunting, etc.* (New York: Derby and Jackson, 1859).

18. Clarence Gohdes, *Hunting in the Old South: Original Narratives of the Hunters* (Baton Rouge: Louisiana State University Press, 1967), xvi.

19. As Daniel Justin Herman noted, "within the hunter's heart was a paradox. In engaging in rural sport, middle-class hunters cast themselves as heirs to rustic frontiersmen, yet they also cast themselves as heirs to the chivalrous hunters of England . . . Two images of the hunter — one democratic and native, the other elitist and foreign — coexisted uneasily, epitomizing the classic dilemma of nineteenth century Americans." Herman, *Hunting and the American Imagination* (Washington, DC: Smithsonian Institution Press, 2001), 11.

20. Ibid., 223.

21. See Carl Jacoby's *Crimes against Nature: Squatters, Poachers, Thieves and the Hidden History of American Conservation* (Berkeley: University of California Press, 2001), esp. chap. 4, "Nature and Nation."

22. North Carolina State Board of Agriculture, *North Carolina and Its Resources* (Raleigh: M. I. & J. C. Stewart, Public Printers and Binders, 1896), 282, 296, NCC CR917 N87a, UNCCH.

23. Edward Ayers, *The Promise of the New South: Life after Reconstruction* (New York: Oxford University Press, 1992), 61.

24. "Moving Forward," *Baltimore Journal of Commerce*, quoted in *Edenton* (North Carolina) *Fisherman and Farmer*, April 13, 1888.

25. Environmental historian Albert E. Cowdrey said of Southern natural resource depletion after Emancipation: "What happened to the South's natural wealth depended very largely upon the action of outsiders, who cut its forests, bought up its land, and financed its railroads and many of its nascent industries" (Cowdrey, *This Land, This South: An Environmental History*, rev. ed. [Lexington: University of Kentucky Press, 1996], 103). Indeed the Northern speculators and investors who made their way south between the 1880s and the 1930s included some of the nation's most wealthy and powerful. Along the South Carolina coast, site of perhaps the most famous sporting destinations, investors in sporting tourism included members of the Vanderbilt, Pulitzer, Guggenheim, Field, Whitney, DuPont, Dodge, and Roosevelt families.

26. Harris, *Deep Souths*, 139–41.

27. Ibid., 139.

28. Sam Stoney quoted in John H. Tibbetts, "The Bird Chase," *Coastal Heritage* 15, no. 4 (spring 2001): 3.

29. For the South Carolina Lowcountry, the decline of rice and cotton culture created perfect conditions for wildlife propagation. *Field and Stream* contributor D. J. Hart, who spent a month on plantation lands in the Georgetown area, recalled that the region once had vast plantations of rice and cotton, "but little farming is done in this section at present, especially on these large estates and this old plantation." That change, however, created the conditions that led investors to purchase such lands and invite sportsmen such as Hart to hunt on them. "It is nearly all woodland and a large part of it heavy timber; old-growth long- and short-leaf pine which grow on the dry soil, and cypress, gum, oak, etc., in the swamps." These lands proved ideal for wildlife recovery. Hart, "Wild Turkey Hunting in South Carolina: The Ways and Habits of Meleagris Gallapavo," *Field and Stream*, December 1915, 778.

30. Herman, *Hunting and the American Imagination*, 199.

31. According to Virginia Christian Beach, who chronicled the history of South Carolina's famed Medway plantation, this "second Northern invasion," of wealthy capitalists and sporting enthusiasts, lasted into the 1940s. During that period, "having been stripped of their agricultural wealth by an invading army, plantation owners invested themselves, economically and emotionally, in one of their few remaining assets, the hunting grounds." Beach, *Medway* (Charleston, SC: Wyrick & Company, 1998), 38.

32. Emerson Hough, "The Sunny South—Part VI," *Forest and Stream*, March 16, 1895, 206.

33. Wirt Howe, "With the Quail among the Cotton," *Outing* 33, no. 3 (December 1898): 245–46.

34. "An Old Sportsman," "Shooting in the South on the Gulf Coast," *Field and Stream*, January 1913, 1019.

35. William Bruce Leffingwell, *The Happy Hunting Grounds* (Chicago: Donohue & Henneberry, 1895), 8, NCC Cp799 L49h, UNCCH.

36. "Two Famous Island Preserves," *Field and Stream*, January 1902, 703.

37. "Letter from Elkton, MD," *American Sportsman*, October 17, 1874, 43.

38. "A Sporting Reminiscence of the War," *Forest and Stream*, May 20, 1880, 306.

39. See, for example, Richmond and Danville Railroad Company, *Summer Resorts and Points of Interest of Virginia, Western North Carolina, and Georgia* (New York: C. G. Crawford, 1884), NCC Cp917.5R53S1, UNCCH; The Seaboard Air Line Railway, General Passenger Department, *A Guide to the Famous Hunting and Fishing Grounds of Virginia, North Carolina, South Carolina and Georgia Traversed by the Seaboard Air Line, with a Synopsis of the Game Laws of Those States* (Richmond, VA: A. Hoen & Company, 1898), SCL799Se1g, USC; Atlantic & North Carolina Railroad, *Hunting and Fishing in Eastern North Carolina* (Goldsboro, NC: Atlantic & North Carolina Railroad, 1905), NCC microform CO92S68, reel 81, item 5, UNCCH; and Frank Presbrey, *The Empire of the South: An Exposition of the Present Resources and Development of the South* (Washington, DC: Southern Railway Company, 1898), NCC Cp917P92e, UNCCH.

40. Southern Railway Company, *A Samaritan of the South Is the Southern Railway* (Washington, DC: Southern Railway Company, 1898), 1, NCC Cp917.5S72sa, UNCCH; Presbrey, *Empire of the South*, 33.

41. N. L. Willet, *Game Preserves and Game of Beaufort, Colleton and Jasper Counties, South Carolina: Hunter's Paradise Manly Sports* (Beaufort, SC: Charleston & Western Carolina Railway Company, 1927), 1, 7–8, SCL s.c. p639.1 C38g, USC.

42. George C. Rogers Jr., *The History of Georgetown, South Carolina* (Spartansburg, SC: Reprint Company, 1990), 487.

43. William Page McCarty to Alice Beulah, May 28, 1897, McCarty Family Papers, 1859–1898, manuscripts, Mss2M1278b, VHS.

44. Silber, *Romance of Reunion*, 66–67.

45. Ibid., 68.

46. See, for example, E. J. C. Wood, "Aiken, S.C. as a Winter Resort for Invalids or a Desirable Location for Permanent Residents, with Catalogue of Properties for Sale" (1871), SCL 917.57751 W85a, USC; and North Carolina Board of Immigration, Statistics and Agriculture, *North Carolina: Its Resources and Progress; Its Beauty, Healthfulness and Fertility; and Its Attractions and Advantages as a Home for Immigrants* (Raleigh: Josiah Turner, 1875), 68, NCSA.

47. Silber, *Romance of Reunion*, 68–69.

48. "From North Carolina," *Forest and Stream*, January 27, 1881, 505.

49. Emerson Hough, "The Sunny South, Part IV," *Forest and Stream*, March 16, 189, 206.

50. Hinton A. Helper, *Aiken: A Popular Winter Resort for the Tourist and Health-Seeker* (New York: South Publishing Company, [1880s]), 12, SCL s.c. p917.57751 H36a, USC. Hinton Alexander Helper, who wrote numerous tourism guides, was the nephew of Southern author Hinton Rowan Helper, whose treatise on slavery, *The Impending Crisis of the South: How to Meet It* (New York: Burdick Brothers, 1857), argued for abolition based on slavery's negative impact on poor Southern whites and was widely distributed before the 1860 presidential campaign. Although Hinton R. Helper was no champion of social equality, as demonstrated by his subsequent works outlining black racial inferiority, this book made him one of the most despised men in the South. It is ironic that Hinton A. Helper would play a role in proffering Southern tourism when just three decades earlier his uncle's treatise played such a notable role in exacerbating sectional tensions.

51. "Halcyon Hale," "For the Tourist Sportsman," *Field and Stream*, January 1905, 286–87.

52. Silber, *Romance of Reunion*, 69–70.

53. Willet, *Game Preserves and Game of Beaufort,"* 16.

54. F. W. Eldredge, *Camden, South Carolina as a Winter Resort* (New York: Mook Brothers & Co. Printing, 1880), 1, SCL s.c. 917.57611 E12c, USC.

55. Joseph LeConte and William Dallam Armes, *The Autobiography of Joseph LeConte* (New York: D. Appleton and Company, 1903), 25.

56. Rogers, *History of Georgetown*, 463.

57. Southern Railway Company, *Columbia, South Carolina, as a Winter Resort* (Washington, DC: Southern Railway Company, 1908), SCL 917.57711 C72w, USC.

58. Eldredge, *Camden, South Carolina*, 16.

59. Howe, "With the Quail among the Cotton," 245.

60. Miller, "With Tad and Gosh in Cotton Land," 847.

61. David Franklin Thorpe to John Mooney, June 24, 1866, David Franklin Thorpe Papers, folder 8, "January–June 1866," SHC #4262, UNCCH.

62. Julian Ralph, *Dixie; or Southern Scenes and Sketches* (New York: Harper & Brothers, 1895), 376.

63. Rogers, *History of Georgetown*, 496. Rogers takes this argument even further, suggesting that the popularity of Southern destinations blunted Northern efforts to reform the South in the decades after the war and made whites outside the South more readily accept the region's racial chasm as a necessary adjunct to Old South mythology. For Rogers, the purchase of plantations became part of the process whereby Americans accepted Southerners' revision of their own history. He noted that "the second Yankee invasion of Georgetown County strengthened the national myth about the glories of the Southern plantation past, a movement of which the film *The Birth of a Nation* was an early teaser and *Gone With The Wind* the final statement. It was under this blanket of national public opinion that the Solid South was put together. These Yankees had no desire to reform the South in any way" (489).

64. "The Future of the South," *Southern Cultivator*, January 1893, 23.

65. Fred W. Wolf Jr., "From Virginia," *Field and Stream*, February 1902, 749–50.

66. B. W. Mitchell, "Quail and Duck at Currituck," *Field and Stream*, October 1901, 451.

67. H. F. C. Bryant, "A Southern Fox Hunt," *Field and Stream*, September 1903, 343.

68. "G.A.G." "A Southern Coast Home," *Southern Cultivator*, August 1894, 402–3.

69. Wood, "Aiken, South Carolina as a Winter Resort," 6.

70. Henry Wellington Wack, "The Sportsmen's Elysium of the South, Part II: The Game Animals of Florida," *Field and Stream*, March 1901, 21–22.

71. Ibid.

72. Edward Cave, "A Southern City's Door Yard," *Field and Stream*, December 1904, 193.

73. Herbert K. Job, "The Story of a Game Preserve: Told Chiefly by the Camera, with a Trifle of Supplementary Detail," *Field and Stream*, September 1909, NCC Cp799 J 62s, UNCCH.

74. Robert Pinckney Tucker to R. L. Montague, November 24, 1904, Robert Pinckney Tucker Papers, SHC #1010, folder 99, UNCCH.

75. Such was the case when, for example, a firm of Savannah, Georgia, professionals purchased the Hobonny plantation of Beaufort County, South Carolina, in 1925. The new owners allowed the fifteen African-American families to remain as independent farmers for a rental fee of $12 per year. Suzanne C. Linder, *Historical Atlas of the Plantations of the ACE River Basin—1860* (Columbia: South Carolina Division of Archives and History, 1995), 244.

76. "Description of Altama and Hopeton Plantations," Jackson and Prince Family Papers, Subcollection 2, Subseries 9.2, Miscellaneous Items, SHC #371, UNCCH.

77. In antebellum plantation parlance, "watchman" referred to a trusted employee who served as a lookout or guard during the evening. In field sports, watchmen were responsible for traveling plantation or club lands looking for wildlife, tracking its location and movement, and reporting the results to their superiors. This was typical of Southern sporting retreats, especially the larger ones that ranged over thousands, even tens of thousands, of acres.

78. As supplies of Southern game birds dwindled throughout the late nineteenth and early twentieth centuries, more and more sporting clubs and plantations adopted the practice of raising birds, such as quail and coot, specifically for seasonal hunts. Club agents spent the off-season caring for the birds; some they raised in captivity, others they let loose on club lands, employing bird-minders to track them, cultivate their habitat, and protect them from poachers. This elaborate process was undertaken simply to guarantee visiting sportsmen a fine winter's sport with plentiful supplies of game birds.

79. Kinloch Gun Club Records, 1914–1922, "Payroll, 1914–1922," 25/148/2, SCHA.

80. Ibid.

81. "Rules and Regulations for the Season Beginning November 15, 1914," Kinloch Gun Club Records, 1914–1922, "Correspondence, 1913–1914," 24/47/1, SCHS. The prices quoted by the Kinloch Club are consistent with prices occasionally listed for sporting guides in national sporting periodicals and Southern sporting advertisements beginning in the late nineteenth century. A guide published by the Seaboard Air Line in 1898, for example, indicated that guides typically earned between 50 cents and $2.00 per day, depending on the region. In Southampton County, Virginia, guides could be hired for 50 cents to $1.00 per day. In Northampton County, North Carolina, guides cost $1.00 per day with 50 cents extra for the use of dogs. In Gwinnett County, Georgia, two or three experienced guides could be purchased for between $1.00 and $2.00 per day. Seaboard Air Line Railway, *Guide to the Famous Hunting and Fishing Grounds*, 13, 16, 20.

82. Kinloch Gun Club Records, 1914–1922, "Correspondence, 1916," 24/14/5, SCHS.

83. "Oakland Club, St. Stephens, P.O., Berkeley County, South Carolina" (1908), 5, SCL 799.2026, USC.

84. Kinloch Gun Club Records, 1914–1922, "Correspondence, 1915," 25/147/2, SCHS.

85. Ibid.

86. Archibald Rutledge, *Santee Paradise* (New York: Bobbs-Merrill Company, 1956), 155.

87. Buchanan, *Holt Collier*, 198.

88. "Fees and Tips," Kinloch Gun Club Records, 1914–1922, "Correspondence, 1915," 25/147/2, SCHS.

89. "Oakland Club, St. Stephens."

90. John Edwin Fripp Papers, ser. 1.2, vol. 5, SHC #869, UNCCH. The constant

depredations against Chelsea Club game by African Americans greatly frustrated Fripp. He often had difficulty identifying and stopping such poaching, as demonstrated by an August 30, 1899, entry. Desperate to protect plantation deer until the club season opened, Fripp questioned local African Americans and found them less than forthcoming. "That's three [deer] that have been killed out there in the neighborhood. Saw John Brown. Swears he knows nothing about any deer being hunted or killed there." Fripp often seemed skeptical of such denials. On August 9, 1902, he complained that even though he frequently questioned African Americans about incidents of poaching, "they all lie and pretend to know nothing." Fripp also had difficulty with Kit, hired to help safeguard the club. On August 15, 1899, for example, Fripp heard shooting and was certain it was Kit. The following week he confronted Kit about the incident, but with no success. "Got lot of sass from Kit for shooting on 13th. He don't like being spoken to about his neglect of duty." One problem sporting plantation or club officials had to deal with was keeping their own employees—the people most familiar with area fish and game and best equipped to catch it—from taking too much away from the club's affluent visitors.

91. "North Carolina Game Region," *Forest and Stream,* November 5, 1891, 308. "Porte Crayon" was the pen name of David Hunter Strother of Martinsburg, (West) Virginia (1816–1888). He was a leading illustrator of landscape and sporting scenes before the war and, after the war, depictions of the war itself. In the art journal *The Crayon,* in *Harper's Monthly,* and in his own books, Strother created images of the South that became widely circulated in the North, helping to shape Americans' images of the Old South.

92. Entry for November 23, 1904, Santee Club Records, 1901–1969, 34/423/9, SCHS.

93. Harry F. Lowe, "Our Coon Hunt and What We Got," *Field and Stream,* January 1909, 756, 757.

94. Archibald Rutledge, *Days off in Dixie* (London: Leonard Parsons, 1925), 205.

95. A. S. Salley, *The Happy Hunting Ground: Personal Experiences in the Low-Country of South Carolina* (Columbia, SC: State Company, 1916), 38.

96. Nash Buckingham, "The XIVth of John," in *Hunting the Southlands,* ed. Lamar Underwood (Clinton, NJ: Amwell Press, 1986), 175.

97. So revered was David Gourdine Jr., affectionately referred to as "Davy," that when he died he was interred in the plantation cemetery and the Stoney family placed a remarkable epitaph: "A Keen Sportsman and / Famous Deer Driver / No More His Mellow Horn / Shall Sound / His Echoing Voice Rouse / Flagging Hound." Beach, *Medway,* 85.

98. Ibid., 86.

99. Titus Brown and James "Jack" Hadley, *African American Life on the Southern Hunting Plantation* (Charleston, SC: Arcadia Publishing, 2001), 8.

100. Ibid., 22, 46, 50.

101. Henry D. Boykin II, "Looking back at the Boykin Hunting Club" (Camden, SC, 1984), 34, SCL 799.2B691, USC.

CHAPTER 5: "WHEN HE SHOULD BE BETWEEN THE PLOW HANDLES"

Epigraphs. Colonel Howard quoted in "Proceedings of the State Agricultural Society, with the Actions of the Farmers' Convention and the Agricultural and Manual Association of Georgia" (Macon, GA, 1868), 16, Rare Book Collection, Southern Pamphlet Collection, 6487, UNCCH; Rice quoted in Benjamin Franklin Taylor, "The Audubon Society" (typescript, 1909), 10, Kosmos Club Records, SCL manuscripts, MS R, USC.

1. "Hunter's License Law Is Effective Today," *Progressive Democrat,* July 1, 1915. The law was initially passed on January 31, 1914. According to observers such as the *Georgetown Times,* the bill was long overdue because "anything that would tend to restrict killing of game birds and reckless use of firearms was along the right lines." "Tinkering the Game Laws," *Georgetown Times,* January 31, 1914, SCL microforms, GeT6, USC.

2. "Inforcing [*sic*] the Hunter's License Law," *Beaufort Gazette,* August 13, 1915, SCL microforms, reel BfG2, USC.

3. The seventeen counties covered by the Ziegler Bill were Lexington, Barnwell, Beaufort, Calhoun, Charleston, Chester, Darlington, Dillon, Dorchester, Florence, Greenville, Hampton, Jasper, Laurens, Marion, Oconee, and Orangeburg. Information from the 1910 census is available for only sixteen of these counties. Jasper County was created from portions of Beaufort and Hampton counties in 1912 and population numbers do not exist for 1910.

4. Department of Commerce, Bureau of the Census, *Negro Population 1790–1915* (Washington, DC: Government Printing Office, 1918), cited in William Loren Katz, general ed., *Negro Population in the United States, 1790–1915* (New York: Arno Press, 1968), 829.

5. "Inforcing the Hunter's License Law."

6. "Venatoe," "Pot-Hunting," *Forest and Stream* 8, no. 8 (March 29, 1877): 117.

7. "Louisiana Game Interests," *Forest and Stream,* September 16, 1886, 146.

8. "Shotgun and Citizenship," *Forest and Stream,* August 23, 1894.

9. According to Eugene P. Odom, biographer of noted North Carolina naturalist Herbert Hutchinson Brimley, a lack of concern for fish and game slaughter among Southerners as a whole posed a significant problem. "The reader should remember that prior to 1900 there were virtually no laws restricting the taking or sale of game, or non-game animals, for that matter . . . The average person thought nothing of this unrestricted slaughter because the game seemed so abundant then, an attitude not uncommon today concerning things . . . of which we still have a good supply." Odom, ed., "H. H. Brimley: North Carolina Naturalist. Selections from His Writings," 9, Herbert Hutchinson Brimley Papers, 1861–1940, box 203.3, p.c. 203.1, NCSA.

10. John Ott, "Fish and Game," *Southern Planter and Farmer,* September 1879, 495–96.

11. Numbers cited by South Carolina's chief game warden, A. A. Richardson, in 1915 point to the need for preservation. According to Richardson, about 8,040,000 quail alone were killed in the sixty-seven counties of the state of Alabama. "At ten cents each,

which is a ridiculously low price for the actual food value of quail, the annual quail crop is worth the enormous sum $804,000. When the bag annually made by Alabamians of doves, duck, geese, snipe, plover, woodcock, wild turkey, squirrel and other game, birds, and animals, is computed the aggregate becomes so amazingly large as to astound the experienced and observant mind with the value of the wild life of the State." *Annual Report of A. A. Richardson, Chief Game Warden of the State of South Carolina (for 1914)* (Columbia: Gonzales & Bryan, State Printers, 1915), 12–13, SCL s.c. 799 So8re, USC.

12. T. S. Palmer, "Some Possibilities for Game Protection in North Carolina" (1904), 8, NCC, UNCCH. According to Palmer, wildfowl produced much revenue for North Carolina. In Currituck County, the state's richest fowling region, Palmer estimated the annual game revenue from visitors to the sounds at around $50,000 (8).

13. Ibid, 11.

14. T. S. Palmer and H. W. Olds, *Digest of Game Laws for 1901*, U.S. Department of Agriculture, Division of Biological Survey (Washington, DC: Government Printing Office, 1901), 11.

15. John Sargent Wise, "The Game Law Problem," *Outing* 38, no. 1 (April 1901): 47.

16. Audubon Society of North Carolina, *Fifth Annual Report of the Audubon Society of North Carolina* (Greensboro, NC: Audubon Society of North Carolina, 1907), 7.

17. Odom, "H. H. Brimley."

18. Polk Miller, "Hunting in the South," *Forest and Stream*, December 1, 1900, 426.

19. "Game Fish in Virginia," *Rod and Gun and American Sportsman*, August 28, 1875, 323.

20. "Cosmopolitan," "A Paradise for Sportsmen," *American Sportsman*, July 18, 1874, 246.

21. "Game in Season for January," *Forest and Stream* 1, no. 25 (January 29, 1874): 395.

22. "M," "The Freedman and the Quail," *Forest and Stream*, March 1, 1883, 87.

23. Odom, "H. H. Brimley."

24. "The Working of the No-Sale Law," *Outing* 31, no. 4 (January 1898): 101.

25. For nearly half a century, lacking public enforcement agencies and unwilling to commit state and regional law enforcement officials to the task, states relied on the private shooting and sporting clubs to enforce game laws, even going as far as empowering club officials to make arrests and levy fines against offenders. According to a 1911 manual from the DuPont Corporation, a long-time club sponsor in the South, "Someone has aptly said: 'A sufficient number of gun clubs in a State is better than the best game law'" (E. I. DuPont De Nemours Powder Company, "The Sport Alluring: Trap Shooting" [1911], 11, NCC Cp799 S76 e, UNCCH). Clubs asked members not only to observe the fish and game laws but also to serve as game wardens and, if necessary, initiate suits for trespassing when required. According to the rules of North Carolina's Onslow Rod and Gun Club, "It shall be the duty of every member of the Club to act as a detective, and every member shall have the power to institute suit and

prosecute any one for trespass, in the name of the Club." "By-Laws of the Onslow Rod and Gun Club" (1921), NCC Cp799059n, UNCCH.

26. "Otranto Club: Constitution and By-Laws, 1916–1924," 35, Mitchell and Smith Records, 0152.02.08, box 8, SCHS.

27. Virginia Fish and Game Protective Association, "A Medley of Suggestions to Farmers," *Southern Planter and Farmer*, December 1877, 810.

28. "The Dog Question," *Southern Planter and Farmer* 8, no. 3 (March 1874): 138 (emphasis in original).

29. James Henry Rice Jr., *Glories of the Carolina Coast* (Columbia, SC: R. L. Bryan, 1925), 112, NCC C917.11 R49g, UNCCH.

30. "Louisiana Game Interests," *Forest and Stream*, September 16, 1886, 146.

31. [Editorial], *Southern Planter and Farmer* 6, no. 10 (October 1872): 579–80.

32. "Audubon Society Favors Hunter's License Measure," *Beaufort Gazette*, January 20, 1911, SCL microforms, reel BfG2, USC.

33. G. G. Ford, "Deer Hunting in South Carolina," *Field and Stream*, August 1908, 358.

34. "Unkel David's Letter," *Field and Stream*, January 1911, 1893.

35. Ibid.

36. George Bird Grinnell, naturalist and *Forest and Stream* editor, founded the first national Audubon Society in 1896 after inviting readers to sign a pledge to join a group dedicated to protecting birds. He named this early group, which consisted of about 40,000 people who responded to the call, the Audubon Society for the Protection of Birds, after famed American naturalist John James Audubon. Grinnell soon grew frustrated with the group when it grew too rapidly, and he disbanded the organization. The first permanent local Audubon Society, formed in Massachusetts in 1896, grew out of efforts by Bostonians Harriet Hemenway and her cousin Mirna B. Hall to stop fellow socialites from promoting bird slaughter by wearing feathered hats. National Audubon Society, "Historical Highlights: The Heroes," www.audubon.org.

37. Benjamin Franklin Taylor, "The Audubon Society" (typescript, 1909), Kosmos Club Records, SCL manuscripts, MS R, USC. Page numbers in the following text refer to this source.

38. B. F. Taylor, "South Carolina's Needs," *Field and Stream*, January 1910, 847.

39. James Henry Rice Jr., "As to the Game Law," *Beaufort Gazette*, December 24, 1908, SCL microforms, reel BfG2, USC.

40. M. G. Vinson, "From the Game Fields," *Recreation*, January 1901, 38.

41. "T.H.W.," "Some Southern Needs," *Recreation*, September 1903, 198.

42. "Letter from Thos. P. Devereux, esquire" (1867), Legislative Documents, 1866–1867, NCSA (emphasis in original).

43. K. H. Schuricht, "Is This Fair?" *Southern Planter and Farmer*, April 1896, 179–80.

44. Audubon Society of South Carolina, *Fifth Annual Report of the Audubon Society of South Carolina* (Columbia: R. L. Bryan, State Printers, 1915), 5–6, SCL 586.06 Au2a, USC.

45. Audubon Society of North Carolina, *Fifth Annual Report*, 13.

46. Miller, "Hunting in the South."

47. John H. Wallace Jr., "The Direct Benefits Accruing to the Farmers and to the State as a Resultant Effect of Model and Modern Game Protective Legislation" (Montgomery, AL, 1912), general collection, SK457.C6, VHS.

48. Ford, "Deer Hunting in South Carolina."

49. T. N. Buckingham, "Bob White, Down't Aberdeen," *Field and Stream*, September 1913, 460.

50. Ibid.

51. Frank A. Heywood, "North Carolina Game Region," *Forest and Stream*, November 5, 1891, 308.

52. Marguerite Tracy, "Hunting a Holiday," *Recreation*, November 1898, 353.

53. "Terrapin," *Charleston Evening Post*, January 28, 1897, SCL microforms, USC. As one observer pointed out, this decrease in market terrapin proved a double-edged sword. On the one hand, many whites were relieved that such a potentially lucrative means of employment was closed to former slaves who might better expend labor in the service of whites. On the other hand, as asserted in another *Evening Post* editorial, such restrictions might ultimately make it more difficult for the average consumer to purchase cheap terrapin, since the law would likely "frighten the humble darkey who has been in the habit of supplying the local market with a few bivalves or reptiles . . . thereby depriving the home consumer of previously enjoyed advantages of having a home dish at low cost." "To Protect Terrapin and Oysters," *Charleston Evening Post*, March 11, 1897, SCL microforms, reel 51, USC.

54. "W.L.J.," "Dog Tax," *Southern Planter and Farmer*, May 1875, 268.

55. Dr. Lavender and Colonel Howard, in "Proceedings of the State Agricultural Society," 16, 18.

56. "J.E.W.," "The Game of North Carolina," *Forest and Stream* 2, no. 3 (February 1874): 37.

57. Herbert Hutchinson Brimley, "A Sketch of the History of Wildlife Conservation in North Carolina," Herbert Hutchinson Brimley Papers, p.c. 203.1, NCSA.

58. Virginia Fish and Game Protective Association, *The Virginia Fish and Game Protective Association to the People of Virginia; with the Laws of this Commonwealth Relating to Fish and Game* (Richmond, VA: Clemmitt & Jones, 1878), 7, general collection, SK 457.V5, VHS.

59. "The Absolute Prohibition of Traffic of Game," *Forest and Stream*, February 10, 1894.

60. Audubon Society of South Carolina, *Third Annual Report*, 38–39.

61. "Nigger in the Woodpile," *Georgetown Times*, January 11, 1905, SCL microforms, reel GeT6, USC.

62. Charles T. Otken, *The Ills of the South or, Related Causes Hostile to the General Prosperity of the Southern People* (New York: Knickerbocker Press, 1894), 241.

63. B. W. Mitchell, "The Fishing of Mr. and Mrs. Bias: in Which the Former Discourses upon Angling Ethics and the Latter on Domestic Matters," *Field and Stream*, n.d., 1906, 41.

64. "Sportsmen v. Poachers," *Forest and Stream* 1, no. 15 (November 20, 1873): 232.

65. Ott, "Fish and Game," 496 (emphasis added).

66. "Poachers, Law Officers and Sportsmen," *Cecil Whig*, n.d., quoted in *Rod and Gun and American Sportsman*, October 9, 1875, 26.

67. Audubon Society of South Carolina, *First Annual Report of the Audubon Society of South Carolina* (Columbia: R. L. Bryan, State Printers, 1908), 3, 13, SCL 598.06 Au2a, USC.

68. Ibid., 13.

69. Audubon Society of South Carolina, *Second Annual Report of the Audubon Society of South Carolina* (Columbia: R. L. Bryan, State Printers, 1909), 8, SCL 598.06 Au2a, USC.

70. Audubon Society of South Carolina, *Third Annual Report of the Audubon Society of South Carolina* (Columbia: R. L. Bryan, State Printers, 1910), 36, 38–39, SCL 598.06 Au2a, USC.

71. Audubon Society of South Carolina, *Fifth Annual Report*, 5–6, 9.

72. "The Conservation of Bird Life and Game Preservation in Virginia: Reasons Why the Moncure and Rutherfoord Bill Should Be Enacted into Law without Amendments" (1912), general collection, SK457.C6, VHS.

73. Ibid.

74. Wallace, "Direct Benefits Accruing to the Farmers and to the State."

75. Quotations of Richardson in this and the following paragraphs are from *Report of A. A. Richardson, Chief Game Warden of the State of South Carolina* (Columbia: Gonzales & Bryan, State Printers, 1914), 7, SCL s.c. 799 So8re, USC.

76. *Report of A. A. Richardson, Chief Game Warden of the State of South Carolina* (Columbia: Gonzales & Bryan, State Printers, 1915), 7, SCL s.c. 799 So8re, USC (emphasis added).

77. "Audubon Society Favors Hunter's License Measure."

78. "Report of W. H. Gibbes, Chief Game Warden of the State of South Carolina, 1919," *Reports and Resolutions, South Carolina, 1921*, vol. II, SCDAH.

79. N. B. Landy, "A Fair Crop of Virginia Quail," *Field and Stream*, January 1919, 704.

80. George Rawick, "Kentucky Narratives," in *The American Slave: A Composite Autobiography* (Westport, CT: Greenwood Press, 1972), 16(4): 96.

81. Wallace, "Direct Benefits Accruing to the Farmers and to the State."

CONCLUSION: CONTRADICTION AND CONTINUITY
IN THE SOUTHERN SPORTING FIELD

1. M. E. Ravenel, "Opening the Hunt," St. John's Hunting Club Manuscripts, SCL R1236, USC.

2. Archibald Hamilton Rutledge, *Hunter's Choice* (New York: A. S. Barnes and Company, 1946), 22, 21.

3. Henry Wellington Wack, "The Sportsmen's Elysium of the South, Part II: The Game Animals of Florida," *Field and Stream*, March 1901, 21–22.

4. C. W. Boyd, "Winter Shooting in South Carolina," *Outing* 8, no. 5 (February 1889): 401.

5. Henry D. Boykin II, "Looking back at the Boykin Hunting Club" (Camden, SC, 1984), 34, SCL 799.2B69l, USC.

6. U.S. Fish and Wildlife Service, *National Survey of Fishing, Hunting and Wildlife-Associated Recreation* (Washington, DC: U.S. Fish and Wildlife Service, 1996).

7. U.S. Fish and Wildlife Service, *Participation and Expenditure Patterns of African-American, Hispanic and Women Hunters and Anglers: Addendum to the 1996 National Survey of Fishing, Hunting and Wildlife-Associated Recreation* (Washington, DC: U.S. Fish and Wildlife Service, 2000). Page numbers in the following text refer to this source.

8. According to the Fish and Wildlife Service, African Americans in 1996 were less than one-third as likely as whites to hunt, with 7 percent of white respondents age sixteen or older, compared with 2 percent of African-American respondents, participating in these activities. Moreover, of the $10,674,456 spent on hunting by Americans in 1996, a mere $174,186 was spent by African Americans. Ibid., 5.

9. Responsive Management, *Women's, Hispanics', and African-Americans' Participation in, and Attitudes toward, Boating and Fishing: Submitted to the Fishing and Boating Partnership Council* (Harrisonburg, VA: Responsive Management, 1998), www.responsivemanagement.com/focusgroupprojects.html. Page numbers in the following text refer to this source.

Essay on Sources

Research into hunting and fishing in the post-Emancipation South required a great deal of digging through a broad range of sources. This essay provides a brief tour of the most important primary and secondary sources that informed the study. It is not intended as a comprehensive guide, but rather as a focused discussion of the key materials that most aided my work.

Contemporary Magazines

The most useful sources were the national sporting periodicals. By the 1880s, the South had become more a part of the national outdoor sporting culture and the region became a more frequent topic of discussion in these periodicals. The most important sporting publications of the day, *Forest and Stream* (New York), *Field and Stream* (St. Paul, MN), and *Outing* (Albany, NY), provided excellent discussions of Southern natural environs, sporting destinations, and race relations. In addition, *American Sportsman* (West Meriden, CT; this later became the *Rod and Gun and American Sportsman* [New York]), *National Sportsman* (Boston), *Outdoor Life* (Denver), and *Recreation* (New York) often discussed the South, proving extremely helpful in identifying the central role of race in national debates over hunting and fishing.

In addition to sporting magazines, other national and regional periodicals helped identify the many links between hunting and fishing and such topics as Emancipation, labor, tourism, and agriculture. Agricultural journals such as *American Farmer* (Baltimore), *Southern Cultivator* (Atlanta), and *Southern Planter and Farmer* (Richmond, VA) were the best sources for tracing attitudes toward the Southern "labor question," as well as its connection to African Americans' customary rights, over the period studied.

Memoirs, Guides, and Interviews

Memoirs of Southern life after the Civil War provided critical material for the study. Only a few dedicated, elite sportsmen made hunting and fishing a major emphasis of their recollections, but memoirs that include discussions of these sporting activities and African Americans make the perspectives of elite whites clearer. Some of the more helpful memoirs, readily available through the Documenting the American South Collection at the University of North Carolina (UNC) at Chapel Hill, are Frances Butler Leigh, *Ten Years on a Georgia Plantation since the War* (London, 1883), an account of the Butler family's Georgia plantations; Elizabeth Allston Pringle, *A Woman Rice Planter* (New York, 1914), an account of plantation life near Georgetown, South Carolina, written under the pen name Patience Pennington; Susan Dabney Smedes, *Memorials of a Southern Planter* (Baltimore, 1887), an account of post-Emancipation life in Mississippi; and Edward J. Thomas, *Memorials of a Southerner* (Savannah, 1923), an account of life and labor in and around Savannah, Georgia.

The published sporting memoirs and accounts of Southern natural history, though much more scarce, offer critical information on sporting culture and conservation that helped establish the contours of Southern hunting and fishing. Among these are Horatio Bigelow, *Flying Feathers: A Yankee's Hunting Experiences in the South* (Richmond, VA, 1937); William Elliott, *Carolina Sports by Land and Water* (New York, 1859), probably the best known of all antebellum sporting accounts; William Templeton Hornaday, *Thirty Years' War for Wildlife: Gains and Losses in the Thankless Task* (Stamford, CT, 1931), the naturalist's assessment of the early conservation movement; James Henry Rice Jr., *Glories of the Carolina Coast* (Columbia, SC, 1925), a valuable account of natural and sporting matters by the long-time secretary of the South Carolina Audubon Society; many books by South Carolina's poet laureate and novelist Archibald Hamilton Rutledge, including *Days off in Dixie* (London, 1925), *Home by the River* (New York, 1955), *Hunter's Choice* (New York, 1946), *Santee Paradise* (New York, 1956), and *Those Were the Days* (Richmond, VA, 1955), accounts of Rutledge's South Carolina upbringing that made hunting and fishing central parts of the story; and A. S. Salley, *The Happy Hunting Ground: Personal Experiences in the Low-Country of South Carolina* (Columbia, SC, 1916).

Published accounts of Southern visitors' impressions of the region, which often include discussions of both hunting and fishing and race relations, proved another essential source. Travel accounts with occasional commentary on hunting and fishing and related topics include Clifton Johnson, *Highways and Byways of the South* (New York, 1904), a photographic and textual exploration of the Southern countryside; Edward King, *The Great South: A Record of Journeys in Louisiana, Texas, the Indian Territory, Missouri, Arkansas, Mississippi, Alabama, Georgia, Florida, South Carolina, North Carolina, Kentucky, Tennessee, Virginia, West Virginia, and Maryland* (Hartford, IL, 1875), an account of the *Scribner's* correspondent's travels in the Reconstruction South; Frederick Law Olmsted, *The Cotton Kingdom: A Traveler's Observations on Cotton and Slavery in the American Slave States: Based upon Three Former Volumes of Journeys and Investigations* (New York, 1861), one of the most famous antebellum memoirs; and Julian Ralph, *Dixie; or Southern Scenes and Sketches* (New York, 1895), a record of the New York journalist's journey through the South.

Published guides promoting Southern tourism or extolling the region's virtues for potential visitors and investors helped establish both the economic importance of the natural environment and the central place of hunting and fishing in luring Northerners to the South. Representative publications include Frank Presbrey, *The Empire of the South: An Exposition of the Present Resources and Development of the South* (Washington, DC, 1898), published by the Southern Railway Company; and Richmond and Danville Railroad, *Summer Resorts and Points of Interest of Virginia, Western North Carolina, and North Georgia* (New York, 1884). Both are found in the extensive North Carolina Collection at UNC Chapel Hill. Also useful are Seaboard Air Line Railway, *A Guide to the Famous Hunting and Fishing Grounds of Virginia, North Carolina, South Carolina and Georgia Traversed by the Seaboard Air Line, with a Synopsis of the Game Laws of Those States* (Richmond, VA, 1898), at the South Carolinia Library (SCL) in Columbia; and Southern Railway Company, *Hunting and Fishing in the South: A Book Descriptive of the Best Localities in the South for Various Kinds of Game and Fish* (Washington, DC, 1904). These guides helped both in tracing the immense changes occurring in the Southern landscape and economic structure and in locating hunting and fishing in those processes.

Sources that capture African Americans' voices, especially important since so vastly outnumbered by whites' publications, proved indispensable to uncovering the long relationship between former slaves and hunting and fishing. Unsurprisingly, the most valuable documents are published former-slave narratives. George Rawick's *The American Slave: A Composite Autobiography* (Westport, CT, 1972) provides scores of Federal Writers' Project (Works Progress Administration, WPA) interviews with former slaves who discussed hunting and fishing, sometimes in great detail. Some particularly useful interviews included in *American Slave* are those with Holt Collier ("Mississippi Narratives," in suppl. ser. 1, 7[2]), Heywood Ford ("Alabama Narratives," in 6[1]), and Josh Horn ("Alabama and Indiana Narratives," in 6[1]). The Horn interviews are also compiled in Alan Brown and David Taylor, eds., *Gabr'l Blow Sof': Sumter County, Alabama, Slave Narratives* (Livingston, AL, 1997), 69–70.

Besides the WPA interviews, numerous published slave narratives discuss hunting and fishing. Examples of these are Charles Ball, *Slavery in the United States* (New York, 1837); William Hayden, *Narrative of William Hayden, Containing a Faithful Account of His Travels for a Number of Years, Whilst a Slave, in the South* (Cincinnati, 1846); and Peter Randolph, *From Slave Cabin to the Pulpit: The Autobiography of Reverend Peter Randolph* (Boston, 1893). While rarely spending substantial time on hunting and fishing, these narratives occasionally provide important accounts of how former slaves used those activities to survive the transition from slavery to freedom.

Archival Sources and Unpublished Material

Archival research provided much essential information for the study. Among the most useful records were those of sporting clubs and resorts. These records, while not as numerous in the archives as I had hoped, nonetheless provided some of the study's most valuable information. The records of the Kinloch Gun Club and Santee Gun Club, both housed at the South Carolina Historical Society (SCHS) in Charleston, for example, contain invaluable details about African-American huntsmen and sporting laborers. The same is true of the records of the St. John's Hunting Club and the Kosmos Club, housed at the SCL in Columbia, although these records are not nearly as comprehensive. The John Edwin Fripp Papers, including records of Fripp's time as overseer of the Chelsea Plantation Club, a Beaufort County, South Carolina, sports-man's association, are housed in the Southern Historical Collections (SHC) at UNC Chapel Hill; these helped establish the connection between hunting and fishing and elite Southerners' sporting and racial identity. In addition, the SHC also contains the David Franklin Thorpe Papers, with their unfortunately brief records of the St. He-lena Island Rifle and Sporting Club—wherein can be found the sad story of the maimed sporting laborer Isaac Polite.

Surviving records from state and private wildlife protection agencies were also very useful. The annual reports of the South Carolina Audubon Society, in the reading room of the SCL, allowed me to follow the evolution of natural conservation in South Carolina and to connect African Americans to elite sportsmen's concerns about wild-life and labor problems. Perhaps the most important of such records for this study were the annual reports of South Carolina's chief game warden. These detail the connec-tion between controlling black labor, protecting elite sporting privilege, and guaran-teeing white supremacy. The collections of the Virginia Historical Society (VHS) in Richmond contributed invaluable material linking wildlife protection and race rela-tions. The pamphlet "The Conservation of Bird Life and Game Preservation in Vir-ginia: Reasons Why the Moncure and Rutherfoord Bill Should be Enacted into Law without Amendments," for example, helped establish that race was used to justify wildlife protection beyond the Deep South.

At the SCHS in Charleston, the Mitchell and Smith Records, particularly the in-complete "Alston v. Limehouse Case Records, 1892–1902," provided evidence of the conflict engendered by the competing interests of whites and blacks in commercial fishing. The Mitchell and Smith Records also contain brief records of the Otranto Club, a Berkeley County sporting organization founded in 1872. In addition, the SCHS contains the Conner Family Papers, which include fascinating correspondence between F. C. Ford and Audubon Society Secretary James Henry Rice Jr. document-ing whites' anger over supposed sporting abuses by blacks.

The SCL in Columbia also has numerous archival collections, beyond those dis-cussed above, that contributed to my research. The rules and regulations for the "Oak-land Club, St. Stephens, P.O., Berkeley County, South Carolina" (1908) helped es-tablish the cost of labor at sporting plantations. Henry D. Boykin's unpublished "Looking Back at the Boykin Hunting Club" (1984) provided useful commentary on biracial hunting in South Carolina from someone with deep sporting ties to the re-gion. The SCL also houses the Henry Edwards Davis Papers, the surviving business and personal records of this renowned turkey hunter and sporting author.

The SHC at Chapel Hill led me to letters in the James Philip Jones Papers, which discuss the postwar labor problem. In addition, the James Lee Love Collection con-tains a multi-volume typescript that occasionally mentions hunting, fishing, and prob-lems with labor; the Robert Pinckney Tucker Papers, which contain a wealth of ma-terial related to hunting, fishing, and other land uses, left by Tucker, the South Carolina land and lumber speculator; and the Jackson and Prince Family Papers, which contain typescript descriptions of sporting plantation land for sale in Glynn County, Georgia.

The NCC at Chapel Hill holds many travel and tourism broadsides produced by railroads, resorts, and land agents, and informative pamphlets on wildlife protection in North Carolina, such as T. S. Palmer's "Some Possibilities for Game Protection in North Carolina" (1904) and "Prospectus of the Shocco Game Association" (1894). The NCC also contains the valuable study of farm tenant life by the North Carolina State Extension Service, J. A. Dickey and E. C. Branson's "How Farm Tenants Live" (1922), which helped establish the importance of fish and game to laborers' diets even as late as the 1920s.

The VHS in Richmond possesses a wealth of useful information on Southern hunting and fishing. The broadside collection contains *The Virginia Fish and Game Protective Association to the People of Virginia* (1878), a pamphlet in which the association announced its intention to aggressively pursue wildlife protection in the Old Dominion. Most importantly, the VHS general collection contains the essay "The Direct Benefits Accruing to the Farmers and to the State as a Resultant Effect of Model and Modern Game Protective Legislation" (1912), written by Alabama Game Warden John Wallace Jr.; this was Wallace's attempt to convince Virginians of the need to pass wildlife legislation as a check to African Americans' abuses. The VHS also contains the Kelly Walker Trimble Papers, including the letter to George Washington Trimble complaining of the flight of the laborer William Carter after he reacquired his hunting dog Jack.

SECONDARY SOURCES

Despite the frequency with which accounts of hunting and fishing appear in narratives of blacks' life before and after slavery, these activities have received comparatively little attention from scholars of Southern or African-American history. Most works that discuss these topics either do so briefly—such as the classic plantation studies: George Rawick's *From Sunup to Sundown: The Making of the Black Community* (Westport, CT, 1972); Eugene Genovese's *Roll, Jordan, Roll: The World the Slaves Made* (New York, 1974); and John W. Blassingame's *The Slave Community: Plantation Life in the Antebellum South* (New York, 1972)—or do so in short articles in which hunting and fishing are not the central focus. The latter include John Campbell's "'My Constant Companion': Slaves and Their Dogs in the Antebellum South" (in *Working toward Freedom: Slave Society and Domestic Economy in the American South* [Rochester, NY, 1994]); and David K. Wiggins's "Good Times on the Old Plantation: Popular Recreations of the Black Slave in Antebellum South, 1810–1860" (*Journal of Sports History* 4, no. 1 [1977]: 260–84). Aside from these works, none of which address the post-Emancipation period, few scholars have addressed the role of hunting and fishing in the lives of African Americans in the nineteenth century and beyond.

Most studies of hunting and fishing in the United States between the eighteenth and twentieth centuries have focused primarily on such topics as how elites used field sports to reinforce class distinctions; how hunting and fishing reinforced or redefined

American masculinity; and how such activities fit into the ebb and flow of American evangelicalism. Two essays—Gary Kulik's "Dams, Fish and Farmers: Defense of Public Rights in Eighteenth Century Rhode Island" (in *The Countryside in the Age of Capitalist Transformation: Essays in the Social History of Rural America*, ed. Steven Hahn and Johnathan Prude [Chapel Hill, NC, 1985]), and Harry L. Watson's "'The Common Rights of Mankind': Subsistence, Shad and Commerce in the Early Republican South" (*Journal of American History* 83 [1996]: 13–43)—discuss conflicts over dambreaking strictly in terms of class. Ted Ownby's *Subduing Satan: Religion, Recreation and Manhood in the Rural South 1865–1920* (Chapel Hill, 1990), a study of how male Southern recreational culture changed after the Civil War in response to growing Southern evangelicalism, is far-reaching and comprehensive. But it does not address hunting and fishing in extensive detail and does not devote significant attention to black Southerners. It must be noted, however, that while Ownby spends little time on race relations, his work is extremely important because it does establish that African Americans' hunting activities threatened both white landowners' economic prosperity and white sportsmen's sense of sporting superiority.

Most studies mentioning Southern hunting and fishing give little more than passing notice to how such activities, which were common for nearly all groups of Southerners, black and white, rich and poor, reflected larger and longer-lasting racial conflict. There are several notable exceptions to this trend. Nicholas Proctor's *Bathed in Blood: Hunting and Mastery in the Old South* (Charlottesville, VA, 2002) is perhaps the best and most useful work in laying out the antebellum antecedents to messages of race and racial control developed in late-nineteenth-century accounts of African Americans' hunting and fishing. Arguing persuasively that slaveholders used hunting to cultivate mastery over nature, over their own emotional impulses, and, most importantly, over slaves, Proctor presents hunting as an activity used to reinforce the social order. He compares the meanings of hunting by white slave owners and by slaves to great effect, clearly establishing hunting as an important way in which Southern elites defined and conserved their class privilege and racial identity.

Studies of hunting have become more popular in the past decade, thanks, in part, to the increasing popularity of environmental history, the history of sports, and the history of tourism. Some of these studies demonstrate the connection between the social structures of field sports and the construction of cultural values and institutions. The work of Mart A. Stewart, Albert Cowdrey, David S. Cecelski, Daniel Justin Herman, Jacob F. Rivers, and other scholars has demonstrated that the social meanings ascribed to field sports, particularly in justifications for and written narratives of these sports, give excellent insights into American cultural, intellectual, and social life. Stewart's *What Nature Suffers to Groe: Life, Labor, and Landscape on the Georgia Coast, 1680–1920* (Athens, GA, 1996), and Cowdrey's *This Land, This South: An Environmental History* (Lexington, KY, 1996), are among the best environmental histories of the South and help make plain the general plenty that initially made the region's fish and game such a valuable source of subsistence and income for poor Southerners and later, as the nineteenth century wore on, the source of increasing conflict over environmental use between the races and classes. Cecelski's fine *The Waterman's Song: Slavery and*

Freedom in Maritime North Carolina (Chapel Hill, NC, 2001) outlines the general importance of long-standing customary rights such as fishing for whites and blacks living in coastal North Carolina in the nineteenth century, but does not address the topic in terms of race relations. Herman's *Hunting and the American Imagination* (Washington, DC, 2001) is a fascinating study of how popular images of hunting both reflected and reinforced American ideals of manliness, racial identity, and nationalism. It is effective in locating racial attitudes in sporting narratives, but does not address the South or African Americans in any substantial way. Rivers, in his *Cultural Values in the Southern Sporting Narrative* (Columbia, SC, 2002), provides primarily a literary analysis of Southern sporting narratives, which, although allowing him to tease out some aspects of whites' attitudes toward African Americans, deals only briefly with the decades after Emancipation. Taken together, these works provide excellent pointers for future scholars in their attempts to locate aspects of American social, cultural, and intellectual development in various groups' visions of field sports. But scholars have yet to make a detailed attempt to do so for the postwar South.

None of the above works, even though each deals with race to some degree, attempts to connect the culture of Southern hunting and fishing to race relations from the late nineteenth through the early twentieth centuries. One notable exception is Steven Hahn's "Hunting, Fishing and Foraging: Common Rights and Class Relations in the Postbellum South" (*Radical History Review* 26 [October 1982]: 36–64), which demonstrates how Southern elites' loss of control over the lower classes, especially African Americans, proved an incentive for restricting, from the 1870s, the general right to hunt, fish, and forage and put animals to graze. Hahn's work, which first established elite Southerners' wide-ranging assault on plebeian customary rights, is central to my study. Another work that attempts to connect Southern hunting and fishing to race relations is Stuart A. Marks's *Southern Hunting in Black and White: Nature, History and Ritual in a Carolina Community* (Princeton, NJ, 1991). Although focusing to a degree on race, it gives little attention to the late nineteenth and early twentieth centuries and, despite the title, does not make a broad argument about Southern race relations. Aside from noting the differences between the hunting habits of slaves and their masters and suggesting that Emancipation played a role in the growing sentiment for wildlife restrictions, Marks does not deal much with the many connections between hunting and race in the postwar South. Hahn and Marks argue for a general connection between hunting and fishing and race, but neither gives the topic detailed analysis.

Several scholarly monographs dealing with American hunting and fishing, although not focusing on the South, help demonstrate the importance of such activities to poor Americans across the country and the omnipresence of conflict created by these customary activities. Karl Jacoby's *Crimes against Nature: Squatters, Poachers, Thieves, and the Hidden History of American Conservation* (Berkeley, CA, 2001) documents the criminalization of the hunting, fishing, and foraging traditions of the lower classes that attended development of three national parks, making clear that elites' assault on plebeian subsistence methods was truly a national process. Likewise, Louis Warren's *The Hunter's Game: Poachers and Conservationists in Twentieth-Century*

America (New Haven, CT, 1997) analyzes the conflict created by emerging government efforts to regulate wildlife in the twentieth century. Together, these works help locate the struggles in and over the Southern sporting field in a larger context.

There are several valuable studies of the post-Emancipation South that proved helpful for situating hunting and fishing in the lives of Southerners after the Civil War. Studies of economic development and tourism, for example, which are central to any understanding of Southern sporting traditions, help us understand how both nostalgia and economics underlie the importance of hunting and fishing. J. William Harris's important book *Deep Souths: Delta, Piedmont, and Sea Island Society in the Age of Segregation* (Baltimore, 2001) provides a clear picture of the economic, particularly agricultural, transformations occurring in three regions of the Deep South between Reconstruction and the 1930s. It includes a fine discussion of the growing importance of Northern sporting tourism to the region as changes in the agricultural economy, particularly in the Mississippi-Yazoo Delta and coastal Georgia, made more lands available for Northern investors.

Other studies reveal the clear links between tourism and growing national nostalgia for a mythical antebellum South, particularly the key place of race in that relationship. Nina Silber's *The Romance of Reunion: Northerners and the South, 1865–1900* (Chapel Hill, NC, 1993), although not addressing hunting and fishing, is important for identifying the strong connection between race-based nostalgia and the emerging tourism industry—which, as Silber demonstrates, became an important factor in sectional reunion. David W. Blight's influential *Race and Reunion: The Civil War in American Memory* (Cambridge, MA, 2001), again not dealing with hunting and fishing, makes clear the concrete relationship between idealized, racialized memories of the Old South and the physical and symbolic reunion of North and South—both of which became central to the emergence of hunting and fishing as a key site for drawing the color line.

These works collectively indicate the potential usefulness of customary activities such as hunting and fishing for studying both African-American life and Southern race relations in general, but they also demonstrate a lack of attention to the critical post-Emancipation period and the construction of the Southern racial divide. By clearly establishing the impact of hunting and fishing on African Americans' lives, we can view the South's fields, forests, and streams as contested arenas that reflect crucial tensions in Southern life. The work that scholars have done to date suggests that a further examination of Southern hunting and fishing can reveal as much about race and race relations as about class conflict, masculinity, and American religiosity.

Index

Page numbers in *italics* refer to photos and illustrations.